D1522113

FILMMAKERS SERIES

edited by
ANTHONY SLIDE

HOLLYWOOD HOLYLAND:

The Filming and Scoring of
The Greatest Story Ever Told

by
KEN DARBY

Filmmakers, No. 30

The Scarecrow Press, Inc.
Metuchen, N.J., & London
1992

British Library Cataloguing-in-Publication data available

Library of Congress Cataloging-in-Publication Data

Darby, Ken.
  Hollywood Holyland : the filming and scoring of The Greatest story
ever told / by Ken Darby.
      p. cm. — Filmmakers ; no. 30.
  Includes index.
  ISBN 0-8108-2509-0 (alk. paper)
    1. Greatest story ever told (Motion picture)   I. Title.
  II. Series: Filmmakers series ; no. 30.
  PN1997.G6893D37   1992
  791.43'72—dc20   91-47501

TO

Vera	Martha
Peter	Lucy
Tina	Fred
Abel D.	David
Lorin	Tommy
Clara	Maria

In Memory Of

ALFRED NEWMAN

CONTENTS

FOREWORD

by J. E. Wallace Sterling (1906-1985)

My acquaintance with Ken Darby began vicariously as I listened to radio's Royal Quartet, "The King's Men." And how they could sing! A rare blending of voices sang Ken's harmonious arrangements, most of which were spiced by an unexpected change of key and tempo.

Many years passed before I met The King's Men in the flesh. It was in July 1949 at the Bohemian Grove, and with them was John Charles Thomas, with whom they had done many programs and whom I had heard sing in several concerts. It was instant chemistry at work, as if we had been destined to meet and become fast friends. My inauguration as president of Stanford University was scheduled for the following October. Imagine my presumption! Before I left the Grove, I had asked The King's Men to sing at a reception which my wife and I were to have for students after the formal inauguration ceremony. The King's Men came and brought their wives. And sing they did, drawing on their vast and varied repertoire. The students were loath to leave, and my aged and ailing father refused to retire until long after his prescribed bedtime. The King's Men came twice again to Stanford during my presidency of almost twenty years, once on my tenth anniversary, and once to do a benefit for the Students' Institute for International Affairs.

That is how my ever deepening friendship with Ken Darby began. The reader of what follows should not be faulted if he senses in what I write my difficulty in being completely objective about this man and his remarkable talent and career. "Liberty" as a word is an abstraction; only individuals can give it life and meaning. So it is with objectivity, an ideal ardently to be pursued, but in real life always fugitive, if not unattainable.

Ken was kind enough to ask me to read the first draft of the manuscript for this book. I did so with pleasure and interest, taking the liberty of making a few editorial suggestions. I wondered as I read this draft, about the accuracy of what Ken had written, even though I was well aware of his extraordinarily retentive memory. I am now satisfied with its accuracy because I have learned that he kept a diary when on location, he took notes on or tape-recorded conversations, and, being a superb photographer, he has a pictorial record of the rugged beauty of the location site and of those who worked there. Similarly, working back in the MGM studio, Alfred Newman's secretary, Elaine Thompson Dabick, took notes on or tape-recorded what was said at meetings and who attended. When Elaine was not free to do this, Ken did it himself. The care and consistency with which this record was made and used, backed by Ken's memory, has removed any doubts I may have had about the accuracy of the story told in this book.

At one point in my life, I "moonlighted" on radio as a news analyst and conducted forums. It was on one of these forums that I first met Alfred Newman, but I did not come to know him well until later when Ken invited me to luncheons at the studio. I can testify to the good times we had together at our several lunches. Perhaps more important, I can testify to the care, hard work, and more than a little frustration which attended the editing of the film. I have sat for several hours by Ken's side as he worked to cut and splice the film in the formidable tasks of matching the music to the dialogue and matching the transitions from Alfred's beautiful original music to that other music on whose inclusion the director had insisted. I know as a fact of Alfred's chagrin and trauma as some of his music was thus cast aside.

If one knew as I do of Ken's sensitivity to and perception of delicate situations or of his love of the majesty of nature, one would not be surprised that he took long walks while on location or that he sustained accord with his fellow workers under circumstances which were frequently difficult. Ken Darby—as did Alfred Newman—has a penchant for perfection. It shows in his writing, to which he brings an appreciation and wide knowledge

of the English language. This may be attributed, at least in part,
to his omnivorous reading and his retention of what he has read.
I have also witnessed this penchant as we have prepared for our
campfire shows at the Bohemian Grove. He will rehearse the
choir and those who do special numbers until he is satisfied that
they are ready to do their best. This may involve changing a key
or rearranging an entire number. But he does it, applying the
same discipline to himself as he tries to inspire in others.

Although much of his work had been in the field of popular
music, a few years ago he began to organize the symphonic music
of Alfred Newman into a cantata. To this cantata, Ken added
his own lyrics, based on the King James Version of Holy Writ,
and entitled the completed work for mixed chorus and orchestra
Man of Galilee. The final "Hallelujah" movement was performed at Brigham Young University in October 1982 and was
greeted with an enthusiastic ovation.

I must add one other tribute: he has versatile hands. They are
as much at home on the keys of a typewriter as on the keys of a
piano, or at carving chessmen, or doing cabinet work, or building
and keeping up-to-date his own sound recording and production systems.

I confess that our correspondence has become prodigious.
My indispensable secretary occasionally informs me, in a mina-
tory tone, that unless I reduce the size of our files by culling out
"dead wood" to make room for the Darby-Sterling correspondence, we shall have to acquire another filing cabinet, the cost
of which might strain our office budget. A letter from Ken
brightens my day, and he claims that my letters to him are eagerly
awaited.

As I warned at the outset, it is not easy to be completely
objective about such a friend, but I would not have it any other
way. I congratulate Ken on his many accomplishments which
have brought him, among other tributes, three Oscars and three
other nominations for that award; and I thank him for allowing
me to have been a part of his life and work.

J. E. Wallace Sterling
Stanford University

PREFACE

Film director George Stevens (1904–1975) stands among the great innovators who brought distinction, artistry, and originality to the medium of motion pictures. The list of his directorial output is not long, but from it many classic films emerge: *Gunga Din, Penny Serenade, Shane, A Place in the Sun, Giant, The Diary of Anne Frank*—acknowledged by his peers to be masterworks of the cinematic art form.

The Greatest Story Ever Told should have been—and was intended to be—his magnum opus. Lovingly prepared over a period of more than six years, beautifully costumed and photographed, it would have become the crowning achievement of his career had he not fallen under the strangely hypnotic influence of those he chose to counsel him in the matters of editing, casting, and musical scoring. Outstanding artists in each of these fields had been engaged to work on the picture, yet he permitted the opinions of less discriminating people to abort the efforts of all those experienced craftsmen and to subvert his own better judgment. The ultimate disillusionment he suffered was a cruel blow to Stevens, and he never quite recovered from the anger at having to butcher his beloved creation.

It was the near-unanimous negative critical reviews that crushed his expectations and awakened him to the realization that he had been betrayed . . . by his own misplaced faith. All of us who worked closely with him shared an empathy for him but could not escape the weight of his—and our own—deeply felt and lasting disappointment.

The events described herein actually took place. Dialog was recorded on tape or taken down in shorthand at the moment of utterance, and the emotional responses to the various activities were noted in my daily journal of "happenings."

With gratitude I acknowledge the important suggestions, contributions, and encouragement offered by musicologist and colleague Fred Steiner, whose scholarly dissertation on the life and music of my late associate, Alfred Newman, is a work of inestimable value in the annals of cinema history. That he would even consider writing the beautiful Interlude between Book One and Book Two is a compliment to a friendship beyond any attempt of mine to adequately evaluate it.

To the memory of my dear friend, J. E. Wallace Sterling (1906-1985), late president and chancellor of Stanford University, I bow with affectionate thanks for his proofreading, editorial comments, letters about nearly everything under the sun, and for honoring Alfred and me with his generous Foreword.

The Prologue to this book, by Page Cook, came as an explosive surprise. He lives in New York, I in Los Angeles, and we have never met! Yet our correspondence would fill a trunk. From his first letter—and my enthusiastic response—there has burgeoned a kinship of great value. I do not deserve all the accolades he has bestowed upon me in his column "The Sound Track" (*Films in Review*), but I accept them with humility and thanks. He has never called a spade anything but a spade!

Ken Darby
Sherman Oaks, CA

Editor's Note: During the final stages of production of this book, Scarecrow Press received the sad news that Ken Darby had died on January 24, 1992. We would like to extend our appreciation to his assistant, Robin W. Holman, for compiling the index and completing the last details for the book to be published.

PROLOGUE: ABOUT KEN DARBY

by Page Cook

One fine day early in 1958, Samuel Goldwyn sought the services of his old friend and former musical director, Alfred Newman[1] to supervise the scoring of Gershwin's *Porgy and Bess*. Newman had known and worked with Gershwin in the 1920s and had, in fact, directed George's last film score *The Goldwyn Follies*. Sam knew that Newman was a natural for *Porgy*. Newman, however, was overloaded by his duties as Musical Director of 20th Century-Fox and unhappily informed Goldwyn that he could not undertake the huge job. "But," he added, "if I *could* do it, I wouldn't—not without Ken Darby." Goldwyn assumed his classic posture, laying a finger on his nose and asking, "Who is this Ken Darby?" Darby was signed the next day, and again through Newman's recommendation, so was Andre Previn.

In 1958, despite Sam Goldwyn's ignorance, Ken Darby was already Hollywood's finest vocal/choral arranger/conductor, having won his first Academy Award in 1956 with Newman for *The King and I*.[2] He had appeared with his King's Men Quartet in many Westerns, had accompanied Bing Crosby in more than twenty Decca records with his Ken Darby Singers (including "White Christmas"), had been Walt Disney's favorite choral arranger, had been associated with some of the greatest films ever made, and was responsible for some of the most thrilling and innovative choral sounds to emanate from the silver screen. There had been fine vocal/choral arrangers in Hollywood. Bobby Tucker and Charles Henderson were two of the best, but Darby was clearly in a class by himself; not only was he an unsurpassed Kapellmeister who, according to Donald Bishop,

Jr., "brought the dimension of the human voice into film music with new and refreshing insight," he was also a top-flight lyricist, singer, and all-'round film musical marvel.

Kenneth Lorin Darby was born on May 13, 1909, in Hebron, Nebraska, to Lorin Edward Darby (1876–1959) and Clara Alice Powell (1884–1979). Lorin met Clara on a train. Clara had gone for a drink of water; the train gave a lurch and threw her into Lorin's lap. Ken's first recollections were of the time when he was four years old and Clara, sitting at an Ellington upright, played Chopin's *Military Polonnaise*. He loved it! Clara Powell was a graduate of music at Cotner College near Lincoln, Nebraska, and started teaching her son piano when he was five years old, Ken recalls, "and there was no way out." Clara had other pupils, and Ken took his turn with the rest. Clara never gave up her music. She became the organist at Veteran's Chapel in West Los Angeles and, after twenty-five years of service, retired on a pension but played every day in her apartment on a Thomas electric organ Ken gave her for her birthday. Ken had a deep bond of understanding and love with his mother. His father was an agile, gentle, ambidextrous and unambitious man—barber, butcher, carpenter, hotel manager, electrician, telegrapher, telephone linesman (he helped string the first copper wires between Cheyenne and Denver), ending his career by purchasing a grocery store in Ocean Park, California, in a poor neighborhood where people needed credit in order to eat. He was often heard to say, "We can always eat the stock." When Lorin was unable to help Ken with his pipe organ lessons, money was borrowed from a doctor friend and Lorin paid him back in groceries. He was a rare companion and taught Ken every handicraft he knew. "He never wanted very much for his family except a roof, clean clothes, a seat in church every Sunday, and enough to eat," Ken recalls. "You can't buy security," Lorin told him, "that comes from inside." It was a profound blessing to Ken that he was able to ease and comfort the declining years of his parents' lives with the apartment he built for them in Santa Monica.

When Ken was nine, Lorin presented him with a cornet. Practice doubled, and the piano lessons never faltered. When the family moved from Nebraska to California, Ken's teachers were multiple: John Hughes, first chair trumpet with the Los Angeles Philharmonic; Mae Nightingale, who taught him sight-singing, music appreciation, and vocal arranging—a woman of great dedication; Doris Moon, a pupil of the great Carolyn Alchin who wrote the book on *Applied Harmony* and taught him harmony, composition, and counterpoint in Santa Monica High School; Edgar Eugene Eben, pipe organist who opened Grauman's theaters, one by one, and who gave the last show for Ken to score on the enormous four-manual Kimball then at the Forum Theater in Los Angeles.[3]

After his graduation from Santa Monica High (for which he wrote the Alma Mater still in use today), Ken took a postgraduate course in advanced composition with Doris Moon, together with classes in Junior College.[4] He worked at a job in a gas station from 2 to 8 a.m., slept from 8:30 until 2 p.m., attended classes until 5, practiced till 9, played the pipe organ at the Forum Theater from 9:40 till closing, and on Sunday evenings, scored the silent flicks at the swank Uplifters Club[5] on an outdated Skinner organ. Ken recalls: "I'm not a little appalled by the effrontery of that skinny youth who dared match his improvisations to the films shown there. Such is the naive confidence of the young. It was heady stuff to be tolerated by those celebrities. They never complained, but they never increased my salary: $10.00 a film, no questions asked."

In 1928, Ken enrolled in California Christian College (now in Orange, California, and called Chapman College) with the tentative idea of entering the ministry. It was classes by day, the Forum Theater by night. Those long years of study on the trumpet, which had seen Ken soloing in every concert hall in Los Angeles, were gone—completely engulfed by the magnitude of the organ manuals under his hands. One night in 1929, as he was scoring a Greta Garbo film, a hand touched his back and a voice whispered, "Can you sing bass?" Ken caught an important cue, then turned and whispered back, "I don't know. I never tried."

When the curtains closed and he had played the theater empty, there were three of his college classmates sitting in the front row. They climbed over the rail, and the four rode down on the console elevator to the dressing rooms under the stage. Bud Linn said, "If you can sing bass and we can learn this song tonight, we've got a job in a picture at Paramount tomorrow." The four gathered around the piano. Ken rehearsed the parts, and made a couple of voice leading changes. They discovered they sounded good together and learned the song, "Sweeter Than Sweet." Next morning they appeared at Paramount, and The King's Men Quartet was born.[6]

The film was titled *Sweetie* and starred Nancy Carrol and Jack Oakie. The King's Men were photographed in the film, and Paramount liked them well enough to put them in *Only the Brave* with Mary Brian and Phillip Holmes. Then came *We're Not Dressing*, where Ken first met the great pianist, Ray Turner . . . and then, nothing. But it was too late to stop—they had savored the taste of fame, and it was good. Darby says, "After two semesters majoring in comparative religion, music, philosophy, psychology and drama, it seemed to me I could do better with music than I could by haranguing other poor sinners from a pulpit."

Ken began making arrangements, and they started rehearsing a growing repertoire until the chance came to make a couple of recordings with The Happy Chappies: "When the Bloom Is on the Sage" and "Make Your Mind Up to Wind Up in Sunny California." They were, Ken admits, "lousy", but they sold, and the group began singing for clubs, banquets, radio stations, in churches and Rotary meetings—"anywhere they'd feed us," Ken recalls.

Sound had come to films, and the pipe organ was quieted forever. In the summer of 1930, The King's Men Quartet was engaged for three plays written by John Steven McGroarty, then Poet Laureate of California. In "La Golondrina" they were swarthy Spaniards and sang convincingly in Spanish. In "Osceola" they were bewigged Indians; in "El Dorado" (which starred Handley Stafford of Baby Snooks fame) they were rough and tumble miners. The huge tent on the grounds of McGroarty's home in Tujunga was packed every night, and it was there that a famous radio personality of the day heard them and offered the quartet a permanent spot on his program, "The Bill Sharples Breakfast Club." There they became the Gold Medal Freight Quartet, and Clarence Muse was "Jackson" the chef, singing his brand new song "When It's Sleepy Time Down South." Sharples was a very slick sharpy: he sold his sponsor's contracts, at a discount for cash, to a gentleman who later became a U.S. Senator,[7] then spent the cash for cars, horses, women, whatever; when it came time to pay the cast, no money was forthcoming. The program sputtered and fizzled completely. But The King's Men had been heard, and they set their goal on Warner Brothers' radio station KFWB, from which the Boswell Sisters had graduated to the big time in New York. They made it. KFWB signed them at $30 per man per week—as sustaining artists; they became known as "Radio's Royal Quartet." They did everything: answered the phone, held the musicians' music, swept the visitors' foyer, and hung onto the microphones when an earthquake hit in 1932. Ken filled a filing cabinet with hundreds of arrangements, and the group gained in popularity, singing, and gaining a name.

Paul Whiteman heard them on a transcription they had recorded. He sent for them and gave them a five-year contract in 1934 at $100 a week each. Up to this point, Ken had been sharing equally with the other three boys; arrangements and accompaniment had been free. It remained so on the Whiteman program, but outside work expanded; as Ken started making arrangements for mixed groups, his arranging fees were added to his regular salary. These groups appeared with Lennie Hayton and Eleanor Powell on Mobil's *Flying Red Horse Tavern*, with *Burns and Allen* for White Owl Cigars, with Ed Wynn on the *Plymouth Program*, and as guests on the *Hit Parade* with Johnny Green and *Kraft Music Hall* with Bing Crosby. "I began to have that feeling of happy Nirvana that it would never end," Ken recalled. "But it did . . . Whiteman went on the road, and we went along with him, singing all over the country."

They spent the summer of 1936 in Fort Worth, Texas, at *Billy Rose's Centennial* extravaganza, broadcasting Whiteman's weekly program from a night club. It was there that Charlie Teagarden, brother of the famous trombonist, discovered that Ken could play trumpet, and the brass section wheedled an instrument from Vega. Ken became a utility man: first, second, and third "relief" trumpet! Then, when pianist Ramona left the band, Ken was asked to play second piano with Roy Bargy . . . without compensation. When Darby approached Whiteman about this, Paul said, "Read your contract." This so disturbed the quartet that when 1938 dawned, they decided they'd had it. Leaving their wives[8] in New York, they returned to California where newspaper headlines bannered "THE KING'S MEN ARE HOME." But Whiteman had beaten them to the punch, and their contracts with him were not only "for hire" but for "management" as well, a practice no longer legal in the United States. Paul sent letters to every studio, radio station, and club stating that any business done with The King's Men would have to be handled by the Whiteman Management Service. However, through the intercession of Whiteman's wife, Margaret, the quartet was given a release upon payment of certain commissions they had withheld.

Meanwhile, Darby had not been idle. The wives were sent for, new homes were found, and Ken began making arrangements for an assault on the studios. He put together an octette (adding four to The King's Men), recorded four fifteen-minute transcription programs (for peanuts), and started off with the transcriptions under his arm for an interview with Herbert Stothart at MGM. That's as far as he got. Stothart listened to *all* the discs, put Darby under contract that same day, and started him on Stothart's next project, later to become one of the greatest film musicals ever made: *The Wizard of Oz*. This is where Darby's career began as a vocal coach, arranger, and conductor of voices in films.

Among his other duties on *The Wizard of Oz*, Darby had to create the voices of the Munchkins. This required a bit of invention. Of 124 midgets, only about a dozen could sing. Today, with magnetic tape, all sorts of effects, such as the voices of "The Chipmunks," are possible, but in 1939 there was no way of achieving this effect in films. The recording machines were sprocket driven optical photographic soundtracks running at 90 feet per minute (fpm). Darby asked Doug Shearer, head of the sound department, to cut a gear that would reduce the speed to 60 fpm, one third slower. Guided by a piano track on earphones, forty mixed voices sang at this slower speed with concise articulation. When played at 90 fpm—behold, *The Munchkins*! Reversing the process (a gear to record at 110 fpm), and using all bass voices, the playback at 90 fpm produced *The Winkies*.

Since there was no such thing as a soundtrack album at the time, Victor Young then worked with Darby and his singers to recreate the songs from *Oz* for the first record "album" Decca ever made. The composer, Harold Arlen, sang the role of the Coroner! Jack Kapp, head of Decca, was Darby's champion. He used him and his singers with Bing Crosby, Danny Kaye, Loretta Young, Ronald Colman, Burl Ives, and for four albums by The King's Men alone. Between recordings, the quartet was in a couple of Jeanette MacDonald/Nelson Eddy films; in *Ice Follies of 1939*, with Jimmy Stewart and Joan Crawford (they skated and sang nursery rhymes); and in *Honolulu*, with Gracie Allen, they clowned a song as Chico, Harpo, and *two* Grouchos. Then came the most famous of their recordings with Bing Crosby: Irving Berlin's "White Christmas." This recording was made on a "gravity" machine, the engineer winding up a heavy weight below the turntable which, when released, spun the beeswax platter. Years later, when tape evolved, Kapp assembled the same group, with John Scott Trotter and Bing, to record it again exactly as before, obtaining a permanent master.

In 1940, after appearing on Rudy Vallee's *Sealtest Hour*, the *Fred Allen Show*, and the *Marx Brothers House*, The King's Men replaced Donald Novis on the *Fibber McGee and Molly* radio show for Johnson's Wax. It was strictly on a trial basis, but the engagement lasted almost fifteen years! In 1942, while working for Walt Disney, another big radio opportunity opened up when John Charles Thomas started his weekly broadcast for Westinghouse. Victor Young conducted a full symphony orchestra, Darby conducted a double octet of men, John Nesbitt told tales from his "Passing Parade," and John Charles sang. This program ended when World War II did.

Ken's association with Walt Disney lasted from 1941 to 1948, and in those years he wrote songs, coached singers, sang, arranged, and conducted units that became part of cartoon/live action feature-length films, including *Make Mine Music, Pinocchio, Dumbo, Fun and Fancy Free, Melody Time, Song of the South,* and *So Dear To My Heart*. During the summer months, Darby had his own radio broadcasts. One year it was "Top of the Evening," for which he initiated the use of an echo chamber for the solo voice of Sally Sweetland backed by sixteen men and two pianos. Jerome Kern heard the broadcast one night and rushed straight to the studio. "You've been keeping big secrets," he told Darby. "You have created a marvelous new musical sound."

Another replacement show was "King For a Night," on which Darby was M.C. and sang with the quartet, each program featuring such guests as Dan Dailey, Dorothy Kirsten, Hoagy Carmichael, Johnny Mercer, Jo Stafford, Bob Crosby, and Burl Ives.

The appetite of the King's Men's for being "on screen" had been whetted when they appeared in the mammoth Berlin extravaganza *Alexander's Ragtime Band* (1938), with a score supervised and conducted by Alfred Newman—already recognized as the most exciting and brilliant music director in Hollywood. But their big break as actors came through another film music pioneer of the day. Victor Young recommended the group to Harry "Pop" Sherman, whose pet package at Paramount was producing the Hopalong Cassidy series starring William Boyd. "Vic Young did most of the scores," Ken notes, "quick and easy," and the King's Men became Hoppy's pals, singing around campfires, in bar rooms, and at the end of the trail, sandwiching in some pretty good cowboy songs. They did their own riding among the Alabama foothills near Mount Whitney at Lone Pine, and for the most part, were "good guys." However, in one film, they were cast as singing outlaws; when a barroom piano presented a sour note, Ken raised the front and Rad put a bullet into the offending hammer. This excursion into the hills with horses, guns, and "all the twang of the early West" lasted through twelve films with Boyd . . . and then came the draft. They were all classified 1A, but were deferred because of families . . . all except Rad, who as yet had no children. He was inducted into the Special Services group at San Diego, but was allowed some freedom to join The King's Men when they toured the many training camps with Fibber and Molly or were called to join the stars of *Command Performance* often conducted by their good friend and supporter, Meredith Willson.

In 1948, Ken was sitting at his desk putting the finishing touches to Walt Disney's *Johnny Appleseed* when the telephone rang. It was Alfred Newman calling from 20th Century-Fox, asking for an interview. Ken took this news to Walt who said, "This may be a big opportunity for you. Go for it."

Newman offered Darby a contract at 20th for seven years with options; it called for a minimum of $26,000 for the first year with appropriate increases thereafter. Darby remained at 20th for eleven years, and this is precisely where his talents and unique gifts flowered in association with Alfred Newman. They continued the collaboration for another eleven freelance years, creating some of the finest scores and adaptations for the screen. "Darby's twenty-two year association with Newman," wrote Donald Bishop, Jr., "was cause for celebration."[9] Darby himself has written: "Those years tied together many great moments, both in the work I had been given to do, and the friendship of a man whose generosity, talent, and creative critical faculties surpass any I will ever know. Quite unexpectedly, my name appeared with Alfred's on the title card of *Carousel* in 1956 as 'Associate Musical Supervisor.' I hadn't asked for it, no agent had badgered anyone to put it there; Alfred had quietly taken the matter up with Zanuck and put through the credit strictly on his own . . . and it threw me. I made a remark in front of the assembled crew, director, producers, that this kind of generosity was unique in the film industry and could only have come from one man! Alfred overheard me and mumbled, 'The hell with that! Nobody gets credit they haven't earned!' And that was that."

One of Darby's earliest collaborations with Newman was the rollicking sea chanty for *Down to the Sea in Ships* (with Lionel Barrymore and the young Richard Widmark), which can be heard today in a fairly new recording by the National Philharmonic Orchestra and Ambrosian Singers ably conducted by Fred Steiner.[10] It gives a fine accounting of one of the earliest Newman/Darby efforts. (The song is "Old Father Briny.")

In the 1950s Darby worked on virtually all of 20th Century-Fox's biggest and brightest musicals, working closely with such stars as Betty Grable (*My Blue Heaven*), Marilyn Monroe (*Gentlemen Prefer Blondes, River of No Return, There's No Business Like Show Business*), Elvis Presley (*Love Me Tender*), and Jane Russell (*The Tall Men*). Darby also worked with non-musical performers required to sing in non-musicals, *e.g.,* Joanne Woodward, Richard Burton, Cameron Mitchell, and Humphrey Bogart.[11]

Some of Ken's recollections and comments about these and others are quite revealing. On Elvis and *Love Me Tender*, for which he co-wrote the score under a pseudonym[12]: "Teaching him a song is all you do when coaching. He learns by listening, and he has an ear like a ten-ton magnet. Then, when he knows the song well, he records with everything he's got. And that's a lot! And with all his fame he's a total gentleman."

On Joanne Woodward and *The Three Faces of Eve*: "Joanne Woodward is a most startling person to work with; she affects the senses like an euphoric drug. I found myself racing to the studio just to be in the same general location where she was having wardrobe fittings, makeup tests and publicity interviews. It was nothing like infatuation, although I adored her and still do. It was more of a mesmeric delight in watching her moods, her sparkling asides, her intensities as she studied with me the kind of person she would be when she slipped into the character of the dancing, singing extrovert. She was shy at first when using her singing voice, but not for long. She learned quickly, and with the growth of confidence came steadiness of vocal ability. After two weeks she was singing too well, and we had to back up not to destroy the 'housewife' simplicity. She recorded easily, and our tracks proved to be exactly what Nunnally Johnson, our director, wanted. I believe this period in Joanne's life was the most expressive, and her Academy Award for *The Three Faces of Eve* was justly given."

On Marilyn Monroe: "She recorded all of her songs with earphones to an already recorded orchestra track *except* 'That Old Black Magic' in *Bus Stop*. She did that live on the set! But for the rest, it was line by line, note by note, phrase by phrase, then editing all the 'right' phrases into a whole. But when she was great, she was fantastic." On Fabian in *Hound Dog Man*: "Very shy, insecure, a terrific young man filled with sad wonderment that he should find himself in front of a microphone. I styled and recorded one of his ballads, then put my voice on his headphone to help guide him through 'This Friendly, Friendly World,' and he got the hang of it quickly, staying in tune and maintaining freedom."

On Mitzi Gaynor: "Like lightning! She loves to rehearse and wrings the last ounce out of a song. She grabs a lyric like a lover and goes to work on it with devotion. Wonderful to work with, an energetic powerhouse of vivid histrionics. I flatly condemn the singer who chews, swallows, gargles, and destroys the words of a song. You can hum to a baby, or to yourself, but the essential quality of a song, whether by one voice or two thousand, is to bring to the ears of the listener the composer/lyricist's message. Mitzi never left anyone in doubt; she was the soul of articulation."

Alfred Newman supervised and conducted the scores of five Rodgers and Hammerstein film musical adaptations.[13] His sensitive expertise and understanding of all the dramatic values gave well-known songs new life, making them appear fresher and more invigorating after countless hearings had dulled them before. Darby's work on these musicals was no small part of this understanding. His choral effects for "Bali H'ai" in *South Pacific* are among the most haunted and haunting sounds ever created for films. The magnificent choral/orchestral welter provided a perfect synesthesia of sight and sound. Very often Alfred and Ken produced in inspired esprit and style that buoyed lesser scores, e.g., their joyous scoring of the 1961 Ross Hunter filmization of *Flower Drum Song*, which transforms a score by Rodgers and Hammerstein with limited appeal into a cornucopia of delights not found on the original cast recording in any form.

It was Darby's collaboration with Newman on the dramatic scores of some of 20th's biggest and most important films that added stature and impetus to both his career and the medium. On *The Robe*,[14] the first feature in CinemaScope and Stereophonic sound: "We were in unexplored territory, every recording was an experiment. Experts came from New York, Paris, and London, with all kinds of directional microphones, and all kinds of ideas on where to place them. Alfred's analytical mind foresaw some of the difficulties, and he persuaded the experts—after they had performed exhaustive unsatisfactory tests—to allow him to discard directional microphones and to place *nondirectional* microphones: extreme left mike over the violins; left-center over more violins including the concert master; center mike moved in and over the woodwinds in front of his podium; right center adjacent to the celli, and extreme right mike covering violas and basses. Percussion and brass were not miked at all, but picked up on the same microphones and recorded in their proper perspectives.

"Listening to Alfred's recording, the dumbfounded experts had to admit his concept was superior (as an ace to a deuce) to their own. Vocal and choral effects were highly successful in this film, with the voices sometimes near the woodwinds, completely meshed into the orchestral fabric. Other scenes were recorded after the orchestra tracks, and it was up to me to wear special headphones and 'chase' the music Alfred had previously recorded."

The score for *The Robe* is one of the greatest scores Alfred composed, and that's saying a lot. It is a standard tool for the study of film scoring in more than one university. Dennis Mann-Riley cited it as "a milestone in film music," and the re-recorded monaural album was one of the first best-sellers in days when film music on records was considered a non-commercial venture. Other masterly Darby choral dimensions imparted real breadth to such scores as *The Egyptian*, with Newman and Bernard Herrmann, *Anastasia, Desiree, An Affair to Remember, Rancho Notorious*, and, later, *How the West Was Won* and *Elmer Gantry*. Who could forget Burt Lancaster singing "I'm on My Way" with the black congregation in a typical Darby exultation? It was Ken's first and only work at Columbia Pictures, and he shared Associate Credit with Andre Previn. "That's when I became utterly beguiled by the beautiful Jean Simmons," Ken admits, "and my congregations fortunately kept me on the sets where I could see her daily."

Darby once noted that the terms "Choral Supervisor" and "Associate Musical Supervisor" implied little to the layman.

"Aside from waving my arms in front of a group of singers, just what is my job? In a 'Musical' that's not hard to identify: there's a lot of singing, dancing, solos, combos, trios yammering, and everybody knows it's my job to write out the notes and get the cast to yammer harmonically together. But in a dramatic film, it's a songbird of a different warble.

"Here's an example: In *David and Bathsheba*, we see a man touch the Ark of the Covenant—and fall down dead. Now comes the scene where David (Gregory Peck) stands before the Ark, stricken by guilt at having taken the wife of another man whose death he has machinated. We *know* David is going to put his hands on the Ark, and there are only a few minutes left before the film reaches its climactic conclusion. How does a choral supervisor figure in such a scene?

"In this case, Alfred and I huddled together and decided it would have to be a 'classic' adaptation of David's own work, and we picked the 23rd Psalm because it had all the elements of a dramatic scene that would lift the picture, and hopefully the audience, to a thrilling ending.

"Alfred never felt comfortable when trying to set music to an author's words. He always wrote a melody, and a lyricist would battle to fit words to it. He backed away from 'setting' the 23rd Psalm, and suggested a collaborative solution. He asked me to write a 'dummy' model on manuscript paper, a map setting a singable 'pattern' of notes, accents, expression dynamics, bar lines, and tempo guides. When I had finished this, he pored over it for about two hours and came up with a haunting mode-enhanced melody for me to harmonize as I saw fit.

"Right away I wanted to start it in unison without accompaniment, using a chorus of mixed voices. He agreed, but suggested that an accompaniment in low woodwinds and strings enter on the line 'Thou preparest a table before me,' etc., in preparation for what would grow into the End Title. After a little thought, I said, "Is there enough in the budget to hire eight of the best classic baritones in town to stand still and do nothing until the words 'Surely goodness and mercy shall follow me all the days of my life' and on to the end, bolstering the melody while the chorus gets up in the stratosphere?"

"Do it," he said, "it's a powerful idea."

"The voices were cast from my beloved first-call singers, then my vocal contractor found eight legitimate opera baritones. I rehearsed them for four hours, quieted my goose bumps with a light lunch, and went on the stage with the orchestra, which was set up in its usual position beneath the projection screen at the south end of the studio. My chorus was on risers at the other end of the stage with our own microphones. We took our pitch from the orchestra and I relayed the a cappella portion to Pap, holding my breath that we'd be on key when the accompaniment joined us (we were, thank heaven), then he relayed his beat to me and we synchronized perfectly. Those are great moments for a Choral Supervisor, no matter what you call him."

By 1959, 20th Century-Fox was on the list of endangered species. Zanuck was gone, Buddy Adler (Zanuck's replacement) was ill and would die in June, 1960. The music department had been totally dissolved and television had fixed its gluttonous electronic eye on the entire movie industry. Mr. Skouras put all but the southeast corner of the huge 20th lot up for sale, to become Century City! While Ken was doing *Elmer Gantry* at Columbia, Alfred was doing *The Diary of Anne Frank* with George Stevens in what was left of the 20th lot. They would rejoin forces again at Universal and never be separated after that.

Darby won his third Academy Award (Alfred's ninth) for *Camelot* at Warner Brothers in 1968, one of the longest and most arduous tasks either man had ever faced. Josh Logan explained an astonishing approach: "We will record all the songs *live*, that is, in front of the camera. I want no pre-recorded playbacks, and no lip synchronization. *Spontaneity* is the key word."

Alfred and Ken protested that this method of recording had been junked in the early 1930s; it made editing impossible, and keeping an orchestra on the set prohibitively expensive. To use an off-camera piano for accompaniment would prevent ever removing the "piano" sound from the vocal tracks, and the noise inherent in *any* sound stage or outdoor set would be a permanent part of the recordings. Josh said, "You figure it out, that's why I insisted on having you!"

Vanessa Redgrave as Guenevere was a non-singer (although she might be inclined to argue the point); Richard Harris was afraid of nothing, including singing, and he worked hard at the exercises Ken made him practice—"the most eagerly teachable person I ever coached," Darby said, "but Franco Nero, who played Lancelot, was no songbird, and I was extremely fortunate to find Gene Merlino to dub Franco's voice. Not only was Gene of Italian extraction and bilingual, but his name was a good omen: MERLIN-O, and I had the uncanny feeling that the old sorcerer Merlin was looking over my shoulder.

"In order for the singers to have something to listen to on the set while they were recording 'Live,' each song was rehearsed and orchestrated. We'd spend as much as eight hours on one complex song, Vanessa in the vocal booth, or Richard, or both, as the music might demand. Styling, interpretation, expression, rubato passages, accelerandos, all were meticulously worked out and recorded by the orchestra and voices. Then, when Josh, Vanessa, Richard, Alan Jay Lerner, the recording engineer (Dan Wallin), Alfred and I reached an agreement (this was the tough part since there seemed to be no chairman of the committee) we printed the orchestra track only, tossing the vocal tracks into the vault. On the set, I used a directional loudspeaker, pointing straight at the performer. The cameras would turn and Josh would yell, 'Music!' and the orchestra would blast from the loudspeaker. If it was too soft, Vanessa couldn't hear the accompaniment and wandered dreadfully off key. If it was loud enough for her to hear it, her microphone picked it up and buried her voice. After the first day, even Logan realized that we could never get a good vocal performance on the set, so I turned up the volume, let the singers hear the orchestra, and we picked up enough of the voice to hear words.

"This meant bringing all the actors, except Franco (who impeccably synchronized to Gene's playback), into the studio *after* the film was shot, cut, and edited, setting them in front of a screen in an isolation booth, earphones clamped to their heads, and making them synchronize their lips to what they saw on the screen, guided again only by the orchestra track. We did this by sections called loops. Each loop consisted of four to eight bars, then repeated itself after an interval of silence. Each time the loop came around, the performer would sing the phrase. It was my job to listen for intonation, diction and performance as well as the all-important synchronization of lips to picture. The total for Vanessa was 135 takes to complete one song. But Harris should have made the Guinness Book of World Records by going to 173! In the middle of this unnecessary torture, I called Logan to the looping room. After he witnessed a half hour of this, I turned to him and said, my voice drooling carbolic acid: "*There*, Josh is your goddam spontaneity!" He walked out. It took a month to finish looping.

"Those were the rigors; the pleasures were many. I made two trips to England during the preparation period to work with Vanessa, and location trips to Madrid, Toledo, Segovia, and many castles in Spain. Far more than in any other collaboration with Alfred Newman, I was able to assist him in adapting his music for the postscore, notably in Merlin's magic forest and the desperate dance following 'What Do the Simple Folk Do?' "

While *Camelot* was in the editing stages, Darby was assigned the preparation of *Finian's Rainbow*, with Fred Astaire, Petula Clark, Don Francks, Keenan Wynn, Al Freeman, Jr., Barbara Hancock, and Tommy Steele. "Neither the producer (Joseph

Landon) nor the director (Francis Ford Coppola) had ever made a musical before, so they leaned heavily on Ray Heindorf and me. Oddly, it was given as a play in a live performance in one of Warner Brothers' big bungalows on the back lot, witnessed by a select audience, before a camera was unpacked. Fred Astaire was, as always, delightful and charming, singing with his usual flair and elegance. Petula Clark was so easy to work with that I felt ashamed to take my salary. Don Francks was alert and willing to try anything, and did. My 'Rainbow Valley' inhabitants were a successful and cooperative blend of black and white. Tommy Steele took the bit in his teeth a couple of times, but we went on the principle that a leprechaun could do no wrong even when mistaken. I was able to assume duties on the set only when playbacks were involved, being batted about like a shuttlecock from *Finian's* to *Camelot*, to Alfred's home assisting him with a 'sandwiched' score for *Firecreek*, the Jimmy Stewart/Henry Fonda western. But *Finian* remained my principal interest; I had had the pleasure of working with Fred Astaire on *Daddy Long Legs*, and I treasured his friendship and the moments we shared making this zany musical fantasy."

Finian's Rainbow was Darby's last film, and he received, for the first time in his entire career, his own title card. A more well-earned credit has rarely been seen on the screen; Darby infused new life and verve into the great Lane/Harburg score, which was superbly adapted and conducted by Ray Heindorf.

Since retiring, Darby has been active. He established the Alfred Newman Memorial Library at USC; Little, Brown published his tidy investigations into Rex Stout's domain, *The Brownstone House of Nero Wolfe*; he has written two biographies: one on John Charles Thomas, one on Charley Weaver "Cliff Arquette" (both unpublished); but the most ambitious task has been assembling Newman's scores from *The Robe* and *The Greatest Story Every Told* into a symphonic cantata entitled *Man of Galilee*. It was given its world premiere at Brigham Young University on October 1, 1987, and is now published by Bourne Co. Music Publishers, both in symphonic form and in a simpler edition for standard choirs.

In the nearly thirty years I have known Ken Darby, I've been fascinated by his memory for detail, his ready but rarely injuriously cutting wit, and his abilities as a storyteller. We have never met, yet he has been a surrogate father, avuncular confidant, and anxious believer in my writings. His work among the giant directors and film musicians—Hugo Friedhofer, Bernard Herrmann, Alex North, Miklos Rozsa, Herbert Stothart, Franz Waxman, Andre Previn, and especially Alfred Newman—has left him humbly thankful that he lived in their time. His correspondence with me has been voluminous, and I am forever grateful to have gleaned something of the wisdom, sensitivity, and humor with which he has faced his life, his art . . . and the world.

Note: Page Cook is the author of "The Sound Track," an important feature in *Films In Review*, published by the National Board of Review of Motion Pictures, Inc., P.O. Box 589, Lenox Hill Station, New York, NY 10021.

NOTES

1. Newman had composed memorable scores for Goldwyn's *Street Scene, Dead End, The Hurricane, Stella Dallas, These Three, Dodsworth,* and *Wuthering Heights*, among many others.
2. He was to win Oscars for *Porgy and Bess* and *Camelot*, with nominations for *South Pacific, Flower Drum Song* and *How the West Was Won*.
3. Ken returned to the Forum twenty-five years later with Alfred Newman to view the rough cut of *How the West Was Won*. The theater had been taken over by Cinerama as a dubbing room.
4. English literature, composition, musical history.
5. The "in" place in the 1920s frequented by Will Rogers, Snowy Baker, the young Darryl Zanuck, Douglas Fairbanks, Mary Pickford, Bebe Daniels, Norma Shearer, Matt Moore—the "Polo" crowd. The club remains today as a public park with tennis courts.
6. Jon Dodson (Dodson Blunt) was lead tenor, son of Reverend J. Blunt, minister of the First Christian Church of Ocean Park. Born in Joplin, Missouri, he was the eldest of The King's Men; shy, diffident, the clothes horse of the group, he had the most captivating singing voice and wrote many beautiful songs in the folk idiom. He died of acute alcoholism Thanksgiving Day, 1963. Grafton (Bud) Linn, top tenor, was a sociology major from Indianapolis, Indiana, with a tremendous singing range, to high F above high C. He returned to his sociological career with the YMCA after The King's Men ended theirs, and died suddenly of a heart attack in July 1968. Radburn

(Rad) Robinson was born in Bountiful, Utah, son of a bishop in the Mormon Church of the Latter Day Saints. He was the baritone of the group and had aspirations toward opera. Following several years with the Summa Corporation in Las Vegas as talent coordinator, he joined Tibor Rudas and the Resorts International team, promoting concerts by Pavarotti. His death in September, 1987, left Ken the sole survivor.

7. Senator Kramer.

8. Vera Matson was born in Ohiowa, Nebraska, and married Ken in 1932. Dorothy Woodbury was born in Hollywood, California, and wed Bud Linn in 1932; Tensie Hatch was born in Ogden, Utah, and wed Rad Robinson in New York in 1934. Jon Dodson didn't marry until 1941. Each couple became parents: three daughters for Linn, a son and a daughter each for Darby, Robinson, and Dodson.

9. Music Heritage, Vol. XVII, 1974.

10. Entr'acte lp; Preamble cd.

11. Burton in *Prince of Players*, Bogart in *The Left Hand of God*.

12. Vera A. Matson, his wife's maiden name.

13. *Carousel, The King and I, South Pacific, State Fair*, and *Flower Drum Song*.

14. Because of deadline release pressures, the credits of *The Robe* omitted both Ken's name and Emile Santiago's, who went on to win an Oscar for costume design. Producer Frank Ross explained that it was impossible to remake all the main titles but took out ads in all the trade papers, apologizing to both Ken and Emile, and promising that Ken's name would figure prominently on the Decca Records album of the score (DL 9012). Darby was often uncredited for some of his best work, *e.g.*, the finale of *Love Is a Many-Splendored Thing*, but it is to his credit that he was never vocal about it (no pun intended).

BOOK ONE

ONE

The alarm crowed savagely, hawking 1962's sole edition of Wednesday, November 17. My arm flailed out and slammed it silent. One eye peered off into the vast panorama of sky and hills that is always at my bedside. The valley wore a thin belt of mist through which the San Gabriel Mountains arched cold backs to touch pale yellow sunlight. Below, the sheen of countless windshields marked the creeping migration of Sepulveda Boulevard's monstrous commuter traffic jam. For a few moments I watched its spastic inchworm progress, then I stripped off the blankets, ouched on stiff ankles, and went trotting down the hall to the thermostat.

The hot shower stung my back, and I felt my body come fully awake. It was a good body—not too rugged or handsome—but still vigorous and lithe after fifty years. With care, I reflected as I toweled it down, it might be coaxed through a couple of dozen more—perhaps the most important years of my life. Up to now I had used that life as though it was just a practice run. There had been this silly notion in the back of my giddy optimistic mind that I would get a second time around; that one of these days I'd simply turn back twenty or thirty years, as I would the pages in a book, and start doing the important things I had intended to accomplish in the first place. Not so, knucklehead! All those pages are permanently stuck together in the past, and here you are—over the hill—already holding the short end of life's shtick.* Better, I thought as I shaved, that I should focus upon doing something at least remarkable with my remaining days, be they eleven or eleven thousand. There were books to write and

---

*See Glossary for technical terms and show-business vernacular.

music to compose and games to invent and antigravity to discover. . . .

"Do you want your coffee in there, or out here?"

. . . and there was my wife to unravel and Europe to see and museums to explore and art to appreciate. . . .

"It's nearly seven. Will you have time for eggs?"

. . . and chicken fat to avoid. "I'll just have coffee and toast," I called, "out there". . . perhaps I could convince the citizenry that the IRS would some day be employing half of the U.S. population to confiscate the property of the other half—or I might find a substitute for fossil fuel, or a way to depollute the sea, or prove that Prejudice and Bigotry were more deadly than any H-bomb, or poke a camera into the future and take photos of the morons our kids would become after being addicted by the boob tube to its idiotic commercial jingles—all seeing alike, smelling alike, thinking alike, totally voyeuristic, ready to commit any noxious act to get their lookalike faces in front of a TV camera. Or maybe I should just splash on some after-shave lotion and get a move on.

The coffee was right, the toast and jam landed gently. As I brushed my teeth I suddenly realized that I was almost the perfect target for my own crusades. My toothpaste would give me 21 percent fewer cavities, my slacks and jacket were woven out of Madison Avenue platitudes, my tie was nationally advertised, I carried the right luggage, pen, antacid, credit cards, and a partridge in a pear tree!

"Let's go," I said, and followed my wife through our split-level home to the three-car garage, loaded my bags into the status symbol of all time—a black Continental—glanced at the silver Fury alongside and said guiltily, "Maybe you can have the dent in that fender repaired while I'm gone . . . and don't forget to deposit those royalty checks."

Then I gave myself and my phony noble thoughts a mental razzberry.

We rolled into the Burbank airport at seven-forty. I kissed Vera, told her I would telephone on arrival, and watched as she slid under the wheel.

"I'm going to miss you," she said.

"I'll miss you, too. Don't let the kids get you down, and call me any time you need to get them off your chest."

The shiny black beauty pulled away from the curb. I stood for a moment watching it muscle aside a taxi, then picked up my bags and walked briskly into the terminal. Les Warner was waiting for me at a desk conspicuously identified as GEORGE STEVENS PRODUCTIONS.

He shoved papers at me, saying, "A necessary formality, Ken. According to Mr. Davis, you'll only be in Utah for a couple of days, but everybody on this project has to be insured."

I signed the forms, wincing as I thought how blank would be my future pages should this particular airplane tumble out of the sky. "This particular airplane" turned out to be an old DC-3, and Frank O'Neill was the only other passenger.

"I'm a film editor," he announced as we boarded. "Harold Kress sent for me to assist him—good thing, too—I'm down to my last bread; had no work for months. Do you know Harold?"

I nodded. "We're working on the same picture right now."

"Hey! Then you must be doing *How the West Was Won.* I hope you'll pardon my ignorance, but in what capacity?"

"Music. Composing, lyricist, choral director. I'm working in collaboration with Alfred Newman. We'll be scoring the film next year. We like Harold very much. He's a great editor."

"Are you and Newman doing the music on *this* picture?"

"It will be Alfred's score. I'll do the vocal chores and the coordinating." I found a seat and fastened my safety belt. Frank gave me a funny look and started to giggle.

"You're gonna make a *musical* out of the life of Christ?"

"Don't laugh. Somebody will do just that some day."

The engines coughed and roared into sibling argument, cutting off further talk. I looked around. Two stewardesses were on board, one with an incipient case of flu if I ever saw one, red-eyed and runny-nosed; the other was a blond with a face sharp enough to cut wood.

"Your seat belt fastened?" she screamed. I nodded.

We lifted off at five minutes after eight. San Gorgonio Pass was packed with winter fleece and we flew slightly over it at eighty-five hundred feet, bouncing a little, but not anything like the battering I had experienced before in that turbulent and windy gulch.

Frank began yelling at me from across the aisle—how he had left Dick Powell's Four Star Theatre to join the staff of "Peni-

tentiary Fox," only to have that ill-starred company fall out from
under him (or *on* him, I couldn't understand which).

"I made the wrong move at the worst possible time," he
shouted. "But I was sick of TV, and the stories were so rotten
they made me ill. I'm a writer too, y'know, and it just killed me
to see some of the shit they bought—when they wouldn't even
look at mine."

I shouted back, agreeing that the junk being broadcast on the
tube was one of my own pet peeves. Then I strained to hear
more of his personal history, how he had married late to a
woman with a child by a previous marriage and how fate had
compounded his problems by adding two children of their own.
I wondered after a while how much mileage he was good for.
My own voice was growing hoarse from yelling, "Yes; uh-huh;
is that so?" So I opened my briefcase and pulled out my small
Bible. "If you see me reading this for the rest of the flight, it is
not because I am a coward; I've got some research to do."

He goggled at me from behind round lenses, sighed with
disgust, and picked up a newspaper. I turned to the Book of
Luke and read the entire Gospel while the time and the miles
slipped by. All the old familiar phrases were as fresh and beautiful as they had always been through the years.

"That's a helluva sight, isn't it?" Frank bellowed.

I looked out. Deep broken terrain lay below—the huge,
fiercely eroded walls of the Grand Canyon.

"Fasten your seat belts," shrieked the blond, "it may be
rough."

And then we were settling below the mesa tops, jerky and
unsteady in the uncertain air, descending lower and lower to
make a smooth circle above long curving lines of metal houses—
arranged in rows—like giant parentheses glittering on the desert floor. The engines softened their voices as we glided over
the square-topped crenelations of the burgeoning Glen Canyon
Dam, and a tire squealed as we touched down on the asphalt
strip of Page, Arizona.

"Ten forty-five," I said.

"Correction," said the blond. "*Eleven* forty-five. We're on
Mountain Time here."

I stood up, tapped the feverish girl on the shoulder, and said,
"You take care of yourself."

She was testy. "Take care of your own self, friend. This location is known as Gonad Gully. When the Assistant Director begins to look like Gina Lollobrigida to you—or vice versa— you take the next flight *out!*"

Thick red mud clung to the tires of the station wagon. Harold Kress was just climbing out of it wearing heavy boots, corduroy pants, fleece-lined jacket, and a big smile.

"Welcome to Muddy Mesa," he quipped. "It rained all night, and every road to the set is washed out this morning, so there'll be no shooting today. How was the flight?"

We all shook hands and Frank started a hop-skip-and-jump prattle about airplanes, Hollywood studios, Arizona mud, and station wagons, but when he got to his family problems Harold headed him off and became our tour guide.

"This bridge is the highest single span in America. Once across it we're in Utah. Down below on the right is the dam. When it's finished, our entire location will be under the water of Lake Powell. That dome of rock up ahead has been sacred to the Indians for generations. Look at it now—dynamited and sliced in half. The Navajos say bad spirits were locked inside; now that it's been cracked in two, those evil spirits are free and will take destructive revenge on the white man."

"It's about time," I said.

Frank gave me a sour look. Harold went on. "There's the haul road. It goes from the gravel crusher, in a straight line, to the concrete mixers—about seven miles. The trucks wind up to eighty-five, full or empty, back and forth, twenty-four hours a day. And when the wind is right, they sound like they're coming right through the middle of our camp. That little grouping of shacks is called Wahweep. Over there, by that far red butte, you can make out our set of the walls of Jerusalem. Hang on, now."

He negotiated a tight turn in the road, guided the wagon through a small river of mud, and up to the top of a wet hillock beyond. Ahead was the location camp, and Harold was grinning at our surprise. "Impressive, isn't it? Welcome to Galvanized Galilee. Ken, you have a bungalow somewhere—I don't know which one—and Frank, you'll bunk with three technicians. That house trailer is the Production Office, and my new cutting room is here." He swung the car to a skidding halt beside a partly completed frame structure. "Just leave your bags in the wagon till you check in at Operations."

The sun was warm, and I wondered why I'd bought four hundred dollars worth of woolens. Frank walked on ahead with Harold; I shucked my jacket and checked in with Lee Lukather, and within twenty minutes I had met twenty old friends from Hollywood, transplanted here in the middle of Stevens' Holyland, friends I had worked with on *Carousel, The King and I, South Pacific, Porgy and Bess,* and *Flower Drum Song.* They were glad to see me, and in that few minutes I began to feel at home.

Harold and I ate a box lunch together in a huge circus tent filled with rows and rows of long tables covered with oilcloth, with benches for seats, and area heaters hanging from the big top to warm the air. Harold apologized for the fare.

"Tonight will be different. We've got a great chef, and the coffee is always good."

After lunch, Jack Lacey, the host of Tin City, escorted me and my luggage in his electric mini-truck to cabin C-3.

"I got a hundred and seventeen of these shanties to look after," he grumbled. "Four hundred and fifty honest-to-god residents, and only He knows how many poaching extras from Hollywood, or how many whores of one sex or another smuggled in from Page. You got it lucky. Michael Ansara left for L.A. this morning so you're by yourself—except on weekends. On Saturday and Sunday you'll have to share it with Professor Dan Vandraegen, our speech coach. Here's your key. If you need anything, just holler."

I moved in, hung up my clothes, checked the windows, picked up my camera, and stepped out into blazing sunshine. Carpenters were swarming over Harold's new cutting room; young men with beards were playing touch football in the "town square" around the flagpole. I toured the area, acquainting myself with the main office, the make-up tent, the leach field with its faint but unmistakable odor, the haul road and its rifling trucks, the buttes across the canyon, and the French jet helicopter sleeping on its pad. I met Mary, Stevens' secretary, and Tony Perris, youthful sergeant-at-arms-messenger boy, and then—because of an abrupt weariness—I walked back to the cabin, lay down on a butt-sprung bed, and fell into a doze.

Hazily, I was behind the camera with Stevens, watching as Jesus climbed into a boat at the edge of the lake of Galilee, and suddenly I was saying, "I'm sorry, George, but that's not the way it was done."

"And just how *was* it done?" he asked. I took him by the hand and led him to the water's edge. "Like this," I said, and walked out on the water a few steps. "Of course," he said, and went straight to the boat, walking on the water.

It was dark in the room and my feet were cold. I lit the wall furnace and turned up the flame. The sun's departure had dropped a cold curtain. Thankful now that I had brought them, I changed into my wools, lit a pipe, and started down the path between the bungalows.

Coming out of the theater next to Harold's cutting room was George Stevens with a group of company technicians. He glanced at me perfunctorily, without expression, and moved on. Harold left the group and joined me.

"He didn't see me," I said, "or he looked right through me."

"He does that to everybody," Harold muttered. "It makes you feel transparent and expendable—if you let it."

"Maybe he doesn't know I'm here."

"Oh yes he does. I told him you had arrived with the tape recordings you and Al made at the studio last week. He just nodded and said he was too busy to hear them, but would have Tony Vellani schedule a meeting in a couple of days."

"I'm only supposed to *be* here a couple of days," I said.

At that moment, Saul Wurtzel—a friend for many years and a topflight assistant director—joined us and said, "Multiply that by ten, Darby. And let's get the hell in out of the cold."

It was three steps to the cabin he and Harold shared. Inside, Harold poured Scotch. Saul was overburdened, and he let go. "Stevens isn't Preminger or Hathaway. George doesn't yell or get red in the face or make people weep. He just very quietly and methodically skins your ego down to the bare bones. That kind of a wound rarely heals without leaving a scar."

Harold nodded. "He tried that on me the first day here. I ran the daily rushes with him after I had cut them together on my Moviola. He stopped projection almost immediately and told me I was *never* to edit any film he shot—that *he* would edit the entire picture—and when I asked him what he needed *me* for he said, 'I really don't know!' I got so upset that I didn't speak to him for three days. I spent day before yesterday out on the set with him and we never exchanged word one. Last night I wrote a note to him. In it I said, 'If you need me, send for me. I'm remaining in camp to supervise the completion of my cutting room and to prepare the dailies.' He left a note in my post office box that night telling me I was *not* to prepare any dailies, and to leave the film alone."

Saul smacked his lips. "Typical. It's a technique he tries on everybody. He strips away all your self-esteem and confidence. Whatever you are an expert in, he makes you feel like a rank amateur. Once he knocks you down, he can be as benevolent as an angel, helping you back up, but in between he's a rough customer—all antagonism and attrition."

I ventured a comment. "Perhaps he's trying to rub off some of our Hollywood habits, expose a few nerves, and sensitize his people to new and fresh ideas, like Jimmy Valentine filing his fingertips before cracking a safe."

Saul snorted, spilling his drink. " You show me a man who can do his best work while his nerve ends are waving around in the breeze and I'll show you a masochistic, psychopathic sonof-abitch who should be written up in Krafft-Ebing* No, sir! I think Stevens has a God complex."

"Hi. Are you guys going to talk all night?" asked a voice from the doorway.

Harold said, "Ken Darby, meet Mary, our Mother Superior."

"We've met. Only she looks a lot better outside Stevens' office and away from her typewriter."

She grinned. "Let's all eat and drive into Page. The stores are open till nine-thirty, and if I don't get some shopping done a lot of people I know are going to find nothing but Navajo beads under their Christmas trees."

"How come?" I asked. "No time off for Christmas?"

"This company works a six-day week *every* week, with no time off for Thanksgiving, Yom Kippur, New Year's, *or* Christmas. You'd think Stevens would honor His Son's birthday." Saul downed the last of his Cutty Sark.

---

*Author of *Psychopathia Sexualis*.

"Signals over," Mary said. "While you've been out on the set, new word has come down from on high. We fly everybody home the morning of Christmas Eve, and fly them back to start shooting again on the day after Christmas."

Saul slammed his fist on the table. "Just what I needed. Another exercise in logistics. Oh well . . . let's eat."

The soup was hot and good, the salad was crisp and cold, the baked potato was mealy and delicious, but the veal was 100 percent Florsheim. I sent it back and got a medium rare New York steak plucked out of a gourmet's dream: tender, well-charred, and flavorful. On the other side of the table was a sharp-eyed, gluttonous gent lecturing the camera crew on "white-light" printing versus "standard development" of modern film, masticating furiously between sentences. He spoke with such intense authority that I guessed him to be Eliott Elisofon (which Harold confirmed), the man who had achieved the lovely Lautrec palette in the film *Moulin Rouge*, and now the color consultant on Stevens' payroll. He was so imbued with his subject, and his delivery was so fascinating, that I absent-mindedly consumed two slabs of blueberry pie à la mode before I discovered that Mary, Saul, and Harold had departed.

Having missed the ride into Page, I walked back alone across the compound to my shimmering bungalow, wrote a quick letter home, got into pajamas, visited the john, swallowed a sleeping pill, lowered the furnace, opened two windows, and folded myself into the cold sagging bed, thankful that I had put on an extra blanket.

Outside, the gravel trucks made their hissing crescendo-de-crescendo patterns in the night. Again . . . again . . . again. . . .

TWO

The persistent blatancy of the public address system dragged me from sleep. I tried to move, but the icy fingers of the sheets jerked me back into my prescribed orbit of warmth, and I realized how foolish I'd been to open *two* windows. Reaching up, I closed the louvres of both, yanked the body out of bed, and twisted the knob on the furnace. From the trio of fanned loudspeakers perched on top of a post in the compound I could hear—even over the stutter of the hot shower—that a Mr. Lukather was wanted in the office immediately, and that the shuttle bus to Page would leave in ten minutes. I had slept twelve hours.

Harold Kress and the camp projectionist, Charlie McCleod, were leaning on the rail outside the new cutting room gazing off to the northeast. Ominous clouds hung there trailing long plumes of rain, and, as I watched, a horizontal streak of lightning bolted westward over the flat mesa, twisted sharply back upon itself and hooked into the butte. Thunder grunted.

"KEN DARBY, ATTENTION. KEN DARBY, PLEASE COME TO OPERATIONS—"

Harold grinned at me and said, "Stevens is sending out messages by thunderbolt now, just like Zeus."

"Hasn't he always?" quipped Charlie.

The message waiting for me at Operations was from Tony Vellani, Stevens' associate producer, Bible expert, and story advisor. "Please be at rehearsal tent 2 p.m. to play Newman prerecorded tape for screening committee and to discuss other location recording projects." Suddenly, I felt uncomfortable. Location recording projects here in the desert had never been mentioned to me before, and I began to suspect that my mission of three or four days might turn out to be that many weeks.

I lunched with Harold, Charlie, and a man who until two days ago had been Stevens' assistant director—Ray Gosnell. Ray had been trounced and humiliated, demoted to what he now termed "assistant chief of confusion." He was unhappy.

"Oh, sure, I'm on the payroll, but I don't know what's going on and Stevens won't talk to me, and I don't know what I'm supposed to be doing. I'm just riding the plane back and forth from Page to L.A. every day; all I am is ballast!"

I invited him to the two-o'clock meeting but he demurred, muttering something about being a fifth wheel, and walked out.

"There's no skin on *his* ego left to heal," Harold said.

When I left the mess tent, wind was snapping the canvas and rudely chasing battalions of ragged clouds around the sky. I dashed to the cutting room, picked up the tapes, and barely had regained my shelter when the first volley of rain hit the metal roof. No fireworks, please, I prayed. Lightning could play these shacks like a giant vibraphone.

It poured, and abruptly the torrent became hail—tapioca at first, then marbles—slamming slantwise into our tin city with such a din that I began to feel like a small bug trapped inside a field drum on the way to battle. But then, out of the north, came a slashing scythe of wind, sweeping the downpour off to the south and buffeting me roughly across the compound to the meeting tent. Inside, Tony Vellani introduced me to Tony Van Renterghem, and it became obvious that these two Tonys comprised the "screening committee." Without any preamble, Vellani asked to hear the rebel chant Alfred and I had written for Barabbas; Van Renterghem operated the tape deck, and the chant was punctuated by blasts of wind.

> The Romans came across the sea
> To bring us peace, to set us free,
> And now we're free to be Roman slaves.
> The only Roman peace is in our graves!
> We do not want the Romans here
> To rule our lives with sword and spear,
> To tax the poor and make us bow the knee.
> Oh, send the Romans back across the sea!

Vellani pulled at his lip two or three times and said, "This kind of musical comedy material is more at home in *The Vagabond King* than in *The Greatest Story Ever Told*. I know Mr. Stevens asked for this song, but I'm not sure he's right."

Tony Perris came in just then, making the third Tony in the tent. I handed Van Renterghem the tape of the 136th Psalm, and its playing evoked an immediate reaction. Vellani got up and started pacing—whether from cold or enthusiasm I couldn't be sure—until he said, "That's good. Just right—and a very beautiful blend of voices. Stevens will like this."

I said nothing, but I thought his tendency to predict the reactions of George Stevens was a dangerous habit to get into and one I would certainly avoid.

We started to play the delicate instrumental soundtracks, but our attention quailed before the noise of the wind, and we postponed further listening.

I walked with Vellani to Stevens' office and telephoned Alfred. The long-distance line snapped with static, then his voice came through. "Ken? How's the weather around George Stevens? He always makes his own, you know, and it can be sunny or stormy depending on who he thinks you are. When will you escape from that ersatz Holyland and come home?"

I told him I had not yet met with Stevens, but had played the tapes—under weird circumstances—for a trio of Tonys.

"To hell with *them*!" he interrupted. "Your job there is only with Stevens. Make a point of *that* with your Tony pals. See George as soon as you can, then come home. Don't let anybody trick you into giving any opinions on anything—except to George. He'll trick you anyway. It's his nature. I went all through the Stevens baptism on *The Diary of Anne Frank*—and before that on *Gunga Din*—and I don't mind telling you it was like being circumcised *twice!* I'm hoping I won't have to go through another one on this picture." The line went suddenly dead, but returned a few moments later as Alfred was saying, " . . . so I'm at loose ends while you're away. I need your critical ear. Hurry home. Now, let me speak to Vellani."

Vellani had little to say because he had a lot to listen to. Once or twice his face grew pink; he used a lot of curt affirmatives: "yes . . . fine . . . good . . . right . . . understood . . . goodbye," and returned the phone to me. Alfred was chuckling. "He knows who you are now, and why you're there. What's next?" I told him about Vellani's plan to do some direct recording of vocal chants and lamentations, all of which Tony wanted me to prepare, arrange and supervise. He moaned that such an extension of my absence would not help his disposition any, and, at length, we said goodbye. His last words were, "You call me anytime, day or night, if they give you a bad time. My moral support is damned effective even at long distance."

I hung up thoughtfully, recalling how through the years Alfred's insight and prophetic evaluation of circumstances and people had invariably been uncannily precise. I hoped his uneasiness about this film would be unfounded; the story of Jesus was so meaningful that I prayed there would be no crucifixion in it for him or for me, and I felt sure that Providence would guide us, inspire us, and save us from catastrophe.

Before dinner, the 25-member Inbal Dance Theater group— imported by George Stevens from Israel to lend authenticity— held their Sabbath service in the rehearsal tent. All men sat to the left of an improvised altar, all women to the right. Fourteen flickering candles were held aloft by twin menorahs on a cloth-covered table, and four tumblers of Mogen David wine were placed at the corners. Chairs had been assembled for the congregation: mainly actors, artisans, and orthodox celebrants. Stevens passed me on the way in and stopped to shake hands. His voice was gentle and friendly. "Hello, Ken. I've been told Al's music is interesting, and that he is anxious for me to hear it. Is there any particular rush?"

I smiled, thinking how quickly Vellani had reported our meeting. "Yes . . . and no," I said. "He would like *your* reaction as a guide to further composition, and there *are* questions which only you can resolve—but no hurry."

"Perhaps tomorrow. Are your quarters comfortable?"

My reply was forestalled by Madam Sarah, the fussy little mother figure in charge of the Inbal Dancers, who descended upon him with smiles and chatter, reaching up to place a blue satin yarmulke on his head—a feat made impossible by her four-foot, ten-inch height. George stooped to receive the little cap, and followed her meekly to the seat of honor behind the improvised altar. On his left sat Margalita, a lovely tiny woman with a sweet voice and light milk-chocolate skin. Next to her was a curious Yemenite composite of Mickey Rooney and Cantinflas! I learned later that this was Yehuda Cohen, a professional comic, but tonight he was not cracking jokes; he was the cantor. Next to Yehuda was a tall, broad-shouldered Scandinavian wearing a white silk yarmulke on his short blond hair. Overhanging his deep-set eyes was a massive monolithic brow. This, and the protruding lower jaw, gave him an aspect of slight distortion, as though reflected in a cheap mirror. He was Max von Sydow, the Jesus of this film, who was already imbuing his role as Christ with extraordinary strength and virility. With makeup, he became the almost perfect personification of man's most popular conception of the Saviour, but *not* wearing a yarmulke as he was tonight. The white cap on the wispy hair made him look like an elongated Harpo Marx.

Any kind of hat, I discovered, was permissible so long as the head was covered before the altar of Jehovah. Many, including my own, were simply draped with paper napkins.

The songs were awesomely ancient; their authenticity was undeniable. They were modal, antiphonal, and definitively Hebrew, and I was impressed. After the second song, the tiny exquisite girl next to Stevens floated from her seat as though by levitation and, with closed eyes, enunciated a strange and wistful ceremonial prayer in perfectly executed intervals. The group answered her with an exotic "Amen," and she drifted down into her chair.

During the next musical offering I kept my eyes on George Stevens' face, watching the curious interplay of expressions: paternal serenity—"I love these graceful naive children"; sharply focussed interest—"this music comes straight out of racial memory"; frowning preoccupation—"how much of this documentary-type material can I ever use?" solemn inscrutability—"this is all fine, but it would go better with another Beefeater martini"; whimsical amusement—"Harold Kress looks like an idiot with that paper napkin on his head. . . . "

The cantor stood up and nervously grasped the wine bottle, which still contained several ounces. He emptied it into one of the tumblers, filling it to the brim. Carefully, he balanced it on the flattened palm of his left hand, blessed it with his right, and began a quavering tenor chant, here and there inserting a florid embellishment and spewing droplets of saliva across the table. At several points during his recital, the men of the Inbal chorus put a musical period on the end of the wandering phrases as he toured through a forest of unrelated keys.

Having sufficiently expectorated in the sacramental wine, he leaned forward and sucked in an audible sip, still without spilling a drop, and handed the tumbler to Max on his left, who looked bewildered at having it thrust upon him. After a whispered coaching from Madam Sarah, von Sydow gingerly sipped from the glass and passed it on. By the time it reached *me* I was happy I'd had my flu shots, and was wondering what else might be contracted from the common goblet, and how would I explain *that* to Vera.

The moment the last swallow was down, the shouting began. "Sab*bath* Sho*lom*! Sab*bath* Sho*lom*!" they called. My hand was gripped by everyone, and smiles of tolerance and love shone in the tent brighter than the guttering candles. Madam Sarah stilled the babbling by tapping her glass with a spoon. They all sat down again and Ovadia Tuvia, the Inbal composer-conductor and expert on ancient Yemenite folk music, gave a long curving downbeat, in the middle of which the group began to sing his latest English tune.

"Wa-a-atch-man, what of the ni-i-eeght? The maw-r-ning com-eth, and al-so the ni-i-ee-ght."

The tune was fair, the words scanned properly, but it was not folk music. Then as I watched the eager face of Madam Sarah, I became aware that Stevens & Company were being given a commercial pitch. She was acting as Ovadia's song plugger. And when Stevens began tapping his foot to the following rhythmic phrase, she knew the song was *in*—and so did I. The Inbal performers finished to applause. Service was over.

Dinner followed, and it was entirely social—the mess tent filled with laughter and conversation. Harold, Mary, Frank O'Neill and I joined Florence Williamson at a long table where she was sitting alone. Harold introduced her as George Stevens' script consultant, and I pulled my first stupid boner by remarking that the tip of her pink nose made her look like a happy, perky clown.

"I get that from working all day long on the set," she snapped. "You should try it sometime, paleface."

"I do need some color," I admitted lamely, wishing that I'd kept my mouth shut. Wasn't that red nose a bit veinous for sunburn? Couldn't it more probably be an alcoholic glow? I polished my glasses, trying to find a way out, then added, "How is the work progressing on the set. Is Mr. Stevens happy with what he is filming?"

She softened, and her eyes grew dreamy and remote. "Yes, I really think he is. I watch him closely all day, wondering where he gets his enormous reserves of strength and patience. He has the ability to create word pictures that are visible. All of us on the set can practically *feel* the emotions he is drawing from the actors just by listening to his instructions. And sometimes . . . he seems godlike. He has hypnotic powers I swear, because the set becomes totally quiet—even the grips and the electricians—and nobody speaks. He's wonderful."

I hadn't taken a bite through all of this; I was being spellbound myself. This pink-nosed woman was positively idolatrous, and from the cut of her sweater and the fit of her stretch pants I had to assume that a good healthy libido was hiding somewhere in that idolatry, making her judgment of George Stevens something more than purely intellectual. I knew how to talk to Florence now, and I was prompted to push my luck. I chewed, swallowed, and said, "Has George ever mentioned any musical treatment of the Last Supper? There is a mention in the Gospels that a hymn was sung in that upper room just before Jesus and the disciples went to the Garden of Gethsemane."

"I don't think anything like that is in the script."

"Well, Mr. Newman and I had been thinking that if Mr. Stevens planned to use such a musical moment, we could adapt a Hebrew phrase to fit the words of the Mizpah."

"What's that?" she asked. "What's a Mizpah?"

I quoted: " . . . and now may the Lord watch between me and thee, while we are absent, one from another."

"That's beautiful," she said. "Where did you find that?"

"It's in the Old Testament, somewhere in Genesis I think."

She put down her knife and fork, took out a pencil, and scribbled in a notebook. "See if you can get me chapter and verse . . . and how do you spell Mizpah?"

I spelled it for her and said, "I'll locate it tonight before I turn in." We ended up friends.

Back in my cabin, I adjusted the furnace, lit a pipe, took out my Bible and prepared for a search. The Book fell open at an old-fashioned illustration of Noah greeting the return of his leaf-bearing dove, and I started to turn the page. But a line opposite the picture caught my eye.

"And when Rachel saw that she bare Jacob no children ... " and I couldn't stop reading. Here, in a single column of 18 verses (Chapter 30 in the Book of Genesis), was the sweetest bit of procurement any man could wish: a wife making arrangements for her husband to have sex with Bilhah, her handmaiden, who subsequently gave Jacob two sons. Then it was disclosed that Jacob had another wife named Leah. She, like Rachel, also was barren, and, taking her cue from Rachel, she sent Jacob to bed with *her* handmaiden, Zilpah.

At this point I began to hope that these two handmaidens were more attractive than their names, but they appeared to satisfy Jacob, because in the course of time—and many such beddings—Zilpah also bore two sons.

Rachel had been watching all this undercover activity, and now, when it came her turn to "go unto her husband," she grew apprehensive lest she fail, so she bartered with Leah (for a few mandrakes and other good and valuable consideration) for Leah to bed him instead. This Leah reluctantly undertook, and miraculously surpassed even the fecund and talented handmaidens by bearing two sons and a *daughter*. The peeping wife, Rachel, now was swept by a wave of righteous eroticism. She hurried Jacob off to her boudoir and wrung him out like a rag, becoming belatedly pregnant in the process—and a good thing, too, or we would never have heard of Joseph and his coat of many colors.

Jacob, now the head of an enormous woods-colt family, sought to better his wages with his employer, Laban. He asked for this pay raise in the form of "all spotted and ringstraked" animals born to Laban's flocks. This would purify Laban's herd and give Jacob a start on a flock of his own. But now a rare and curious thing occurred: none of Laban's ewes, dams, mares, and sows gave birth to any *but* ringstraked offspring. Jacob got them all, but while growing rich he also grew fearful of Laban's wrath. Finally, he gathered his army of wives, children, herds, flocks, camels, and horses, and scurried across the river into Canaan.

Of course, Laban came roaring right after him, but when he caught up with the runaways he saw he was outnumbered, so he decided to parley. After all, he said to himself, hadn't Jacob given him twenty years of faithful service? Didn't he owe Jacob a little something for taking his two unmarriageable and unmanageable daughters off his hands? And wasn't he, Laban, still a wealthy man, much more affluent than before because of Jacob's steadfast service? Of course he was!

I was about to flip the page—having completed the main plot of the story—but my eyes read on out of curiosity.

"And Laban said, let us make a covenant, I and thou, and let it be a witness between me and thee. And Jacob took a stone and set it up for a pillar. And Jacob said unto his brethren, Gather stones; and they took stones and made a heap, and they did eat there upon the heap. And Laban said, this heap is a witness between me and thee this day, and *Mizpah*. For he said, *the Lord watch between me and thee, when we are absent one from another.*"(!) (Genesis 31:49)

I sat for a long moment, then looked slowly over my left shoulder, half expecting to see a transparent figure pointing a long glowing finger at the verse. I saw only the graying head of a mystified old Gentile peering back at me from the discolored mirror in the bathroom.

I had found it on the first try. Was it childhood memory? Was it the course in comparative religion I had taken in Chapman College?

I was still questioning the odds as I drifted into sleep.

THREE

My prefabricated sanctum resounded under the rapping knuckles of the maid. I yelled for her to come back in an hour, then threaded my way through the obstacle course of morning ablutions, escaping just as she was about to pound on my door again.

The mess tent was not crowded at 8:30, most of the actor population having departed for the set. The orange juice was fresh, the coffee hot, and I breakfasted lavishly on eggs, bacon, pancakes, and real maple syrup. Afterward, from the office trailer, I telephoned Vera, learning that she had made a purchase of three etchings from Raymond Lewis of San Francisco. She sounded happy.

Having lost a button from my thirteen-year-old Sportsman wool shirt, I wandered around the camp until I found the wardrobe master's tent, set up near the helicopter pad, and chatted with a seamstress as she replaced the button and sewed up a tiny moth hole under the collar.

At ten, I picked up the soundtracks from Harold's cutting room, wished him a good day as he sat disconsolately winding film through his Moviola, and went to the motor pool where I found a stretchout that would take me to the bridge set. My driver was a smallish, deformed man of unguessable age, who talked continuously through the entire journey. All I did to get him started was to ask one question: "How far is it to the set?"

"It's thirty-two miles by car, eight miles by air, but I don't mind th' long drive. Y'see, I was a race driver oncet. I had a bitch of a car. Indi'napolis frame with a blown Buick engine an' a Corvette gearbox. She'd do a hund'rd'n'seventy on th' straightaway. I beat Phil Hill one day in a trial heat an' he was so mad he didn't even stop when we finished, just drove his car onto his trailer an' took off f'r home cussin'. Kinda sore loser, dontcha think?

That was th' car that nearly killed me. Didn't hurt th' car much, but th' centrifugal spin I got into, plus th' sideways slam against th' wall purely pulverized my damn kidneys. I was nine months flat out on my back. I guess I shoulda been used t' that, though, because I spent th' first ten years o' my life in bed."

He pulled onto the shoulder so a car from the set could pass us on the narrow one-way road. "See this scar?" He hiked up his pant leg to reveal a thin white line down the shin. "I was born missin' one vertebra in my back; when I was nine months old they took a piece o' my shin bone an' made th' first successful spinal graft in medical history. I was in a cast clean over my head and out t' my elbows an' down t' my knees f'r too long t' even think about. Oh, sure, they kept changin' th' cast as I grew, but—" he chuckled, "I didn't do much growin' as you c'n see. Kinda humped my back, too, but th' worst part was when they finally cut off part o' th' cast. My ears, arms, an' upper legs dam-near froze. I was cold all th' time, an' I was twelve years old before I learned t' walk! My name's Hal. What's yours?" He stuck out his hand, shook mine vigorously, then put the car back in gear and we bounced from the shoulder down into the well-worn ruts.

"Mine's Ken," I said. "Music Department."

He hardly took a breath. "Y'know, I used t' read music better'n I could English. Yessir, when I got my arms free o' that cast I asked Mom if she'd get me a violin, an' she went right down t' the secondhand music store an' bought me an old Stradivarius." (Here I coughed to keep from choking.) "I used t' play that damn thing all day long. Never did care a lot f'r book readin' though, just music. Say, it must be a trick puttin' music int' pictures. How d'ya do it? It's always been a pure puzzle t'me how anybody c'n write it anyway."

I opened my mouth but he went right on.

"All this here land we're goin' through'll be under a billion gallons o' water when they finish th' dam. A lake about ninety miles long with a hundr'd'n'eighty-odd miles o' shoreline'll be settin' right here where we're drivin'. Me an' my Mom bought a piece o' land over younder there near Wahweep. It'll be only a couple o' hundr'd feet from the water's edge when th' lake's full. We paid near fifteen hundr'd f'r that one acre but it was a good investment. Y'oughta buy a piece before th' prices go up.

Well, we're gettin' there. Enjoyed talkin' with ya. I'll drive ya right on down t' the set so ya won't have t' walk in th' mud."
And for the last thirty yards he was as silent as a stone.

The last rising turn of the road brought us to the crest of a mesa that revealed a breathtaking view of a wide valley. On all sides were magnificent wind-sculptured castles forged in red and brown stone. Magenta, lilac, and lime-green shrubs carpeted the vast floor and crept up the far slopes, making a scene of flowering spring in the November wilderness. Nearer, and to my left, a painter with a portable pump gun was spraying orange stain on a towering rock formation.

Stevens and the camera crew were in a quiet huddle on one side of a fairly deep gully. A sturdy but crude bridge had been built across it, and carpenters were still working on the supports. Under the bridge, the figure of Jesus crouched on his heels, gesturing to "Little" James, Peter, John, and Andrew. The loudspeakers announced, "This is a rehearsal," the carpenters moved away, and a squad of seven Roman soldiers marched across the bridge—two of them woefully out of step.

Tony Van Renterghem met me as I got out of the car, his shushing finger pressed to his lips. In whispers, he gave me an explanation of the problem.

"All of our Roman extras are really Indians from Wahweep. Saul hired a captain from a nearby training camp to drill them so they'd look like the cream of Rome's legionnaires, but it isn't working. Stevens and Saul Wurtzel are going around and around about it right now."

The loudspeakers demanded quiet. I saw Stevens give a signal to Bill Mellor, the camera rolled, and on "action" the septet of Romans marched onto the bridge—the same pair still out of step. Four takes later, Saul averted pandemonium by escorting the arrhythmic pair away from the set, and on the next take the RomaNavajo quintet marched solidly across the bridge in perfect cadence. Stevens let them march right on into the desert before giving the signal to "cut."

Tony said, "That's that. Now he'll move in for two or three scenes with Jesus and the disciples under the bridge, but the principal shot he and Mellor want to get will be at or near sunset, when Jesus and his small band cross the bridge on their way to

Galilee. They want long, flat light and dark clouds in the background."

He noticed the film can in my hand. "If you're looking for Wally Wallace, the sound truck is just around that curve there. I'll walk you down."

We started off, made the curve, and nearly stepped on two technicians who were crouched in the pathway. One of them had a walkie-talkie, and both were staring off into the far distance.

"That's the one," said the man with the walkie-talkie. "Now go to your right . . . up the hill and away from us."

I peered in the direction of their concentration, and saw a clump of heliotrope vegetation slowly moving along the rim of the valley toward a vacant spot among the other polychromatic foliage that covered the hillside.

"Whoa! That's good. Hold it there."

The clump stopped its movement, and two small figures detached themselves from it and walked away.

Tony said, "It took sixty-eight thousand gallons of paint to create that background, some of it sprayed by helicopter."

"At six bucks a gallon," I whispered, "that's over four hundred thousand dollars!"

"Four hundred and eight thousand to be exact. Here's the sound truck; I'll check with Stevens to see if he wants to hear any of your music between setups."

I joined Wally Wallace, the recording mixer, in his truck. It was dark inside, and we chatted in low tones, he with a headphone over one ear to keep track of what was going on out on the set. I gave him a typed copy of the music titles contained on the tape, and he promised to have them ready should Stevens ask for them.

On the way back to the car pool, Tony caught up with me.

"Wally's got the tapes," I said.

"Q U I E T !" boomed the loudspeakers.

Tony wrote quickly on a piece of paper: "Stevens won't be listening to music today."

An hour later I was back in camp.

My cabin door was hanging open and there was a stranger bending over my living room table, studiously perusing something in a black notebook, his nose a scant four inches from the page. I backed off in confusion, thinking I'd wandered into the wrong aisle, but he heard me and raised his head.

Barren and sparse on top, the rest of his square Dutch face was topographically opulent. His smile was set on a bit crooked, and the heavy-rimmed glasses he quickly slapped on his monumental nose held thick lenses that failed to hide the laugh wrinkles at the corners of his sharp, intelligent eyes.

"Come in, come in," he barked. "You must be Darby. I'm Dan Vandraegen, your house guest for the weekend. I come under a warranty to be nonintrusive, completely cooperative, and a paragon of artful coexistence."

I grinned delightedly as we shook hands.

"Welcome to Galilee," he said. "I'm an ambulant gazetteer from U.C.L.A., and I coach the actors in the art of speech. While you are getting used to the idea of joint occupancy, I shall take myself off to see the dailies which have been filmed in my absence. Perhaps I'll see you at dinner?"

He left quickly, his scarf and professorial aura waving behind him like a banner.

I went to the cutting room and started preparing a place for the tapes I would record with the Inbal Dancers, wheedled two empty top shelves from Frank O'Neill, and labeled 21 reels of blank tape. While I was doing this the sun went down and the crew came in from the set. Frank put down his *Esquire* and said, "Let's eat."

The mess tent was crowded. Spirits were high, and dinner was a wordy affair. I listened to Robert Bush, the Assistant Dialog Director, discourse through fumes of brandy and an elegant gray beard on the beauties of fornication. His mouth released syllables as though he resented losing their flavor, although many of them were hardly savory.

"The words, 'cellar door,' " he was saying, "have been called the most beautiful in the English language, but they paint no emotional picture—unless you happened to slide down one as a child and came up with a sliver in your ass. My favorite words always define an emotional sensuality, like *promiscuity, mammalian nudity, mound of Venus, erection, fructification.*"

I left him still spouting profundities and poked my head into the rehearsal tent next door where a 16-millimeter projector was delineating the vagarious life of *The Birdman of Alcatraz*. I

remained long enough to see Burt Lancaster gently fondling the
feathers of an impudent sparrow, realized it was freezing in the
tent, and fled back to my room. I was just beginning to thaw in
front of the wall heater when a timid knock announced a visitor.
I opened the door, and there stood the tall cloaked figure of
Max von Sydow. I couldn't resist; I said, "Knock and it shall be
opened unto you."

He was startled. "Oh! I beg your pardon. I was searching for
Doctor Vandraegen." He gave the name a musical Swedish
mordent. "I must have the wrong cabin."

"The right cabin, but the wrong man. I'm Ken Darby—in
music." He gripped my extended hand. "Won't you come in?"

"No, thank you. Vhen he returns, yust tell him I'll be in my
room across the way here. Pleasure meeting you."

He turned away and I closed the door. Two minutes later,
Vandraegen came in, stomping dirt off of his boots. I gave him
Max's message and he said, "Good. Now I can go to work."

"So late?" I asked.

"Yes. Max is going with the Inbal Dancers tomorrow morning
to watch a marathon dance contest between the Yemenites and
the Navajos on a nearby reservation, so I *must* see him tonight."

"But you've had such a long, weary day," I remonstrated.

"Ah, the best defense we have against fatigue is the enthusiastic practice of cast-iron persuasion called teaching. And I'm a
teacher! It has fabulous rewards."

"You sound exactly like Dr. Nelson in the U.C.L.A. music
department. Do you know him?"

"All of twenty years. My wife and I have known Bob and his
family since 1941." He looked down in sudden embarrassment,
fumbled with his glass case, half withdrew the glasses then
pushed them back. "My wife—" (It was a soft, concerned pair
of words) "—has just undergone radical surgery for that obscene
malignancy." He saw me flinch and hastily added, "But we have
hope. She must have cobalt treatments at U.C.L.A. and the
doctors say she will recover, but . . . "

I looked at this Daniel, standing there in the midst of his own
fiery furnace, felt the radiance of his devotion, and could only
say, "Keep hoping. The cure is near, and if prayer will help, you
both have mine."

He put on his glasses and gave me a straight, warm gaze.

"Thank you," he murmured. Then, in complete contrast: "Now! I must go rehearse Jesus."

I closed the door behind him, pulled off my wool-lined boots, clothes, and long johns, got into my flannel pajamas, and sought my bed, hoping he would leave the furnace turned up and not rake me out at six a.m.

A riot of raindrops dancing on the tin roof overhead brought me up out of a dream. The lights in the cabin were still on, the furnace was purring comfortably. I curled a little tighter on my side, clearing my throat, and the hoarse croak that emerged sent a charge of anxiety through my gut. Damn, I thought. I've known this old bronchial enemy of old. But before I could generate any real panic, I sank back into my dream.

Vandraegen stormed in soon after and shuffled back and forth between bedroom and bath in hushed pianissimo. Not wanting him to know he had wakened me, I feigned sleep so artfully that I departed the scene before he snapped off the light.

In my dream, I was lying on a windy beach watching the crest and fall of angry waves. Slicing the water was the dorsal fin of a great white shark, moving toward shore. Suddenly, Nellie Forbush sped past me, running into the surf, directly in the path of destruction. I tried to shout, but I couldn't move a muscle or make a sound.

FOUR

Vandraegen was up before seven. The floor moved and grumbled under his feet as he started another series of trips to and from the bathroom. My chest was so thick and tight I felt as though I had swallowed Gertrude Stein and she'd only gone halfway down. After Dan had tiptoed out, I hurriedly showered and shaved, inhaling the steam from several hot moist towels. Suddenly he poked his head in the door.

"Ha! You're up. How about some food?"

We breakfasted and talked, then walked back from the mess tent in a mist of snowflakes too buoyant to fall. We lunched together in a tide of expanding conversation, and I learned much about this courageous and well-disciplined man.

He had been a prodigy on the violin at age ten. His high school football career destroyed parts of six ribs, left him without the use of his right arm, and ended forever his active performance in music. He is still plagued by muscular spasms after thirty-five years. Raised on an island of three hundred families in Vancouver Bay amid cattle and sheep and good neighbors, educated at Northwestern University, taking his Doctorate in English Literature while on an Art Scholarship, he emerged a total person with never a doubt as to what he would do with his life.

Religious, yet shunning the panoply and rituals of any formal church; authoritative, yet avoiding demagoguery, he has become eminent as a master of speech and the allied arts, combining his academic work with the lucrative avocation of Dialog Director for motion pictures.

"It all began with *The Brontë Sisters*," he said, between large mouthfuls of roast turkey. "They gave me three actresses who hated each other: Ida Lupino, Olivia De Havilland, and Katherine Somebodyorother. Ida discovered that the paternal

28

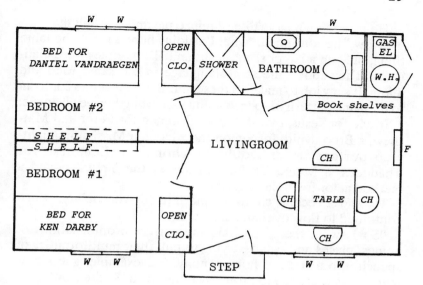

Typical of all the cabins. This is Cabin C-3. The gas and electric meter connections are in an outside closet with the W.H. (water heater); F = wall furnace. Louvre windows throughout.

Brontë was from Ireland, so she insisted on using an Irish dialect which she could enunciate perfectly. She became even more insistent when she learned that Olivia could neither speak it, mimic it, nor endure it. Katherine, sensing the stronger personality, sided with Ida. Added to this improbable linguistic stew was an actor named Montagu Love, whom you may remember as being large of lip and oral cavity, pretentious and diaphragmatic of speech, and totally devoted to Shakespearian English.

"These four unlikely people were handed over to me to wed into a family. Since they had no physical resemblance whatever in common, there remained only the medium of speech. I listened to their arguments and complaints for a couple of days, then hit upon a lucky solution. I pointed out that in the England of the Brontës, *any* form of dialect was abhorrent to the middle class because it belonged solely to the Cockney, the guttersnipe, and the criminal. This argument, in one shot, ended Ida's superiority, Olivia's inadequacy, Katherine's partisanship, and Love's aristocratic pomposity."

He forked up a large bite of mince pie and relished it.

"Now," he continued, "what I'm doing here is much the same thing, only on a larger scale. Jesus and His disciples were Galileans. They spoke the same language in the same tone and idiom. It's my job to make all these multiloquent actors conform to the same pattern of speech—and look what they've given me: a Swede for Jesus, two stilted Englishmen for Peter and Matthew, a Brooklynite for Simon the Zealot, a Mississippi nightclub performer for Doubting Thomas, a Lebanese for Thaddeus, a Maine Yankee for James the Younger, and a method actor for Judas Iscariot!"

He slid a second chunk of pie into his vocabulary, which continued to flow over and around it.

"So I sweat them, teaching the correct pronunciations of names, places and events, trying to pull their multiformities of speech into a state of homogeneity. For example: guess how many ways there are to pronounce the word 'Sanhedron'."

"I've always used the broad "e" with the accent on the second syllable, and so have my sisters and my cousins and my aunts."

"Plagiarist!" he chuckled. "Seriously, there are no less than six. Depending on the country and the century, it has been pronounced San-hĕd'-run, your choice; San-hĕd'-run, in the Arabic; Sän'-hĕ-drin', in Hebrew; San-hĕ-dreen', in Yemen; Sahn'-a-drĭn, in Aramaic—and Săn'-hĕd'-drĕ', in Jerusalem at the time of Christ. And that's the way we're using it in the film. I've researched every place name and title that appears in the script, repeated each one five times into my tape recorder, and then pounded the entire list into each actor."

He swallowed largely and lifted his glass unsteadily in that right hand, spilling it as he drank because of a slight spasm. "Excuse me," he apologized, mopping buttermilk from his chin. "Do you know with whom I've had the most trouble?"

"Jesus," I answered instinctively.

"Point killer," he laughed. "And you're right. When I first went to work with Max, he couldn't speak a simple line of English without singing it in that lilting Swedish dialect. Can you imagine how the Sermon on the Mount, or the Beatitudes would sound? We have rehearsed, and are still rehearsing all the lines he has in the script, sometimes even rewriting some of the dialog. Fortunately for the project, Max is an indefatigable worker."

He ordered another piece of pie and went on.

"They all are hard workers. There's a spirit among the members of this company that amounts almost to Messianic devotion—especially so in the case of David McCallum who plays the role of Judas."

"Speaking of Judas, what do you think of the way Sandburg has softened his character in the script?"

"Do you have strong feelings about Judas one way or the other?" he countered.

"Yes, I have, although those feelings must have been inculcated by Sunday school teachers, preachers, and parents. Judas, as described by them, and as I read it in the Gospels, was a traitor; a weak man anxious to obtain substance, favor, and a lot of notoriety by betraying The Man. Then, seeing how little he obtained, and how cruelly the Jews and the Romans treated Jesus, his remorse was so keen that he killed himself rather than face the hatred of his former comrades."

"Of course. You are another victim of the people who would paint Judas *all* evil, and the other disciples *all* good. Think a moment. Jesus called *all* of the disciples, seeing in each something strong and necessary to the propagation of His ministry— and he loved them all, told them so repeatedly. One of those men had to be sufficiently loyal to commit the most important and repulsive act, one that had been prophesied for generations, the act of betrayal at a moment of fearful emotional crisis. Jesus *might* have seen that kind of devoted loyalty in Judas, mightn't he? Isn't it possible that Jesus saw He could rely upon Judas to perform the one disloyal act that would fulfill the Scriptures? At the Last Supper, both He and Judas knew what the other must do. Jesus said, 'One of you will betray me.'

"The word '*will*' in that sentence has been assumed by some to mean a prophecy, but from a translation standpoint, it is equally correct to use the word *shall*, or *must*. Jesus was not merely prophesying. He was stating that one of them *must* betray Him. He was also telling them that the act would cause pain, suffering, personal revilement, and an agony of guilt and self-loathing. Now, observe what happened. All of the other disciples remonstrated, saying, 'No, not I. I could never do such a thing. Not I, Master.' And Jesus said nothing. But when Judas quietly inquired, 'Is it I?' Jesus gazed upon him and said, 'Thou sayest.' Judas already knew!

"I want you to read a book by Robinson Jeffers called *Dear Judas*. I knew Jeffers for a time; he became Cassandra-like in his old age, and he really lived too long—or, at least, he wrote too long—badly rehashing in his declining years some of the pet ideas which were much better stated in his youth. However, his treatment of the relationship between Jesus and Judas is both logical and stunning. You'll like it, especially if you love Jesus, as I see you do. One more word. The Jesus you love would never have selected as one of his chosen disciples a villainous, conniving, cunning, money-worshipping, homicidal hypocrite, now, would He?"

"Nnnoo," I admitted cautiously. "And anyway, Judas could not have remained *any* of those things once he touched Christ."

"Exactly!" Vandraegen was triumphant. He gave me his crooked smile. "Now, I want you to go back and read the betrayal scene in the Gospel of Mark. Notice particularly that Judas betrayed Jesus to the Priests of the Jewish Temple, *not* to the Romans, and when he kissed his Master in the Garden, he said, 'Take Him away *safely*.' Consider that last word. Was it not Judas who was really betrayed?"

Vandraegen's car left for the airport at 7 p.m., and that evening the cabin was silent. Sleep was a futility. The longest day had nothing on this, the longest night. The tight grip on my throat had given over to spasms of coughing, and my nasal passages were growing spiny cacti of irritation. Forty times I twisted up out of an ugly dream, and forty times I fought my way back into it.

Mankind! The highest, noblest creature of all, host to lofty ideals, grand philosophies, great theories, transcendent inspirations—and to every vicious virus, fungus, bacillus and ravenous bacterium let loose by creation. Man: a bug house of skin and water, bone and ligament; home for bugs, haven for pests, and generations of staphylococci! Who is master here, Lord, bug— or man?

FIVE

I awoke to a double realization: Monday had arrived, and an army of staph had erected a bilateral bivouac in my chest. The invasion force was well established, and I declared war on them with sprays, pills, gargles, lozenges, hot towels, syrups, gallons of water, and all the psychological weapons I could muster. And suddenly I recalled that George Stevens had promised to have a meeting with me on Sunday. That was *yesterday.* No meeting. I'd been stood up.

While I was breakfasting, the loudspeakers in the compound began calling, "KEN DARBY, ATTENTION. YOU ARE RE-QUESTED TO COME TO THE SET IMMEDIATELY." On the way to my cabin, I stopped at Operations, told Jack I was on my way, gathered the warmest gear I had, and jumped into a special bus with a couple of other late-goers. The car radio was on, and as we snaked across the desert it played five consecutive tunes without interruption. Then a female voice announced the call letters of the station, said it was 10 a.m., and that the temperature was 38 degrees. This was followed immediately by more music, and I turned to the driver. "Aren't there any commercial sponsors in Page, Arizona?"

He pulled us out of a nasty skid and said, "Nope. No commercials at all except for the armed forces. They manage to put in a plug every couple of hours hoping to induct a few Indians." He wrestled with the steering wheel. "This road was frozen solid this morning; she's melting into a slippery mess now."

We careened and lurched, sliding on every curve, until at last he swung the bus around the final corner. A flock of sheep, nervously guarded by a scurrying dog, was inching its way through the green, gold, and henna shrubs of the Jordan Valley. Roman soldiers were gathered around a steaming coffee urn munching doughnuts, and white-robed Galileans were standing—coldly motionless—on a distant pathway. Overhead, a B-57 was etching the neo-Holyland heavens with a stiff white contrail.

I stepped from the car into deep red goo and started for the camera. Tony Vellani detached himself from the group and came to meet me.

"I'm really very sorry, Ken," he whispered. "I thought George would have time to talk with you this morning, but he just told me it was impossible. However, he *will* see you this evening right after dinner. You may as well go back to camp."

Before I could reply, he had turned and gone, but I yelled a sarcastic "*Thanks*" at his departing rear.

My return driver was Lou Tate, who had once worked for Spyros Skouras. He kept me so entertained for an hour that I didn't notice the cold until my breathing equipment slammed shut. Lou drove me straight to the camp hospital where the nurse checked my temperature, gave me some sulfa pills and a bottle of croup remedy, and told me to go to bed. After a hot bowl of soup, I spent part of the afternoon in Harold's cutting room watching him assemble the baptismal scene between Jesus and John the Baptist. What he was doing seemed pointless to me since Stevens would simply make him undo it. I must have dozed then, because I didn't hear the crew come in or the loudspeakers calling my name. Harold shook me.

"Hey, wake up. You and Tony Vellani have a long-distance call. Get your tail over to the Production Trailer."

I stumbled out into a dark gigantic refrigerator. I'll freeze solid tonight, I thought, as I shuffled the fifty feet to the trailer. Mary greeted me when I came in. "It's Frank Davis on the line from the studio. Tony's already on the phone."

Whatever Davis had to say was easily interpreted just by listening to Tony's replies. " ... yes, Frank, he's standing right here beside me." (pause) " ... I know what it's costing, but he has had no opportunity to see Mr. Stevens. ... No, it's not his fault, Stevens has been too busy and too tired." (pause) "Yes, we have a meeting set up for tonight, but we may not get to play *all* the music ... okay, I'll try."

He hung up, looked at me and said, "Let's go. If you have the tapes ready we can set up the equipment in the rehearsal tent."

"Everything's ready," I said, "but surely you're not intending to play all our tracks in that drafty igloo. We'll freeze our balls off, and His, too."

"Gad, you're right. But where will we go?"

"Send Tony Perris to fetch Van Renterghem's Wollensak tape recorder while I bring the tapes. We'll move right into Stevens' cabin."

He sighed. "I should have thought of that. Good."

I gave him a double take, thinking he was being sarcastic, but he wasn't. He was bone tired. There was a dazed, blank oyster look in his eyes. He started up. "I'll alert Perris," he said, and left the trailer as though sleepwalking.

Ten minutes later, armed with tapes, notes, script, the Wollensak, and a Bible—and having gargled myself raw—the three Tonys and I invaded Stevens' sanctuary. He was sitting with his arms folded on the table, and made no comment as we set up the machine. I began cautiously.

"You've had a long day, and it isn't my wish to prolong it unnecessarily, so rather than play all of the tapes, let me start with the setting Alfred wrote for the *136th Psalm* which, the script indicates, the disciples are to sing at the home of Lazarus. Then, if that meets with your approval, I can start rehearsing the actors tomorrow even though we discuss nothing else this evening."

"Good, Ken. I am weary."

The taped voices began softly. *"Oh, give thanks unto the Lord, for He is good; for His mercy endureth forever."*

Stevens angled back in his chair and closed his eyes. Now and again his head moved slightly. The psalm played for three minutes, then faded out. I didn't look up, just readied the machine for the second version. There wasn't a sound in the room; the Tonys were intent and expectant, waiting for Stevens to give the first word. I broke the stillness myself, explaining that the next recording was of the same Psalm, but this time sung by a solo cantor with men's voices in response.

Again came the voices, and he listened to the end. Then he opened his eyes, heaved a sigh, and said softly, "Oh, I do like this. It's exactly right." He put his elbows on the table and continued. "It's devotional and prayerful, and it will give the scene following the powerful raising of Lazarus a contrasting calm. But can our actors sing it?"

"I hope to find that out when I rehearse them," I said. "But tell me, were you impressed by the voices you just heard?"

"Tremendously."

"Then may I suggest that we use this track as a playback? I'll teach it to the disciple/actors, and they will synchronize their lips to this recording when they are photographed."

"Yes, but don't you think it sounds too professional? I wanted this song to come from people who had never *learned* to sing, but were singing because they needed to express awed devotion not conveyable by any other means. Play it again. Then play *all* the music. I'm beginning to hear things that may be more relaxing and effective than sleep."

So I started at the top. "The Romans Came" was a bit of a surprise to him. He chuckled and said, "Yankee, go home?"

I nodded.

"Teach that to the disciples, too, Ken—just for fun."

I put on the master tape. It began with Alfred's lonely melody played by a shepherd's pipe, and George leaned over to turn down the volume a notch, listening without comment to the end of Salome's dance music. He was obviously stimulated, and when the last note had finished he pulled my script over and spoke rapidly as he turned the pages.

"What kind of a sound can we get for the women when King Herod kills all the male infants? Can we use a similar sound during the crucifixion when the mobs are pounding on the gates of Jerusalem? And here—in scene 485—where we have several psalms being chanted by the multitude—we need an idea for that. And look at the possibilities during Jesus' visit to Capernaum, the second time He goes there. And here, when Mary and Joseph come back from Egypt and must pass through the valley of the crucified—voices must play a part in lamentation."

He looked up at me expectantly.

I took a breath. "Give me the Inbal Dancers for a few days, Mr. Stevens, when you can spare them from the set. I would like to try integrating some of their Hebrew chants with one of the psalms. . . ."

"You mean like 'The Lord is my shepherd, I shall not want'?"

"Yes, sir."

"I'd have to hear it. There's another place where the mourners are weeping and wailing over the death of Lazarus. Jesus should hear that as he approaches. What can we do there that hasn't been done a thousand times before?"

"I've thought about that scene, as well as the others you mentioned, and I brought along an adaptation of material drawn from the Books of Job and Jeremiah. This might do for one of the laments." I handed him a typewritten page. He read it softly.

"Behold, O God, our woe. Behold, O Lord, our sorrow. The joy of our hearts is ceased. Our dance is turned into mourning. (Oh, very good.) The Lord gave and the Lord hath taken away. O, blessed be the name of the Lord. Behold, O Lord, our burden of distress, for we are bereaved."

He drew out the second syllable like a wail, and went on. "Our eyes that hath seen him will see him no more. Our eyes are upon him, but he is not. As a cloud is consumed and vanisheth away, so he that goeth down into the grave shall come up no more. . . . " He stopped. "Good God, I'm glad those words aren't used in funerals today. They're so shockingly final. How would you use them for the scene?"

"This lament should be chanted by the Inbal men with Ovadia Tuvia as the cantor. I'd choose several special women—ones with the voices and the histrionic ability—to perform the keening, the wailing, and the cries of mourning. Blended together on many tracks and reverberated, these sounds would come in waves, as on the wind. With a little experimentation, I think we could achieve the effect of an entire nation weeping for its dead."

"If you can make it sound as good as you tell it," he said, rubbing his arms, "it should be a new sensation."

"Have you definitely given up the idea of using a short musical benediction at the Last Supper?" I asked. "Alfred wanted me to bring it to your attention so something could be prepared in advance should you need it."

He wrinkled his brow. "We've had that hymn in and out a dozen times. At present, it's out. What did you have in mind?"

"There's a famous one-liner in Genesis that goes, '*Now may the Lord watch between me and thee, when we are absent, one from another.*' "

"That's a wonderful way to end a bull session," he said. "If the music is as simple and as beautiful as the words, the hymn is now back in." He turned to the Tonys. "Vellani, tell Chico Day to give Ken the Inbals at the first opportunity so the vocal experiments can begin. Perris, you and Van arrange a place for Ken to record them." He stood up and reached for my hand. "Tell Alfred the musical ideas are good, and give him my best. Tell him it's a wonderful job. It's better than that. It's better than I'd hoped for, but then I shouldn't be surprised. Alfred never fails to be an inspiration with his music, and now that he's found you to do his talking for him—" he laughed. "When Al tries to explain his composition to me I get pretty confused. His musical rhetoric goes right over my head like a foreign language."

I started to chuckle, but it came out a cackle. "You really can't talk a musical score. I can talk about music, but I can't write it. That's my problem, I talk it out of my system. Pappy sits down and writes you a heartbreak, or a miracle, so who needs semantics?"

He laughed again. "Of course. You're right. Thanks again, so much." He patted me on the shoulder as I left, and gave the Tonys a jovial goodnight.

I walked to the trailer with Vellani, wondering—in a floating way—where I'd go from this first summit meeting. Probably flat on my butt, I decided, unless I produced what I had so glibly promised. At least, I had sustained his total interest; our little "15-minute session" had lasted an hour and forty-five minutes.

Vellani was out on his feet, but he ushered me into the trailer and we put in a call to Alfred. When I heard his familiar voice, I stopped floating and felt anchored again.

"Hi, Pappy," I said. I'm calling from the Promised Land."

"You've got a cold," he said accusingly.

"A perfect doozy," I answered. "It's mine, it's contagious, and I'm spreading it around. The cabins are too hot, the weather's too cold, the days are too short, and the nights too long. Everybody is hacking and spitting and running to the can, but we had a good meeting with George tonight—and he *liked* all the music."

"Oy-damn! I was afraid of that. Now I'll have to start rewriting it. When Stevens says he likes something, it almost invariably gets revised. I was almost hoping he'd say that the music stinks.

Are the Tonys giving you any trouble? Don't let them push you around, now!"

"One of them is sitting right here waiting to talk to you. Shall I put him on?"

Tony talked for about five minutes, giving Alfred a good rundown on the meeting, leaving out nothing, telling it all. When he handed the phone back to me I said, "Well, Pap, that's the scoop. I'm going to experiment for a few days, the Lord willing."

"Don't you stay up there and catch pneumonia. If you're sick, you just knock off and come home. Oh—tell Harold that I told him so. He'll know what I mean. And don't you stay there a minute longer than absolutely necessary. Check?"

"Check."

Dinner was late, light, pleasurable, and relaxed, and my appetite was okay. Vellani and I made a few tentative plans before he fell asleep in his plate, and Tony Van Renterghem told me I could keep the Wollensak in my cabin. I roused the drowsing Vellani, walked him back to his shanty. Once inside my own domain I wrote a few letters, trekked to the trailer with them, phoned Vera, and slipped into bed about 1 a.m., noting that the maid had left me an extra blanket. It must have been made of love, for I was almost completely comfortable. I began searching around in my mind for some way properly to reward her, but all I could find was the mnemonic sound of Stevens' voice repeating "bereaved ... be-reeeeved ... bee-reeeeeeeved ... " blending and interweaving with the hissing of the trucks along the haul road.

SIX

Jack Lacey banged on my door and barged right in. "I brought you a sheet of plywood for your bed. C'mon, we'll tuck it under your mattress. I wouldn't take a hundred bucks for mine. It makes a helluva big difference in the way you sleep, and besides, your bed stays solid if you ever happen to get two people in it."

He guffawed, and we pulled and hauled, finally getting it to suit him. "You'll thank me for this tomorrow morning—about ten times."

"I won't wait. I'll start now. Thank you, thank you, thank you . . . "

"Knock it off." He was grinning as he jumped in his golf cart and rolled away.

Seven of the disciples were in camp that day—not needed on the set. I spent the morning setting up the Wollensak, getting extra chairs from neighboring cabins, and preparing for an early afternoon rehearsal. Hal Weinberger, Chief of Operations, put the loudspeakers to work for me right after lunch: "ALL DISCIPLES, ATTENTION. THERE WILL BE A REHEARSAL OF ALL DISCIPLES IN CABIN C-3 AT ONE-THIRTY SHARP. SEE KEN DARBY IN CABIN C-3 AT ONE-THIRTY."

Half an hour after lunch, here they came, crowding into the living room and overflowing into both bedrooms. I introduced myself and explained the scene in which they were to sing. Then without further preamble, I played the recording of the *136th Psalm*.

They all began to talk at once. David Hedison (Philip) shouted down the others. "Why can't we all sing the song ourselves right on the set when they shoot the scene? We could do it, couldn't we, guys?"

40

They all agreed, and I grinned at them.

"Oh, sure, you *could* sing it," I said, "providing all of you can carry a tune in a respectable key, and with the same kind of calm devotion you just heard on the tape. You could sing it four, five, or even ten times—as many takes as Mr. Stevens requires—and then he'd want to change the angle. After the new camera setup was ready and the lights were in place, you'd start to sing it all over again, this time at a different tempo and probably in a different key. Tell me, how would you cut those two shots together and come out with a whole song, and who wants me to go on with this boring explanation anyway?"

They had been studying me. Now Tom Reese (Thomas) said, "You're right. There's nothing as dead-ass as a bunch of bored disciples. So what's the answer?"

"All you have to do is memorize the song. Then you can synchronize your lips to this recording."

Jamie Farr (Thaddeus) said, "Sho' nuff, let's learn'er."

So I rehearsed them, pointed out the places to breathe, prodded them to sing along with the record, and they soon had the words memorized.

At three o'clock, I distributed copies of "Barabbas' Song" and told them that Stevens wanted them to learn it even though he had doubt that it would be used in the picture. They had it down pat in less than twenty minutes, and the cabin resounded to "Send the Romans back across the sea." There was rude laughter, initiated by Robert Blake (Simon the Zealot), over the line, "The only Roman peace is in our graves," and Gary Raymond (Peter) said, "Blake, you're a necrophiliac!"

That broke up the session and I let them depart. "We'll rehearse again," I called after them. "But next session will be with individuals, one at a time, so do your homework."

I'll record them, too, I thought, just in case Stevens actually does want some of them to sing on the set. At least, I'll know which of them *can.*

The sun was bright, heavy and warm, but the air was cool. I slipped on my windbreaker, hung my camera over my shoulder, and started walking up the western slope leading away from the camp, stopping to watch the roaring trucks slashing away at space on the haul road. VrOOOm . . . and two minutes later, VarOOOm. I crossed the road and ventured into the wilderness beyond. The earth was sandy and red, wind-riffled into waves; ancient starved vegetation crumbled underfoot, and the sorry clumps of tiny cactus looked stunted and unfinished. I walked slowly in this desolate place, breathing quietly, hoping the smells and flavors of sky and canyon, air and sunlight, would enter my occupied lungs and make me well and whole again.

As the shadows grew long, a chill of apprehension crept over my skin. I stopped—stood still—feeling eyes upon me. Was I being watched from the butte top? Were there mud hogans up there behind the bluff where Indian spirits frowned upon my presence? Nothing moved; no beetle or bird disturbed the vast emptiness. Suddenly, a jack rabbit as big as an Irish setter leaped from the shadows at my feet and bounced across a deep gully, zigzagging crazily up the farther side—and scaring me nearly out of my shirt.

I watched until he had lost himself in the ancestral grandeur and my heart had returned to normal cadence, then turned back, feeling so cruelly alone that I wanted to run. The silvery sheen of Tin City sparkled in the last rays like strands of tinsel ribbon. I walked slowly toward it, thinking how, in the eye of God, this earth must seem the smallest grain of sand—but a grain swarming with toxic human bacteria whose careless effluence would one day require the superheated scalpel, or a cosmic penicillin. But no, God's intervention wouldn't be necessary. Long before the festering became fatal, the venomous infection caused by man would trigger its own thermonuclear fever, or perish of its own environmental toxicity. Then the earth would be lovely again, a fine, clean, shining grain of sand.

I took no pictures. Who can photograph loneliness? . . . or introspection? . . . or delirium?

SEVEN

The morning was productive of several things: I coughed, sneezed, gargled, sprayed, and gave endless thanks to Jack Lacey for the solid comfort of my bed. I had slept well for the first time since arriving, and my organs of recuperation were busy ridding my system of the noxious invader. I devoted the entire morning to aiding and abetting.

At lunch, I ran into Tony Vellani, in from the set to get a warm meal. He said, "You can have the Inbals all day tomorrow, Ken. They won't be needed on the set."

I thanked him and reported on my progress with the disciples. Nine of them were eating at the next table, so I took the opportunity to schedule individual appointments for the afternoon.

The first one to arrive was Michael Tolan, cast as James the Elder, and I recorded his speech, his singing voice, and part of the 136th Psalm. He was a bass, a good speaker, not musical, partially tone deaf, but he was able to synchronize to the playback.

So it went for the rest of the afternoon. I recorded Jamie Farr, Roddy MacDowall, Peter Mann, Tom Reese, Robert Blake, Gary Raymond, David Hedison, John Considine. Out of the nine, there were four who sang well, and David Hedison was so enthusiastic that he came back later and sang the whole psalm from memory with good intonation. The rest were really non-singers, but would pass with more rehearsal.

I ate dinner with Harold Kress, who was agitated again. "An editor is supposed to edit," he growled. "Tonight when I ran the dailies with Stevens, I asked him to let me cut some of the reaction shots into the master scenes, and he gave me the frozen stare. He said I was only to cut the dailies together—end to end—and that he and I would *not* edit any film until the picture was completed, which could mean next year, or the year after. He's got me afraid to do anything, and I've already cut three reels behind his back. I wouldn't dare let him know *that*, and I'll never be able to run those reels for him now."

"Not while he has you in the deep freeze," I agreed. "Why don't you wait a couple of weeks, then tell him you have edited together a few ideas—strictly on an exploratory basis—as an interesting experiment? I'll bet he'd listen to that, and would run your three reels. I do know for a fact that he is friendly to investigative experiments."

Harold chewed at a hangnail. "That's *all* he's friendly to; I might as well go home. O'Neill can cut the dailies."

"Take it easy. Just pretend you're a man of leisure. And, by the way, Alfred said to tell you that he told you so."

Harold laughed. "Yes, he did. He told me about Stevens and I didn't believe him. I sure do now."

"Hey," I said, "isn't tomorrow Thanksgiving?"

He pulled out his wallet, frisked it for a card calendar, and slapped the heel of his palm against his forehead. "I've got to call my wife. She was expecting me home. Yes," he added, rising, "tomorrow is turkey day."

Thanksgiving Day came to George Stevens Productions un-edited, untitled, unscored, and as anonymous as any other common old Thursday. The carpenters carped, the mechanics mended their mechanisms, the plumbers fixed forty leaking faucets, and the helicopter crew installed a new jet engine. The only variation was the absence of careening trucks on the haul road. The crew of the big dam would not work today, but Stevens had already made three shots down by the "Jordan," baptizing a few extras in the icy water before I was out of bed. The shower was hot; I soaped and scrubbed in it, feeling no pain. Head was open, no rattlesnakes were in my chest. Was I ready to rejoin the family of man? I gave it a try at breakfast and was accepted. I actually got off a few semi-welcome witticisms. Everyone seemed to love me.

All but the Inbals.

They teamed up against me as though I was instituting a pogrom. I had to enlist Ovadia Tuvia to help me break down their animosity. I tried conveying my intentions to him, and an hour was consumed passing information back and forth—English to Hebrew, Hebrew to English. The spokesman for the group of dissidents declared that they did not want their relatives or orthodox friends ever to hear any sacred words, chants, or davening sounds (Ovadia pronounced it "dahvening" and translated it as "prayerful") emanating from any movie screens anywhere—period! Ovadia patiently explained that I was not asking them for any sacrilegious act, and eventually he convinced them to experiment with me on the tape recorder

An hour later they were performing the most wondrous and compelling sounds, and a large audience had gathered to hear the singing, chanting, sobbing, and keening as they invented spontaneous lamentations of extraordinary impact and fervor. By the time we broke for lunch, they were no longer antagonists.

Afterward, I moved them into the rehearsal tent and put on a fresh tape, auditioning first the women, then the men; rehearsing the combined groups, and finally recording a cantus firmus lament in which each singer started the melody on that note most comfortable to his own vocal register. The result was an emotional experience. Most of the Inbals were in tears, and many of the onlookers—including Vellani—were moved to make extravagant compliments, all of which Ovadia translated to the astonished Inbals. When they heard the playback, they applauded themselves like delighted children.

"This should be spectacular," sighed Tony happily. "I can almost hear it in the finished film—as if upon the wind."

I knew he had lifted that line from someone, so after I had dismissed the Inbals and arrived back in my cabin, I looked in the script—and there it was: "The sound of lamentation is heard as if upon the wind." And I realized, with a jolt, that I had plagiarized and used the same phrase in my meeting with Stevens . . . so why couldn't Tony?

I looked up from the script, and there he was standing in the doorway. "May I come in?" he asked.

"Of course."

He sat down wearily, lit a cigarette and spoke through the smoke. "Do you think you have accomplished everything Mr. Stevens wanted—for now?"

There's a question, I thought, directly from moneyman Davis. "With the disciples, yes," I said. "With the Inbal Dancers, there's more to do. They have a lot to offer—"

Tony interrupted. "Can any of the disciples sing?"

"A few; and all of them can synchronize."

He ran his hand over his forehead. "I think you and I should go over the script again to spot the laments, but I'm too tired to do it now. I'll go lie down for a little while." He looked at his watch. "Bang on my door in an hour. I'm nearly ill with fatigue."

He dragged himself out of the chair and across to his cabin, leaving me to study this odd conversation. Apparently, he was trying to determine whether to take Davis' advice and send me home, or to honor Stevens' instructions for more experimentation. Sending me home would get me off the payroll; with that extra twelve hundred a week they could buy a lot of paint.

I spent the hour going over possible exploratory vocal ideas, making notes and dredging for innovations. Promptly on the hour I knocked on Vellani's door. He looked out at me sleepily—and we both saw Stevens' car drive up.

"We won't have time for the script now," he said. "The company's back from the set early and Stevens will want me in the projection room with him when he runs the dailies."

The air had taken a chill. The sun had gone behind dramatic sprays of black clouds, and my sinuses were aching. I soaked with hot towels, massaged the forehead, inhaled steam, and wondered how to avoid the Thanksgiving cocktail party the ladies were throwing in the mess tent. It should be fun, so why was I resisting? Because I didn't drink? Envy perhaps?

Yes, I concluded in a cloud of steam, I'm plainly and distressingly envious of all the people with stomachs and hollow legs who have the capacity for conviviality under the stimulation of alcohol.

I swallowed a couple of headache pills, put on my wools, and went across the compound under a black starless sky. The cocktail party was going full gallop in the rehearsal tent, and I paused only long enough to see that it was crowded and noisy. Then I went on into the mess tent and sat myself near one of the area heaters.

The turkey, the dressing, and all the seasonal frills were deliciously warming my insides when Stevens came in with the company surrounding him. He was carrying a half-filled glass, and was squiring a dazzling blond woman whom he introduced to everyone as Miss McTavish. His remarks were short and quite deliberately pompous.

"Ladies and gentlemen of the company: Miss McTavish and I—and all of my staff—wish all of *you* a very happy Thanksgiving. Tomorrow we will start shooting one hour later."

The two hundred and eighty people in the tent all stood up, shouting "Yay!" applauding, and clinking glasses. I was overwhelmed by greetings of "Happy Thanksgiving" from the Inbals, the disciples, and the crew—and my envy grew. The evening was just beginning for some of them. Couples had paired off for the feast and would probably remain together for the night.

Suddenly I knew it wasn't envy. It was a lousy case of self-pity. I kicked at the sawdust as I left the tent, angry at the silly scruples that kept me from mingling and breaking the rules, and walked rapidly back to my new comfortable bed—alone. On the way, I stopped by the deserted trailer, phoned Vera and Alfred to wish them well and give them my thanks—and fell into bed with their love surrounding me.

Happy Thanksgiving, world.

EIGHT

The sky was still dark when I was nudged awake by an impatient idea clamoring for expression. I got up, jotted it down—with the intention of going back to bed—but while I was writing a bright feminine day looked in on me with such a loving blue eye that I dressed and walked out to meet her. She was radiant and embracing; my gal Friday.

At breakfast, there was a sorry-looking group trying to convince me that the cocktail party had been all fun, and the games following it had been racy and naughty. Somehow, the charade fell flat. Mary, whose moist eyes were mistier than usual, was wearing a coarse hangover, and her lips looked puffed and bruised. She pushed aside her bowl of oatmeal, ordered eggs sunny side up, drank two cups of coffee while waiting for them to appear, gave them one glance, and, not liking the way they looked back at her from their blood-flecked orbs, got up and departed abruptly. Harold and I exchanged glances, and Florence said, "How flagrantly we dissipate our youth. How diligently we pursue false pleasure."

"How philosophical it is this morning," Harold added.

While we were laughing together, the compound trumpets began to bellow with excitement. "ALL HOLLYWOOD EXTRAS AND THE INBAL DANCERS REPORT TO WARDROBE IMMEDIATELY. BUSES ARE LEAVING FOR THE BRIDGE SET IN TWENTY MINUTES. MOVE QUICKLY, PLEASE. THIS IS AN EMERGENCY."

"Two possibilities," Harold said. "Someone is either ill or has been injured, *or*, Stevens has finished the Jordan River sequence and is moving to the other location."

"I'll find out," I said. "The Inbals were scheduled to rehearse with me at ten, and I don't think the Lord would do this to me."

Frank O'Neill snorted. "But Stevens *would*, and it looks like he's done it to you good."

The Operations shack looked like a disaster area. People of all shapes, sizes and professions—and in all conditions—were plunging in and out trying to get information and help. I bulled my way inside and found Hal Weinberger on two phones at once, trying to raise a dentist in Kanab and a surgeon in Page. Jerry Parker, the camp's male nurse and unofficial medic (without degree), was picking his nose and talking on the radio transmitter, trying to treat by remote control a workman who had smashed three fingers while carrying timbers to the Walls of Jerusalem, and he was shouting angrily.

"Ice, dammit! There's got to be ice cubes in the caterer's truck. Get that man's hand in a bucket of ice and hold it there while the driver brings the dumb bastard to camp."

Lee Lukather stomped in behind me holding his jaw, white-faced and furious. "Knock it off, Jerry! Hold y'r temper."

Hal Weinberger's voice was an octave too high.

"Hello, doctor? Could you handle an emergency? We have a man here who's just ruptured himself . . . oh, good—Kanab Hospital. He's on the way, and thanks." He turned to the other phone. "Dr. Randall? Can you see a patient with a broken tooth and an exposed nerve? . . . What? Not till six-thirty tonight?"

A van drove up outside, disgorging two pale workmen. They rushed to the infirmary and brought back a stretcher. Carefully, slowly, they lifted a man from the van whose hands were clutching his crotch. Jerry Parker went outside and I followed. A station wagon was brought up, and the stretcher with the groaning man on it was gently loaded in the back.

"Get him straight into Kanab Hospital," Jerry ordered. "They've got a surgeon standing by."

We walked back into Operations. Hal was still on the phone, nagging at the dentist. "But I'm telling you, doctor, this man is in excruciating pain. . . . What'll we do with the exposed nerve, develop it? . . . You've got to be crazy—you want us to give him chewing gum and aspirin?" He turned to Lee Lukather, palming the mouthpiece of the telephone. "This idiot sonofabee wants us to give you chewing gum and aspirin." Then, back to the phone, "Hey, doc—any particular kind of chewing gum?" (Long pause, during which Hal's face reddened.) "Well, if that's the best you can do, we'll have him there at six-thirty." He hung up and turned to Jerry Parker. "Did you get that man with the hernia to the hospital?"

"He's on the way; left for Kanab a few minutes ago. Also, I sent two of our house maids to Phoenix this morning."

"What now?"

"One of them had a bleeding ulcer—only twenty years old, too. The other had infectious hepatitis. Neither one is compensable, so take 'em off of the payroll."

"I will *not*," Hal shouted. "Now's the time they *need* all the help they can get."

I applauded, and the radio began to chatter loudly.

"OPERATIONS FROM JORDAN RIVER. WE'RE ALL WRAPPED UP DOWN HERE. STEVENS JUST TOOK OFF FOR CAMP AND HE WANTS EVERYBODY INVOLVED AT THE BRIDGE SET IN ONE HOUR. OVER."

Hal snapped on his microphone. "Got the message. Everybody will be there. Over and out."

"Are you going back to L.A. on the plane with me tonight?" It was Lee Lukather and he was talking to me.

"I'm beginning to think I'll never be going back. You'll have to fold up this carnival and ship the whole company to the hospital if the hepatitis spreads around."

"You know it." He groaned, rubbing his jaw. "This damned tooth is murder. I'm going home and have it fixed; to hell with that dentist in Page."

"Why don't you try his chewing gum and aspirin while you wait? What do you like, Juicy Fruit?"

"Get outa here, Darby."

Outside, the helicopter was settling behind the cabins on its landing pad. Stevens stepped out and started for his office. He was obviously pleased with the morning's work.

"Good morning, Ken. When the dailies come back, I'd like you to see what we shot today: a retake of the Lord's Prayer. Max did a marvelous study of Christ in supplication."

I thanked him, and he walked toward the executive trailer while I cut through the bungalow aisles to reach mine in the third row back. As I reached the area between the second and third row, here was Stevens, walking around the corner toward me. He hesitated a moment, then came steadily on. "I'll be sending the Inbal Dancers back to camp early this afternoon so you can continue rehearsing with them. I'm told that their contribution is quite spectacular. Keep up the good work."

Then he turned and started back toward his bungalow, making a complete circle.

George didn't come all the way around just to tell me about the Inbals, I thought; something else is afoot. I did a quick dive into Harold's cutting room. He was making doodles on a pad of paper.

"What bungalow is Miss McTavish in?" I asked.

"B-6, just three bungalows farther down from yours."

"Sh . . . " I whispered. Stevens was again coming around the corner. I could see him through the crack of the open door. He walked straight to B-6, turned the knob and walked in. I told Harold what was going on.

"He probably flew in to check her flight plan," he said. "Miss McTee is going back to L.A. this evening on the DC-3."

Forty minutes later the helicopter took off with Stevens on board. I got a nice photo of it against the dappled sky.

Vellani was waiting for me in my cabin. "Ken," he began, "Mr. Stevens wants you to remain with us for another week to supervise more experimental recordings with the Inbals: the prayers and lamentations. Can you arrange to do that?"

"I'm not sure, Tony. I'll have to make some calls."

"Good." He started out, then added, "Let's get together right after lunch and go over the script as we planned. See you in an hour or so."

I thought about another week. I thought about seven more days in this aluminum uterus. I wondered if it would have any labor pains when I left. But thinking and wondering didn't change anything, and Vellani was coming back in an hour—so I jogged over to the office and put in my calls. When I told Alfred what was going on, he grumbled acidly and rang off. Vera promised she would cheer him up; didn't know why *he* was missing me so much when she missed me with a passion. Then Pappy called back to apologize for being so disgruntled and abrupt, and to give me a word of cheer. "I'm composing music to the script," he said. "When you come home I'll have some material to show you—part of it is fair. Don't let them get you down; stay as long as they need you, then grab the money and run . . . and by the way, your agent got you a big raise."

Vellani was pleased that I had arranged to stay, and we spent the afternoon exploring the script. Dusk was welcome!

Dinner was dull, and so was my appetite. The usual gusto was absent. Intake, I realized, was exceeding outgo. Remedy would have to be applied.

I bought a book of crossword puzzles at the canteen, thinking the solving might make me somnolent, but the longer I worked the quicker and sharper I became. At last, with firm determination, I swallowed pills that would put me to sleep and exercise my viscera.

I have arrived at the age, I reflected mournfully, when regularity is more to be desired than Social Security.

NINE

The morning was blessed with brisk action on all fronts. The Inbals marched into my domain at ten, bearing flutes, shofars, lutes, drums and—a *kanoon*. This strange relative of the zither was held flat on the lap and played with picks and plectrums attached to every finger and thumb.

I handed Ovadia the manuscript of Alfred's "Shepherd Song," and he explained how it should be played to his flutist, whom he called by the strange name Tsifion. I turned on the tape recorder and captured the sad sweet tones of his flute and the exotic improvisations he performed to show off his remarkable technique. Less swarthy than the others, Tsifion was also less taciturn; happily he transferred from flute to tin whistle and had us all laughing at his virtuosity.

When I asked the others to play the same melody, I was told gently by Ovadia that none of them could read; they would learn the melodies by rote. But I did get a recorded sample of all the instruments before it was time for lunch.

At one-thirty, I met with Ovadia to show him the 22nd, 23rd, and 24th Psalms that I wanted him to rehearse for trial recordings next day. He studied the copies for five minutes.

"In Hebrew this will not be difficult," he said peacefully, "but the English lament from the Book of *Job* will require much study and rehearsal." Then, as he packed the music in his case he added, "I will do the best I can."

I walked down to the motor pool and rented a car for a drive into Page. A vast mass of land, air and sky surrounded the little town, which had recently expanded importantly because of the dam. In the liquor store, I had to wait for a few moments while a sporty Navajo, dressed in shiny black leather from boots to hat

53

(including gloves), examined the stock while weighing a heavy decision.

"Hill'n'Hill," he grunted finally. "Two quart." And he paid for his purchase with a crisp fifty-dollar bill.

"Not many of them around here can do that," the clerk said after the Indian had left. "Most of them can't even get enough to eat, and the ones who *do* have the money don't seem to give a damn about the rest of their people going hungry—but they *do* drink a lot of whisky."

I bought Harold a jug of Cutty Sark, Florence a bottle of brandy, and Mary a fifth of vodka. Then I drove slowly back, stopping now and again to take pictures of the town, the dam, the camp from a high angle, the Jerusalem Walls, and the sharp sculptured cliffs that sprang from the desert floor. Majestic.

As I approached the cabin, I heard Vandraegan and David Hedison chanting in unison: "Adage . . . umbrage . . . damage . . . hemorrhage . . . positive . . . plaintive . . . punitive . . . passive."

"Enough," I said, opening the door. You have learned all you need to know about punitive damage, and I take umbrage. Would any of you care to dine?"

"Enthusiastically and abundantly," Vandraegan said. "I need only a few more minutes to put the finishing touch on David's labial attacks and I'll be with you."

I left them enunciating "banish . . . battle . . . bushel . . . " and delivered Harold's Scotch and Florence's brandy. Mary wasn't in, so I put her vodka on a shelf in my bedroom.

The mess tent was not crowded. Dan and I were eating and chatting amiably by ourselves when two grips, ignoring the rest of the table, took seats directly opposite and began a loud conversation of such utter banality that we sat wholly enthralled. The one across from me was in mid-sentence.

" . . . an' most of the single ones are hookers. It used t'be a gal wanted it as much as a man did and it didn't cost nothin' but a few beers and maybe a sandwich. Hey, waitress. Hi, sweetie, you married?"

The tired waitress shook her head and he grabbed her arm.

"You ain't? Well good. How 'bout us goin' inta Page when you're through work and havin' ourselves a time?"

"I'm on duty till midnight, and I wouldn't go anyway."

"Aw, c'mon."

She jerked her arm away. "Forget it! You want to order?"

"You're from Arizona all right. Utah gals ain't so dam'd unfriendly. Gimme a Noo York steak—well done—I mean *well*."

The man opposite Vandraegen ordered his steak medium rare and said, "If you're gonna eat a piece of cremated charcoal, go sit at the other end of the table where I won't see it."

Vandraegen inhaled too quickly and choked. My man said, "*You* move. I tried eatin' a rare steak last night and the goddam blood runnin' around on my plate near made me puke. You eat yours any way ya dam please. Me, I like mine cooked civilized."

Vandraegen's man didn't say anything. He just glanced at us and forked up a bite of salad. Mine directed his next remark to us. "You guys from Hollywood got it tough payin' all them dooz to the unions. Us guys from Utah got a right-to-work clause in our system. We git the same dough, but don't pay the dooz. Catch me gettin' suckered into no goddam union. Hey! Ain't them people down at that table blacks?"

The other turned around, looked and swung his head back. "Naw, they're Jews from Arabia or Egypt—someplace like that. They call themselves Inbals."

"Look more like odd-balls t'me," said mine. "Funny combination, too, bein' both Jewish *and* black. Probably from California. That place is lousy with both of them."

"Yuh ever been there?"

"Hell no."

"Then shut up and eat."

I felt a surge of fellowship for the big man across the table. I wanted to pin a medal on him.

"Whatsa matter?" mine asked. "You one o' them nigger lovers?"

"They're people! An' that's more'n I can say f'r some *whites* I know."

There was an ominous silence. Mine chewed hard on a piece of charred steak. Then, on a widely divergent tack, he said, "Yuh know what I'm gonna do tonight? I'm gonna get a snootful. Then I'm gonna get a nice soft belly to rub mine against, an' it won't cost me a dime."

"You're fulla shit! All you Utah guys are fulla shit."

At this point, Dan and I had been sufficiently enthralled. We didn't bother to excuse ourselves, we just stood up and walked away. Dan went to chat with some of his disciples, and I looked in on the end of the movie next door.

"What's the title?" I whispered to Bob Bush.

"*The Last Voyage of the Clarendon*," he whispered back. "The author should have gone down with the ship before he ever put pen to paper. It's the worst aquatic cliffhanger I've seen come out of Hollywood."

I watched a few scenes—long enough to agree with him—and walked outside, nearly falling over Jack Lacey. He was overflowing with bad news.

"We had a near catastrophe today. The big well that supplies all the water for the camp caved in at the two-hundred-foot level. The damn thing delivered two hours of hot water. I stuck a thermometer in it that went up to a hundred and fifty degrees. We finally pumped it out, along with about a ton or so of mud, but we had to order big tanker trucks from Page to keep us supplied with water while the work went on. Can you imagine what would have happened in all our hundred and seventeen toilets if we ran outa water around here?" He grimaced. "I've had acid in my gut all day just worryin' about *that*. You gotta Tums?"

I was fishing in my pocket when a voice said, "Hello, Jack. Do you know where I can find Ken Darby?"

"Right here. I thought you'd met. Ken, shake hands with Frank Davis."

We shook, and Davis said, "We've never met, but I think we know all about each other by reputation."

He was thin and tall, had a slight widow's peak above a wide forehead, and his face tapered down to a narrow chin. A black briar pipe seemed to be a permanent appendage, and over his business suit he wore an expensive suede windbreaker.

He removed the pipe. "Tell me, Ken, are the Inbal Dancers using any of their own songs or compositions in the picture?"

"Yes, I believe they are. At least, they're using Hebrew melodies which have been adapted by their conductor. I would presume that clearances have all been covered in his contract."

"I really don't know if they have," he said. "I'll look into that when I get back to Hollywood. I want you to keep me advised of any original songs used by them—by title if at all possible. Will you do that?"

"Of course, Mr. Davis."

"I'll be here for a couple of days. Drop around by the office trailer when you can, and we will go over this matter thoroughly—in a warmer climate."

He shivered, said goodnight, and walked back into the tent. I handed Lacey my Tums.

"Davis is the company lawyer, isn't he?" I asked.

"Yep. He's also the Executive Producer—a real sharp guy."

"Yeah, *real* sharp," I said. "Goodnight, Jack; thank you, thank you, thank you . . . ."

"Okay, okay, you're welcome already. Thanks for the Tums."

I watched him walk off toward his cabin, but my mind was on the conversation with Frank Davis. If Alfred had been there with me, we would have had a good laugh. Here was the attorney for George Stevens Productions, who should know every word of the contract signed by the Inbal Dancers—individually and as a group—asking *me* to keep him informed about music rights. I hoped he would do some homework when he returned to Hollywood.

My bungalow was empty. I coughed and blew my nose forty or fifty times, washed my face with steaming towels, and got into bed with a pencil and scratch pad, jotting down a schedule of activities for tomorrow. It would be sweet Sunday, no day of rest for the inhabitants of this imitation Galilee. I would have the Inbals at ten for recording on the Wollensak, rehearse with the disciples at two. Then, at Vellani's quite specific (and peculiar) command, Tony Perris and I were to transfer all the discs of *The Messiah*, by Handel, to quarter-inch tape so George could play it on his big mobile machine. By that time Sunday would be gone. If Vandraegen and I didn't collide head on, it would be a miracle.

He was late tonight. I turned out my light, and didn't hear him come in.

I was lifted out of sleep by a sensing of something paranormal. I lay there for a few minutes, eyes wide open, but I heard only the gentle snore from Vandraegen's bedroom. A small hint nudged at the edge of my mind, and I suddenly had it: the haul road was silent! Apparently, Sunday was also machinery's day of rest.

But that wasn't all that needled me. Why did Stevens want Handel's *Messiah* transferred to tape? Was he going to play parts of it to accompany some particular scene in the dailies? That disturbing thought had me out of bed and into the bathroom in a hurry. I remembered another director who had become so obsessed with a temporary music track that he wouldn't accept anything else. The beleaguered film composer, rather than be accused of such bad taste, quit the picture. Consideration of this nasty possibility kept me awake for an hour or more, and I had to read a murder mystery to wash it out of mind.

Maybe I could sabotage the recording machine. It should have a day of rest, too.

TEN

Sunday began with a baptismal service of rain, as though some industrious saint had decided to cleanse our secular sins. It was a brief ceremony in which we were sprinkled, blessed, and sent on our way to rejoice in the pale glow of a forgiving sun. Vandraegen was furious with himself for leaving his microphone, spare tape, and the electric extension cord for his tape recorder at home. I rifled Charlie McCleod's supply closet and came up with all three items.

"You should be playing Max's role," he rumbled. "He only talks a good miracle; you actually perform them."

I moved all my recording gear into the projection room, turning over the bungalow to Dan, and a short time later the Inbal musicians trouped in. Avraham Cohen, the kanoon player, had learned Alfred's melody. After a number of trials and bad starts, he made an acceptable recording. Tsifion unlimbered his flutes and spoke in sputtery English.

"I broke back—*my* back. I did. I broke my back to learn Avraham playing that music—one note then one note next— the tune. Is not for instrument easy."

"You did very well," I assured him. "No music is really foreign to a musician, just unfamiliar. You taught him well."

"I'm ready play now," he said, smiling.

Tsifion recorded all the music, finishing with the odd shepherd's tune that Alfred had written. He played well.

Ovadia spoke gently. "Those last four notes don't belong to that piece. If I had written such a chromatic and modern melody, I would have written the ending to match, not simply appended a major scale."

"Mr. Newman will be interested in that opinion," I said pleasantly. "He will welcome meeting you and discussing the modalities he plans to work throughout the score."

Ovadia smiled. "I shall welcome equally the opportunity for giving any assistance." He paused a moment. "Is Alfred Newman Jewish?"

"You mean genetically, reform, or orthodox?"

He considered.

"That is a question I think perhaps I should not have asked. I can see that to you it makes no difference at all."

"Thank you, Ovadia. That's a fine compliment. To me, a man is the sum of his intelligence and talents, and his behavior toward others. I like him (or dislike him) for what he is as an individual, not for where he comes from or his color or his religious affiliations. I have been told that you are from Tel Aviv and that you are Yemeni. I know you have a wife and children, and that you would like to bring them to America. I have discovered that you are intelligent, talented, trilingual, and a gentle man. You are also a patient and effective teacher. You have generously shown me much of your culture, your folkways and your abilities, for which I thank you as a friend. Now let me tell you about Mr. Newman, who has been my dear friend for more than fifteen years. He is extravagantly talented, a man of great intelligence, who has invested enormous effort to bring his talent to perfection. I never once gave his religion or birth the smallest consideration until one day he said, 'This melancholy old Jew needs a drink.' "

Ovadia smiled, and I continued. "He is not a devout man in a theological sense, nor does he relish for himself the rituals of any formalized religion, yet he is a deeply religious man, respecting his own gifts, and the needs of others. His mother was born to orthodox faith. His father was estranged when Alfred was young, and the responsibility for a family of eleven fell squarely on Alfred's small shoulders. He supplied the courage and the money to help six brothers and three sisters to acquire the best education then available, and he is now the fountainhead of his own family of seven children. His devotion to that family is steadfast and loyal. For these things alone I would love him if he were coal black or saffron yellow. But beyond all this, he is a truly inspired artist, able to touch the emotions of people in every part of the world with his music.

"He will not compose a score for this film which will be totally Hebraic, or a magnificent research monument to antiquity. No one in the theater will turn and whisper, 'Listen to that lovely Yemen Melody.' If the film itself is fluent and dramatically honest, his music will support and heighten every scene. If the film is dull, badly directed, or fails to involve the audience, no music ever written will bring it to life. But one thing is certain: Alfred is a master craftsman and he has a definite purpose—and an intellectual reason—for every single note he writes on paper. Now, listen again to this wandering flute melody."

I turned on the tape, and as the notes began to form their intricate pattern, I went on. "This oblique melody is a plaint. It cries a little as the shepherd mourns his lonely life so far from home. Yet it does not offend the sheep. It is a reflective, nomadic melody. The restless, dissimilar intervals reveal the shepherd's inner frustration at being ever on the move—from pasture to pasture. It is not a mere exercise on the twelve-tone row. He thinks of the woman waiting in the cottage down in the valley, and his tune alters in mood, becoming a strain of pure wistfulness. He thinks, 'I will be finished here tomorrow, then I will go home, and be renewed, calmed, and comforted.' "

The last four notes came through softly, then silence.

Ovadia looked at me thoughtfully. "There is much to be learned. Some music is a touch upon the mind. It would seem that Mr. Newman's music touches upon the heart. I wish very much to know him." He smiled, then added, "The last four notes have great meaning. I did not hear it before."

"Very good, Ovadia. Now, did you find a musical pattern for any of the psalms?"

"Yes, I have something here." He took from his bag a tablet of music paper. "Shall I sing it for you?"

"Before you do that, tell me again—does any person, while praying or reading psalms in the synagogue, use ordinary conversational speech, such as is customarily projected by orators and preachers?"

"No, no. You see, for thousands of years nobody could write music, nor even the printed word. The people put the words in the throat in such rhythmic and melodic patterns so they could long remember them. Messengers always carried the King's edicts from city to city by chanting them while they traveled. The ritual of reiterated chant was bred into the race for uncounted generations. Even after the words became inscribed on scrolls, the voices continued to chant by themselves when praying or reciting the Torah. Old men, young men, children, and even the women, knew all the risings and fallings of the psalms. Whenever they gathered in Synagogue or Temple, where mass prayers were evolved, they would join with the cantor, intoning along with him in their own easiest vocal register, each adding his own embellishment as emotion dictated: a break in the voice, a tremulous quaver, or a rolling mordent. It was—and still is—a strange haunting sound. So I must say *no* to your question. There was no talking as such, only a rhythmic, sonorous, semi-musical chant."

"Do you think we might capture it in English?"

"We can only try. May I show you?"

I turned on the recorder and he began chanting, reading from the manuscript he had written. After a moment, I realized that what I was hearing had no ethnic validity; it was contrived, pedestrian... and I interrupted him. "No good, Ovadia. It won't work. Let's try another method. After lunch I'd like you to bring two or three of your men back here to chant this same psalm in Hebrew. Will you do that?"

"Gladly. I would much prefer it that way."

"My preference, too. In Hebrew it will be beautiful."

"Thank you. As we say, *Toda rada*." He smiled.

The skies were patrolled by roving sundogs. The ground was sloshy and the air was warmer. Vandraegen was still dragging glottal explosions from his pupils, so I went to the big mess tent alone.

"A hot meal for *lunch?*—"

The lanky woman behind the steam table gave me a look reserved for mice and snakes. "We always have hot food for lunch on Sunday."

"Since when?" I asked impolitely.

"Since *today*," she retorted. "Mr. Stevens' orders."

I asked for prime rib. It came to me under lavender goo—a thin, overcooked shingle of meat with slightly less flavor than a square of cork. However, it was hot and I was hungry. Tony Vellani changed all that suddenly.

"We ought to make a playback of all the laments, particularly the English psalm for the burial of Lazarus. What do you think, Ken? Wouldn't playbacks be a good idea?"

I put down my fork, none too gently. "That word *playback* connotes a finished product, Tony." I tried not to sound as irritated as I felt. "We have neither the equipment nor the studio for making stereophonic playbacks. I intend to make *test* recordings of all the sounds I can, but no playbacks unless Mr. Stevens specifically asks for them, and even then only under optimum studio conditions."

"What if he should ask for them?"

"If he should ask," I said, slapping down my knife, "I'd ask *him* to provide a suitably quiet location, bring in another sound truck—or give me the one he uses on the set—and record monaural *guide tracks*, because we do not have stereo machines."

"What's a guide track?"

"It's just what the name implies. A guide track is piped to the singers on earphones to guide them later in making the permanent stereo tracks for the finished film. We *could* make permanent tracks on monaural tape *if* we could strain out all extraneous noises like airplanes and wind and automobiles, but no playbacks."

"Why couldn't we use quarter-inch tape on machines like the Wollensak?"

"The Wollensak is a toy, Tony. There's no possible way to synchronize it—or any similar machine—with the Cinerama camera. If we record anything we want to use in the picture, it will have to be done on the sprocket-driven tape machines in Wally Wallace's sound truck." I tapped him on the arm. "And what about quality, Tony? You've heard what comes out of the Wollensak."

"I suppose you're right. But, just for the record, how soon could you be ready to record any temporary guide tracks?" He had a calculating look in his eyes.

"Tomorrow morning. But," I added loudly, "Inbal Dancers will have to be adjusted for working overtime both today *and* tomorrow, because I'll have to rehearse them most of tonight."

Saul Wurtzel, sitting two tables away, nearly swiveled his head off at the word "adjusted." Like a bird dog, he came to pointed-eared attention, whirled around and called, "How *many* of them will have to be adjusted?"

"Ten or twelve," I shouted back, pushing away my plate. "I'll give you a list of their names right after I *don't* eat my lunch."

"Sorry," Vellani said, and trotted away.

"*He's* sorry," Saul said. "So am I," and followed Tony.

They left the tent together and I turned to my cold plate. The waitress was standing there with a platter of medium rare prime rib au jus, a mound of fluffy mashed potatoes, and a small dish of Harvard beets. My appetite rejoined me and I kissed the waitress' hand. "Be sure you wash it," I said. "You are a discerning lady, and I love you."

She smiled sympathetically, and I enjoyed the ingestion so much that I almost forgot about Vellani. Almost.

The Inbals worked diligently all afternoon, recording on the Wollensak three psalms and the lamentations from *Jeremiah* and *Job*. They wore their yarmulkes, performed in Hebrew, and I had never heard anything so awesome. They were worshipping! All that reverence fled when we attacked the English texts. They labored, Ovadia tutored, and I coached, but we could not wed the language to the modes of antiquity. The singers did not *feel* the words, nor could they fit them to the melody.

I finally dismissed them at 5:30 p.m. with the admonition—conveyed through Ovadia and Madam Sarah—that they must rehearse together after dinner until they could sing and perform all the material in their sleep. They were tired.

As I started to wrap up the recording equipment, one of the handsome bearded young men shyly remained with his female companion—an intriguing little thing of undoubtedly multilateral talents—to make a request.

"May I," he pronounced carefully, "have use of tape maysheen? I have invent of my own. I wish speech in maysheen for send tape Tel Aviv. It is physical plan for culture of human body. I have Wollensak in Tel Aviv. Please?"

This was a tremendous vocal effort, and I smiled applause.

"Yes, of course. Let me load it for you."

He handed me a fresh roll of tape from his briefcase. "Please welcome and stay for hearing," he offered. "Most interesting body health idea—never get sick."

I thought about Vandraegen sitting in my cabin with his semantic army of occupation, and agreed. "I can stay for a little while, but I have an appointment before dinner, so I may have to leave, but I'll go quietly.

"I know how turning off," he said.

I started the tape and he began speaking into the microphone. His words were incomprehensible, but I understood what the young lady was doing. She squatted, then sat, then lay down full length (all five feet of her) on her back, her knees up and her arms stretched to touch them. Obviously following his instructions, she began to roll her head from side to side. The voice continued—without inflection—monotonously, and I must have dozed, because when I next looked at my watch, ten minutes had passed. Yawning, I silently gathered my things together and tiptoed out. She was doing sit-ups.

Was it still Sunday? Yes, and I had forgotten something. Tony Perris was waiting at my cabin door to remind me.

"Have you got the album of the *Messiah*? Mr. Stevens is hot to have it transferred to tape before dinner."

"We'll make it in time," I assured him and went inside.

Vandraegen was nowhere about. I snatched up the album, my pipe, a box of cough drops, and we rushed to the mess tent where Tony Van Renterghem was waiting for us, leaning impatiently on Stevens' giant triple deck tape/record machine.

"This is Stevens' pet thing of the moment," Tony said. "We call it his *Lease Breaker*—and here's how it works."

He ran through the operating sequence with me, saw that I understood it, and left hurriedly. "I've got a heavy date," he confided, grinning back over his shoulder.

I watched him as he paused near the exit to acquire the company of an attractive young lady, and said, "If there's a woman in camp who hasn't opened her gate for that charming Dutchman it's only because her hinges are rusted shut."

"Yeah!" Perris grinned. "He picks up all the good ones."

We started the transfer from disc to tape, monitoring the tape deck at a moderate level on the twin speakers. On and on went the *Messiah*, right on into the dinner hour, and the early eaters began calling out, "Louder. We want to hear it." So we raised the volume and gave them the full concert treatment. By the time we had finished, Tony and I were famished, so we quickly stowed the Lease Breaker and sought a table.

Five people stopped me on the way, each asking the same question: "Are you going to score this picture with Handel's *Messiah*?" I answered them respectively: "Not this year. Who knows? Why not, it's free. Good Lord, I hope not," and "Absolutely not without Handel's written consent."

But the question echoed my midnight suspicions. I knew what it would do to Alfred if Stevens *was* planning such a sneaky maneuver. Scoring the life of Christ with Handel's oratorio would be like putting a wetsuit on Buddha; it just wouldn't fit.

Vandraegen joined us, starved as usual. I thought he had taken off in the plane long since, but a power huddle had kept the executives busy far past the regular flight time. He asked for a large T-bone steak—rare—and was just putting his knife into it when the voice of Saul Wurtzel—very sympathetic but very firm—said, "Oh, *there* you are! It's past time to leave for the airport. Everybody's waiting for you at the motor pool."

"Doom!" said Vandraegen. "Doom and disaster."

I grabbed two linen napkins and wrapped them around his steak. "Eat it on the way to the plane," I urged. "And here, take this chunk of French bread to mop up the chin juices."

"Most satisfactory solution, Ken. I thank you." And he was off, loping along behind Saul toward the exit.

"Happy landing," I shouted after him.

He waggled his steak at me. "See you next week; be well."

During this, two women had taken the seats across the table from me. One smiled and said, "Aren't you Ken Darby? I met you at Rad's house on the occasion of his wife's birthday. You and Rad were members of the King's Men quartet."

I dug into my memory for a name. She was quite pretty, smallish, with gray blond hair, a bobbed nose and lustrous eyes. I should remember a face like that—and the name.

"I'm Mary Bash, in the makeup department," she said.

"Of course," I lied. "In or out of makeup you're a bash. I'm delighted to see you again, and forgive me that awful pun."

She laughed. "This is Flo . . . and that is Betty."

I turned to look at *that*—who was sitting right next to me—and nearly dropped my coffee cup. Leaning my way, not a dozen inches from my face, was a glistening goon of a woman lavishly anointed with oil. I almost expected her to flap a flipper, like a seal, but she only grinned feebly, sending trickles of oil into surrounding folds of fat, and said, "So nice to meet you," in very cultured English.

"Happier here," I lied again and pried my eyes away.

Mary was saying, "I met you during the years when Leo Durocher was married to Laraine Day, not too long after her divorce from Ray Hendricks."

"That *was* a long time time ago. Funny how we count our acquaintances by the divorces of our friends, isn't it?"

We were still talking about all those friends of The King's Men quartet, their past peccadillos and relationships, when Harold Kress wandered in looking wan and dispirited. He sat across from Tony Perris, who had moved farther down the table when he saw me in conversation with the ladies.

"I've been on the sick list—and that other unmentionable list—all day long with cramps and trots," he said. "I feel awful. But Jerry Parker told me to come up and eat a steak just to give my insides something to do besides hurt."

We all encouraged him, and he was getting on quite well when I sensed, then saw, a faint greenish penumbra steal up from beneath his collar and meet gleaming beads on his brow. He lifted himself cautiously, said a hasty goodnight, and left. I was wondering if he'd make it to his cabin when Mary's voice interrupted my thoughts.

"Have you seen the old Mormon ruins?"

"Several. Anybody in particular?"

"No kidding." She laughed prettily. "The ruins of an early Mormon settlement lie between here and the Jordan River set, and I did so want to stop and explore them. Of course, you can't stop when you're being driven to the set, and it seems that nobody wants to take the trip out there on the weekends. I'm an amateur rock hound, you know, and I really haven't had enough time to go snooping around as much as I'd like. I don't have a car, and no one is much interested in taking me."

She waited long enough so that if I didn't come forth with an offer she could consign me to Harold's shit list. It was a list I didn't care to be assigned to, so I plunged into the breach.

"If I'm still here next Sunday, Mary, we've got a date. We'll take a lunch and have a picnic in the ruins, gather a few rocks, take some pictures, and leave no stone unturned. I'll get you out of stir and into trouble . . . and love it."

She was so pleased that she blushed, and offered me a well-manicured hand. "Please stay till Sunday. It'll be fun." I said goodnight to her and Flo. Then, suddenly remembering the oily one, I said the proper words just in time, and she sent me on my way with a greasy smile.

Forty-eight hours has this Sunday in November. Two days mashed into one. One less to live, one more for remembrance. As I walked slowly toward my cabin, the little quatrain I had composed stirred in my head, the one I'd scribbled last Friday morning. Was it only last Friday? It seemed long ago.

I stopped in the middle of the compound and did a slow 360-degree turn, taking in the enormous semicircles formed by rows of shining metal dwellings. I looked back at the mess tent, with the rehearsal tent attached to it like a tumor, and beyond both to the large trailers that housed the crew that made this city work: the chefs, waitresses, plumbers, and laborers. My eyes scanned past the infirmary, the dark office trailer, the cutting and projection rooms, lingered on the operations shack, and rested on the dim outlines of the wardrobe, makeup and costume tents. I saluted the flagpole, and the tall post holding its lily horns silhouetted against the sky, feeling the immensity of desert, the limitless space above me. I contained it all, totally aware in that moment of every star—every grain of sand.

Awareness, the sublime gift. And I said aloud:

> Will Time write up my final scene
> With quotes of praise from devotees,
> Or give me two parentheses
> With *nothing* written in between?

ELEVEN

Monday covered the camp with a smothering silence. Gray scarves of weeping fluff trailed down from the low clouds in soft folds—a silky stifling cocoon—and I overslept. What made me open my eyes was Vellani belaboring my front door.

"We have the sound truck and the crew," he yelled. "Be ready to leave in half an hour."

We drove to the set of Lazarus' house, a magnificent location placed against a mountain of eroded sandstone, holding sprawling man-made vineyards and specimen cedars in its lap. Leading upward from the quiet house was a rough-hewn stairway carved in the solid rock. It would carry the feet of Jesus to the bleached stone doors of Lazarus' tomb.

Into the hush of this beautiful setting rushed our caravan of trucks, and here the Inbals joined us, pouring from their bus thirty strong. My two physical culture friends were notably absent.

"They are sick," Ovadia confided.

I had to stifle a burst of wry laughter. Most interesting body health idea, I thought. Never get sick? No never—well, hardly ever. I bet myself that they were in the sack together.

I grouped the Inbals in front of Lazarus' house at the place where a large swelling dome of white granite was behind them at stage left, and the tall stucco garden wall was at stage right, making a natural acoustic shell. It was cold, but also very still. We rehearsed, and I placed microphones at several points, until I felt we were beginning to obtain the best results. Wally Wallace, listening on headphones in his truck, opened his microphone and the public address system came to life.

"That's beautiful. You'll never get a better sound than that, but you moved that left microphone too far. Back it up."

Vellani concurred. I moved the microphone back ten feet.

"All right, go ahead and roll it, Wally," I called.

We recorded close-up, medium, and long-shot perspectives of the lamentations. The weeping and mourning sound reverberated among the hills. Tony Van Renterghem came shuffling up from the canyon below us.

"My god! That's the most astonishing earful I've ever heard. You should go down into that canyon and listen. It's weird." He pointed to a sheer escarpment of flat-faced rock. "The voices roll around in that enormous amphitheatre like cosmic bowling balls. It's incredible."

Vellani took off into the canyon. "Sing something," he shouted back.

I started the women keening and wailing. Tony scampered around, cupped his ears, then returned to halt the sounds.

"Put the microphones down there," he commanded the crew excitedly. "It *is* incredible."

I measured the distance between the singers and the canyon wall with my eye and called, "Wait a minute, Tony. Hold it! All we'll get from that distance is a lot of wind noise and tape surface hiss."

"He's right," Wally said, stepping from the truck and joining our group. "Let's walk down there and have a look."

We climbed the long sloping wave of rock together, to a point where it fell away abruptly into the canyon. Across from us was a great slab of granite a hundred feet high and twice as wide.

"As long as we're going to experiment with outdoor echo chambers," I said, "let's try to be technically sensible about it and get a useable result."

"I'm with *you*," Wally said. He clapped his hands once. Five separate and distinct echoes bounced back. "Holy cow," he murmured. "This is the place."

I turned to him. "Supposing I bring the Inbals up here on top of this dome, and you find the best position for your microphones down in that area between here and the wall, do you think it would work?"

"Let's give it a try. I'll have Clint Althouse move around with the mike while I listen in from the sound truck."

The Inbals were costumed for the set, and as they came up the hill they seemed to be floating into the present out of the ancient Galilean past. I positioned them among the rocks and started them on a minor chant while Clint walked back and forth on a distant ledge carrying a microphone fastened to a long pole. On the second trip, Wally's amplified voice said, "Whoa! Back up a little bit, Clint. Okay, hold it right there."

Both Tonys, who had been listening in the truck, shouted with delight while Wally's P.A. mike was still open, nearly shattering the loudspeaker and setting up such a din of echoing shouts that we had to cover our ears. After five minutes the silence returned, and we started recording. There were only two interruptions, caused by convoys of supply trucks on their way to the set by the Jordan River.

The resulting tracks were impressive. Vellani's enthusiasm soared to ecstatic heights as he yelped, "Good. Great. Good! Excellent!" after every take.

Lunch was served on the other side of the mountain, and I rode the bus around with the Inbals who sang, chattered, and rehearsed their English. All morning we had been on the lee side of the mountain. Why they had set up the caterer's truck on the windward side I couldn't imagine. They could have brought the food directly to the Lazarus-house set, but had chosen instead to put us in deep freeze. My respiratory department, which had been quiet all morning, put on a disagreeable performance; I hacked and snorted all through lunch.

Some unthinking supervising dietician had ordered pork chops—of all things—covered with cream gravy, cold before it hit the paper plates, and quick frozen before it got to the table. Most of the Inbals refused to eat the pork and were given scrambled eggs and potatoes instead. I ate part of mine on the hood of a Chevy truck. My wool shirt, cashmere sweater, insulated parka, knee-length sox, muffler, fur-lined shoes, overcoat, and felt hat managed to keep out most of the frigid wind, but some of the poor Inbals were tinged blue.

An hour later, we were back again among the shadowed rocks by Lazarus' house recording the lamentations. I covered "The Infant Massacre," "Mourning in the Temple," "The Crucifixion," and the "Lament for Lazarus," which Jesus and his band of disciples would hear from afar as they approached the house.

I called a halt at four-thirty, sensing the emotional discomfort of the Inbals and not wanting to push them beyond the point of diminishing returns. Vellani came rushing up demanding that we continue. I explained my reasons for terminating the session, but he began making executive noises—wanting to try this, and that. It reminded me of an anxious director who kept shooting every conceivable angle in the hope that some fortuitous combination of accidents would result in his being labeled a genius. I remained unmoved and dismissed the group with an expression of sincere thanks.

Then Vellani did a startling thing. He countermanded my dismissal, and notwithstanding the lateness of the hour, the creeping cold, and the tremendous energy already expended, he grouped the Inbals in Lazarus' garden and proceeded to stage a complete scene!

Clint Althouse was directed to take off his shoes and carry the microphone among the mourners.

"Now," said Vellani, "the microphone will be Jesus. He will enter the gate, stop there a moment to look around, listen to your lament and move among you. Some of you will look up, see him, and stop for a moment. The rest will continue to weep or moan softly, still mourning Lazarus' death."

Ovadia then took ten minutes to translate all this into Hebrew. Vellani didn't tell them when to start, when to stop, who would fall silent, and who would continue mourning. He just asked Wally to roll it, and when the slate had been announced, he yelped, "Action."

Clint, poised like a ballet dancer on the distant rock, started slowly forward as the lamentations swelled inside the garden walls—already too frantic and out of control. I stayed in the sound truck, shaking my head at Wally. It was awful.

Vellani made two of these "perambulating microphone" scenes, then listened to them played back on the speaker outside the truck. "It isn't right. Too much babbling and hysteria. We will make another take, and this time try it in English."

Ovadia, his teeth chattering, said, "Mr. Vellani, we cannot perform the English yet. We need more rehearsal."

"Then we'll make one more the way we did it before, only this time," he raised his voice, "not so much screaming from the women."

Wally shrugged. "It's a waste of time," he said. "We can't use any of this stuff. He's trying to outguess Stevens—and that isn't possible."

Vellani's voice rattled in the head phones, "Okay, Wally, roll 'em."

He made another spiritless take, during which Clint lost his balance, skidded on his ass coming down the rock, and skinned his elbow to save the mike. That broke up the party, and we headed back to camp—tired, cold, and nerve-worn.

I went straight to the infirmary. Jerry Parker stopped picking his nose long enough to shove a thermometer in my puss, puttered around with some papers for a minute or so, yanked it out and said, "Hmmn, you're about two-tenths of a degree from having a chill. Take these pills right now, they'll restore your body heat. I'm giving you something to take every four hours— and keep taking them until they're all gone, d'yahear?" He handed me six Dasin capsules and a bottle of antibiotics. I swallowed the prescribed dosage and thanked him.

"How's Harold Kress?" I asked. "Is he still trotting."

Parker shook his head. "When I can't get somebody out of the john in less than twenty-four hours, I begin to worry about 'em. I'm going over to look in on him in a few minutes, and if he isn't any better I'm going to send him home."

Before I reached my bungalow, my head was clear and the rattles had disappeared from my chest. Miracle drug? Or a dangerous camouflage? Whatever—it made me feel fine and I ate heartily, typed the log of the day's recordings on Saul's typewriter, and sat with Harold for a half hour. He was still in bed, rubbing his belly, patiently imploring his cramps to depart. On top of his cluttered chest of drawers was a collection of home remedies sent by sympathetic members of the company—with appropriate suggestions: a bottle of Kaopectate, three packages of Philadelphia cream cheese, a king-size cork, two boxes of Kotex, and a half-gallon carton of buttermilk. Enough deterrent, I thought, to stop the march of time. But he did look better.

Jerry Parker came in, palpated his belly, checked his temperature and pulse and said, "Gastroenteritis. But don't worry, everything's back to normal. You're going to live."

"Sometimes dying is a better idea," Harold growled.

"Don't rush it," I cautioned. "It gets here fast enough."

   We said goodnight all around, and I peeked in on Saul—who was reading in bed. "Will you do me a favor and bang on my door in the morning at seven? I'm sick of being rousted by Vellani."
   He chuckled and said he'd be glad to oblige.
   Quiet wrapped itself around the camp. The metronomic susurrus of the haul road was no longer a distraction—it had become an expected part of the silence. I wondered, as I climbed into bed, if tomorrow would end up like today—in a flurry of spurious activity. I could have sidetracked all the waste of time and energy if somebody around here had given me a little more authority.
   While I was trying to decide where I would get it, and from whom, I lost even the little bit I had.

TWELVE

"Hey, Darby! Rise and shiver; it's seven o'clock."

And it was—exactly. Saul Wurtzel was both prompt and perfunctory. He had disappeared before I could thank him.

I breakfasted on eggs and bacon, took a Dasin capsule with a cup of coffee, shoehorned myself into a car already packed with Tonys, and we were jounced to the Lazarus set under remnants of a sky left over from yesterday.

The Inbal bus had already arrived. I left the men inside to rehearse the English text of the lament, and took Tsifion and three women up into the rocks of our granite perch where they wept, wailed, grieved, and keened for the microphone. But today was not quiet. Trucks, buses, jeeps, tractors, and huge trailers loaded with boxed specimen trees, interrupted us at regular intervals, rumbling along the 65-minute route to the Jordan River set. When the helicopter flew over, we waited reverently in the frosty morning while Mr. Stevens winged his way through the heavens—disappearing majestically—before we could resume. Then an impudent little breeze raced into the canyon and made playful swipes at the microphone while Tsifion was playing his shepherd's pipe, so I had Clint Althouse creep along the ledge and cover the mike with a windsock, all of which took time, and it was 11:30 before we got good recordings.

I called the Inbal men from the bus and grouped them in Lazarus' courtyard. We rehearsed the English chant, but no amount of coaching could erase the strong accent of people singing by rote outside their native tongue. Still, the odd pattern of musical sound was interesting, and might be of some minor value later on. We recorded it twice before lunch.

Box lunches and hot chocolate had been provided, so we ate in comparative comfort, some in Lazarus' house, others in the bus or in the cars. It was better fare than the gristly pork chops of yesterday: two sandwiches, a piece of fruit, and a cup of good custard. Before the last belch was through echoing, Vellani was back in the garden, preparing for his "perambulating microphone" scene again.

I helped him by conducting the mourners, and Clint didn't fall down, so we got a couple of takes. We were listening to the third performance being played back on the speaker, and a scowling Vellani was about to go for another take, when the walkie-talkie in the truck suddenly announced: "THIS IS THE JORDAN RIVER SET. WALLY WALLACE AND SOUND CREW PLEASE GO AT ONCE TO THE JERUSALEM OUTLOOK FOR IMMEDIATE RECORDING OF MAJOR PHOTOGRAPHY." The message was repeated as Wally began stowing his gear ready to make the move.

"That does it." Vellani grumbled. "We won't make any more recording today—perhaps not ever."

Everyone scampered to the bus, happy to be reprieved, and my relief was discernible to Van Renterghem. We walked to the car together, leaving Vellani behind with Ovadia.

"That business with the moving microphone was a big waste of time, don't you think?" he whispered. "But those other sounds up on the rock—I've never heard anything like them before. Are you pleased?"

"You're right about the recordings made in the garden, but some of the other material is going to be very useful."

There wasn't much conversation in the car as we followed the bus back to camp. Vellani's mood cast a gloom over us, and for me the quiet was a benefaction.

After typing up the log and eating dinner by myself, I dropped in on Harold again. He was still in bed and I could hear his gut churning clear across the living room, but his eyes were clear.

"Under control," he said. "Just a gas factory now. I was up for a little while this afternoon and did some work. Tonight I'm a lot better and should be okay by tomorrow. How did you get along today?"

"You'll be dismayed to learn that in the past forty-eight hours—aided and interfered with by Mr. Vellani—we have recorded over ten thousand feet of soundtrack."

He winced. "That's enough for an entire epic movie. Is any of it any good?"

I nodded and then shrugged. "Only about ten percent."

"About ten minutes, eh? I'd like to hear it."

"Oh, you will—as soon as the print is developed and I can edit out all of the crap."

He winced again. "Don't mention that word."

"Sorry." I grinned. "Now you get some sleep."

Only the rumbling of his stomach answered me.

Moonlight was washing down the sides of the bungalows, making them shimmer. I took a deep breath of the cold air and realized that I hadn't been coughing since taking the Dasin. Maybe it *was* a miracle drug.

I waited in line at the public phone and eventually put through my call to Vera. She and Tina were both on the line and we were a family again for about twenty minutes. They were both fine, they said, and I didn't dwell on any of my ailments. Vera promised to telephone Alfred in the morning and relay my report.

"You were only going to be over there for two or three days," she said. "It's already been twelve, and it will soon be the Twelve Days of Christmas. How much longer?"

"I don't know. But they're paying me well and feeding me well, and all but one of the characters I'm working with are treating me well."

"Well, well," she quipped. "We love you."

Sleep came easily, and I didn't dream of Vellani.

THIRTEEN

I woke up to the pleasant realization that there was not the slightest pressure on me to hustle, bustle or rush. I ate breakfast alone, wrote some letters, checked on Harold—who was back in his cutting room being frustrated—and we ate lunch together, neither of us turning green. Then I made him go to bed for a nap, shouldered my camera, ordered a car from the pool, and rode out to the set, taking pictures on the way.

The Inbals were disgusted and in a funk. They had been called for six a.m., made up and costumed, carted to the set—and totally ignored. They hadn't been needed in a single shot. Now, to relieve the monotony of waiting, they were playing the exotic games played centuries ago by the children of Israel during the 40-year trek through the desert in Moses' time. I watched in fascination.

Ovadia finally said, "Now would be a good time to rehearse if you so desire."

They were quite happy when I gathered them all together in the bus and started the chant bearing the English words of the 23rd and 24th Psalms. They repeated them after me, ever with more enthusiasm, until the sound of their voices disturbed the actors on the set some two hundred yards away and a runner was dispatched to put an end to our ululations.

I left them playing their ancient games, and they let me take their picture.

On the way back, I asked my driver to tour the nearby sets, and I photographed several of them in the waning light, arriving back in camp about five-thirty.

At dinner, I asked Chico Day if the Inbals were on the shooting schedule for tomorrow, and, if not, could I have them.

"Tomorrow?" he asked. "How long would you need them?"

"All day, if possible—for some test recordings in camp."

He consulted his day-book. "You can have all but that little character—the comic. He'll be in the first shot."

Tony Vellani, two tables away, overheard the conversation and called, "Good thinking, Ken. You can rehearse them on the 23rd and 24th Psalms. They need work on the English."

I felt like going over and pulling his cap down around his ears. He was deliberately riding me, and I was resenting being bird-dogged. I gave him a thumbs-up sign, finished my dessert, and plodded back home.

"Home?" I said it aloud. "When this place looks like home to you, Darby, it's time to get the hell out."

I started a book by Heinlein—*A Stranger in a Strange Land*—but the feeling about Vellani didn't leave me until I was well into the second chapter. I thought I had him nicely exorcised, but then the book's plot petered out, so I turned off the light and followed the plot into limbo.

FOURTEEN

My twelve Inbals were waiting in the recreation tent at ten a.m. With the tape recorder running, we started, phrase by phrase, to wed the ancient Hebrew intonations to the alien English words. Even Ovadia, that patient friend, became perplexed and I knew that the experiment would be futile. We had completed only half of the 23rd Psalm by lunch time. The result was discouraging, but we finished recording it in its entirety by early afternoon.

Ovadia, Madam Sarah and I then held a conference, going over the script. It took two long hours, and several modest ideas came out of it. We tried them on the group, recording a "Palm Sunday Chant" with flute, lute, drums and songs to a simple repetition of the word "alleluia." Three samples of pre-Christian synagogue prayers followed—all in Hebrew—all very moving. Avraham Cohen looked so forlorn because he had not been included in anything that to mollify him, I taped ten minutes of his astonishing virtuosity on the kanoon.

"He could make a fortune with that instrument in Egypt," Ovadia said, "but they won't let him into the country."

It was a tiring day; I let them go at five o'clock.

Vellani reported that the company had been thwarted by clouds, and very little had been filmed.

My supply of Dasin capsules was exhausted. Now, as the effects of the medication wore off, whatever I had inside of me started on a rampage again: wheezes, coughing, rhinitis, sneezing—the whole wretched bloody works! Apparently, all the Dasin had done was hold every struggling bug locked up in a kind of status-quo prison. It hadn't cured a thing. What could I say about that? I could invent an epigram:

"A cold, perforce, must run its course; an evil curse could not be worse," I invented. Success. Fame!

One bountiful blessing upheld me as I fell into bed: Tony Vellani was not looking for me.

Today ends my second week, I thought, but it seems more like the fifth. Dozing, I wondered if I would live through the third. Or was it the sixth?

Could I survive?

The trucks on the haul road whispered "Ssshure . . . Ssshure . . . Ssshure. . . . "

FIFTEEN

Before I could finish soaping my joints, the bountiful blessing came to a noisy demise. Vellani was pounding on my door. "Rank invasion of privacy," I grumbled. "Rank."

"We're going to run all the soundtracks," he shouted.

I opened the door, draped only in a towel.

"When you're ready," he amended.

As I dressed, I heard myself growling, "Vellani: a race horse in a squirrel cage . . . an affliction . . . a monkey on my back . . . a gas pain! Maybe if I take an enema he'll go away."

Halfway to the projection room, Harold intercepted me. "Where the hell do you think you're going? You can't go in there. Stalmaster is running casting tests with Eric Stacey. And what's this I hear about you and Vellani running all the soundtracks? Damn it, Ken, I can't give over the whole morning to run ten thousand feet of film. It'll tie up my Moviola."

"Moviola?!" I exploded. "Who said anything about running it on the Moviola?"

"Tony Vellani. Who else?"

"For Lord's sake, Harold, that's ridiculous! I am *not* going to listen to any of that stuff on a Moviola."

"Well, Tony thinks you are. You'd better square him off."

We walked into the cutting room where Vellani was waiting. He wasted no time. "I'm very anxious to hear what we recorded on the Lazarus set. Aren't you, Ken?"

"Not on a Moviola," I said bluntly. "It's too damned noisy, and it's not fair to the tracks. Even if I wanted to waste my time, *and* Harold's *and* yours listening to an hour and forty minutes of clatter, I wouldn't be able to make any editorial selections— and I wouldn't let you either—until we heard it properly in the theater. Give Tony a sample, Harold."

I reached over and connected the sound drive to the shutter mechanism. Harold got the idea and turned the volume up high. The machine started with a whickering din, and from the overloaded speaker issued wails and screams of the Inbals, completely shattered by distortion. I turned to Vellani and shouted in his ear.

"Now, I ask you!"

Tony rubbed the side of his head. "It's pretty bad," he admitted. "How about turning down the volume?"

I reached the knob and lowered it to listening level. The clattering of the picture escape mechanism drowned out the recorded sounds. Tony pulled at his lip.

"I guess we'll just have to wait until projection is free."

The public address system, like the voice of a rescuing angel, intervened. "ATTENTION, TONY VELLANI. PLEASE SEE MR. STEVENS ON THE SET AS SOON AS POSSIBLE. TONY VELLANI TO THE SET."

Tony hurried out, and I turned to Harold. "The Lord moves in mysterious ways, etcetera."

He laughed. "Don't confuse me. I'm not sure whether I should thank the Lord or *you*. By the way, all of this tape must be mounted on reels before it can be run in the theater. Do you want the job?"

"Tomorrow I'll bring my union card," I said.

Frank O'Neill took that moment to stagger in with a big package. "Now, by God, I won't have to take any more shit from those two jerks I've been bunking with." He unrolled a lightweight sleeping bag and hung it on a nail. "Ever since I got here they've been trying to asphyxiate me. They leave the furnace burning all night, and they won't let me open the windows, and along about two a.m. it begins to stink so much in there—what with all the farting and the halitosis—that I can't breathe. But tonight, by damn, I'm gonna sleep right here in the cutting room—on the floor."

"Aren't you afraid you might freeze your wife's jewels?"

"Go shit in your hat, Darby."

"Go try the same thing in your sleeping bag," I said, and left quickly before he could throw something lethal. So, I mused, Frank has a feud going on in his cabin. I wonder who the other two "jerks" are?

I stopped by the mess tent for a quick cup of coffee, then joined the Inbals in the tent next door. The Wollensak jammed, and while a technician was trying to fix it, we rehearsed the 24th Psalm. For two solid hours we struggled with it, but when we came to the phrase, "—*Who has not lifted up his heart unto vanity, nor sworn deceitfully,*" it was just too difficult, and not worth the tremendous effort. I felt that the Inbals had given me all they had, and I stood up before them with my arms outstretched.

"I want to thank you—all of you—for the tireless work, for patience and cooperation and endurance beyond all expectation. I am grateful that you have allowed me to share with you an unusual intellectual and musical experience. You have contributed greatly to this film and I want you to know how sincerely I appreciate your contribution. I hope that you still regard me with friendship after all the grueling work I have inflicted upon you. I know I shall always value yours. Many, many thanks."

Ovadia translated this, and we applauded each other.

When I arrived back at the bungalow, there was a newcomer installing himself and his bags in my domicile. He was airily exuding a phony savoir-faire.

"David Sheiner, New York and points west, recently at large," he announced. "Eminent successor to Michael Tolan, who has been promoted—or demoted as the case may be—from disciple to the role of Lazarus. Ergo, sic transit hoc and therefore, meet the *new* James—the Elder James—that is, if Mr. Stevens approves, and doesn't send me home tomorrow. God, I feel lousy. I hate flying on an empty stomach. It hurts my wheels when we land."

I had to laugh at his fluency, and held out my hand.

"Ken Darby here. May I present you with a Miltown, a Probanthine, one antihistamine, two aspirins, and a roll of Tums? Now, get well, or James will never become any elder."

"Oy, a punster." He extended a palm. "Gimme!"

"DAVID SHEINER, PLEASE REPORT TO WARDROBE AND MAKEUP AT ONCE. A CAR WILL TAKE YOU TO THE SET AS SOON AS YOU'RE READY. MR. DAVID SHEINER, ATTENTION . . . "

"Who could ask for more than that?" he cried. "A loud public reception, free transportation, an audience with the local god—

or the son of god as the case may be—and a medic for a roommate. I'm off! Lousy stomach, headache, and all."

He tripped over his feet as he left, almost a pratfall.

I closed the door and retired to the bathroom, determined to meditate. My meditations were stubborn, but there was one compensating factor: Vellani couldn't get at me here.

"Bang, bang, bang," went knuckles on the front door.

"Ken? Ken Darby!"

"One moment," I shouted. I had to be imagining this. It just couldn't be happening. It took me more than one moment, but there he was. I hadn't imagined him. "What is it, Tony? I was on the crapper."

"Oh, sorry. Mr. Stevens wants you to stay over until next Tuesday so you can edit the tapes, make your selections, and give him a chance to hear them before you leave. Can you work that out?"

I refrained from making a bad joke. "Yes, Tony. I start editing tomorrow right after I run the tracks in the theater."

"Damn! I wanted to be with you, but I have to be on set."

"Don't worry, I'll get along okay."

A car honked at the end of the aisle. "Good. I'll tell Mr. Stevens," he said, and started off, jumped in the waiting car and was driven away—into the depths of the Jordan, I hoped.

What's the matter with me? I wondered. He's only doing a job, and his job at the moment is to be my personal leech. I shrugged him off, counting the days. Ninety-six hours till Tuesday. I telephoned Vera with the news. She was busy; her father had been moved from the hospital into a rest home, and I sensed that a weight had been lifted from her shoulders. I asked her to call Alfred, then cradled the phone and trudged back to my galvanized shanty.

Four more days to edit the tape, select the best material, corner Mr. Stevens for a final meeting, and conclude my sojourn in this lovely land of ersatz antiquity. Or was it ersatz? Wasn't I standing on land that was as old as Babylon?

I ate early, locked up and went to bed with a book. David Sheiner stumbled in about midnight and slouched in my bedroom door for a few minutes, exuding histrionics.

"The powers will notify my discipleship day after tomorrow whether I am to stay—or depart. Apparently there is some bit

of doubt as to my character, my suitability, or my aroma. Thank
God my nationality is right. This is a good picture in which to be
a Jew. But be it yes, or be it no, tonight I shall take my lousy
stomach to bed, lay down my aching head, and sleep the clock
around. I can sing, too—and also dance. Vo-la-re . . . oh,
ho . . . can-ta-re . . . oh-ho-ho-ho . . . " Then he cut a fandango
around the living room table and turned a neat pirouette into
the bathroom, slamming the door.

This guy is some kind of a lunatic, I thought, as I adjusted the
furnace and the windows for the night.

From the inner sanctum came "La la lah, la la la lah," ending
in a loud gargle.

"Arpeggios? Yuk!" I muttered. "Must be retribution on me
for my nasty thoughts about Vellani. Oh, Lord, are You taking
away one plague only to replace it with another? Do please
forgive me."

With this cleansing supplication I went to bed, and the sand-
man came in quietly without banging on the door.

SIXTEEN

David was rudely routed from his bed at seven in the most vociferous terms: "SHEINER TO WARDROBE. DAVID SHEINER, REPORT TO WARDROBE—ON THE DOUBLE."

I grinned sleepily, turned over, and resumed the somnolent position. I didn't hear Sheiner leave, but not more than a few winks later there was a familiar racket on the front door.

"Who is it?" I yelled, knowing exactly who.

"Tony Vellani, Ken. I have to go to the set for the day. I want Tony Van Renterghem to run the tapes with you in the projection room while you make your selections. Okay?"

"Fine. Delighted. Good luck on the set." If you can't lick 'em, join 'em, I thought, and started to sing, "Vel-lani, Oh-ho . . . Won't trust me . . . No-no-no-no . . . . "

After breakfast I hurried to the cutting room and shed my windbreaker. Frank O'Neill was winding huge reels of film.

"How'd you sleep last night, Frank?"

He grinned sheepishly. "Like you said; I should've been more careful with my wife's jewels. I put newspapers down on the floor, then blew up my air mattress and put it on the newspapers, got into my airforce pajamas, and opened the window. Then I crawled in the sleeping bag, zipped her up—and nearly froze my ass off. Cold air came right up through the floor. I didn't rightly wake up this morning, I thawed."

Harold and I were laughing by this time, and Frank gave a short hysterical cackle.

"You're okay, Frank," I said.

"Only when I'm cold," he chortled.

Harold indicated a spare bench. "Are you ready to go to work? The bench is special, just for you, and Charlie has an extra splicer in the booth. The film is stored in that pile of boxes there.

All you have to do is cut the takes together and wind them on reels. Can you work the splicer?"

"Hot or cold, butt-jointed, overlapped, or Scotch-taped," I replied, "I've been splicing film and tape all my life."

"Hey, Darby." It was Jack Lacey. "I'm going to move you out of C-3. Mr. Stevens wants your bungalow for a new member of the cast, so out you go."

"Fine," I said. "Just take all my gear to the nearest airport and I'll go peacefully."

His little golf cart was loaded, and the cabin was emptied in less than ten minutes. We drove off together, bouncing on the toy balloon tires across the compound, past Operations and on to a sunny cabin in the first row, near the mess tent.

"I'm putting you in a V.I.P. cottage, and Vandraegen is in with you. It's a better cabin with better exposure."

"You mean bitter, don't you," I kidded. "They all look alike to me—corroded sardine cans."

"Careful," he chided, "my feelings are delicate."

We pulled up in front of E-7, unloaded my belongings and then remembered that we had forgotten my plywood board. Back we went to C-3, wrestled the mattress and extricated the board, and while Jack was loading it on the cart I took a last look around. Two maids had already started cleaning up after me. One of them pointed into Sheiner's bedroom and said, "You're lucky to be getting away from *that* man."

I peeked in and got a shock. It wasn't exactly vacant. Articles were strewn around as though a tornado had spawned a litter of small havocs. Pajamas were flung rampant on a field of open dresser drawers, pillows lay over the entrails of two disgorged suitcases. It was a nightmare's nest of newspapers, bed clothes, boots, bottles, magazines, and junk, and even the window was plastered over with the remains of an old *Variety*.

The bathroom was equally disagreeable. Shaving and dental paraphernalia were occupying every level surface, and even clinging to the walls. I grinned at the maid.

"Maybe it's just as well that I'm retiring from this hut. A spoiler like that could scatter my marbles."

She grinned back at me. "Jack Lacey should be ashamed of himself, putting anybody who ain't neat in the same cabin with *you.* You're the tidiest man we've got in our section, and we're awful sorry to see you go."

I gave her an appraising look. This woman appreciated me. No, I thought . . . too big . . . and too strong. She'd kill me. But I thanked her and tucked a ten-dollar bill in her hand, adding a second one for her friend. Then Jack whizzed me back across the compound, helped me install the sheet of plywood in my new bed, and drove me back to the cutting room.

I was busily winding and splicing the soundtrack when Frank came in with somebody and said, " . . . and this is the editorial cutting room."

A beloved familiar voice bugled, "OhooOO, this is WONderful. Everything is soOOh organized."

Nostalgia spun me around; I looked up and said, "My loving memories of you will never die—only become more dear."

"What? Well, *well*—oh HO, Ken! I'm so glad to see you again. How *are* you? And what are you doing up here?"

His old head was a bit shaky, but the famous smile was as steady and bright as ever. I grabbed him in a bear hug.

"You beautiful old clown! You know me, Ed. I'm up to my same old tricks—music."

"Of course, *music*. Just like back in 1934. Isn't it lovely still to be doing what you do best? Lovely."

"It gets lovelier every year."

"It does, it *does*! So you're on the music! WONderful."

"MISTER ED WYNN PLEASE COME TO OPERATIONS. A PHONE CALL FOR MISTER ED WYNN."

"Those damned loudspeakers are always interrupting something important," I said.

He grabbed my hand. "Never mind, Ken. I'll be around here for a while and we'll get together and talk and talk."

The years hadn't changed him. On the contrary, I thought, as I went back to splicing and winding, he's spent his life changing the years, leaving his mark on the days of the week, on Time itself. It would be fun recalling our past together.

I tried to finish cutting before lunch but couldn't do it. We had plainly recorded too damn much film.

In the mess tent, I found Ed Wynn and his pretty wife, and we talked and talked and talked, reviewing the busy days in New York, our association when he was the Texaco Fire Chief, and

later, our tours through Vermont, Virginia, Iowa, and Ohio with
the Plymouth Show, when Lennie Hayton had the orchestra and
my job was to supply the jazzy arrangements for the King's Men
and Eight Lovely Gals. Ed was as delightfully puckish as ever,
and even came up with some memories I had forgotten.

"So now we're both together again here in the Utah desert,
and I'm going to play a serious role as the blind man Jesus heals.
You put some beautiful music behind that scene, Ken."

It was a reunion we both enjoyed and would long remember.

Tony Perris came back to the cutting room with me to lend a
hand. On the way, we were intercepted by Vellani, who was
accompanied by Frank Davis, still smoking the black briar pipe.
Tony wore a scowl. "You won't be able to run those tracks in
the theater after all," he said. "Mr. Davis is viewing a film until
four, and Van Renterghem is busy after that, so I guess you'll
have to put off your selections until Monday."

"Whenever," I said. "I'll be ready."

"Good." (Why must he always say "good"?)

They walked away. Perris and I spliced and wound film, reel
after reel after reel, until it was finally all in the can and ready
to roll.

"I've had enough, Tony. It's after four and I'm going into Page
just to get out of camp." I turned to Harold and Frank. "Anything you gents want me to pick up in town?"

As I was taking their orders, Charlie McCleod joined us,
having finished projecting the film for Frank Davis.

"Come on," he said. "I'll go with you. I'm stir crazy too." And
we jumped in a car, picking up Marie—one of the hairdressers—
and Red Starr, head of the electrical department.

Marie was full of chatter—about hair, hairdressers and movie
stars, and she spouted a steady stream of words. When Red
could insert a word here or there, he cursed the Utah/Arizona
Department of Water and Power for failing to maintain steady
voltage to the camp, the fluctuation of which had ruined several
pieces of equipment. Charlie got in a few sentences about the
enormous footage Stevens was shooting "as if film was as cheap
as toilet paper." The rest was all Marie.

I listened.

My purchases at the general store included cough syrup,
Ex-Lax, a jar of seasoned salt for Wally Wallace, a toothbrush

for Harold, bourbon for Frank, and a pair of slacks for Andy Slocum who had left them in town to be cuffed.

On the way back, our driver stopped at the Glen Canyon Motel, Stevens' headquarters for arrivals. The latest of these was Joanna Dunham, who was to portray Mary Magdalene. She was accompanied by her fresh-from-London husband, Harry, who was sporting a luxurious Dickensian beard. Charlie and Red offered to wait and catch the next company car leaving Page, so Harry and Joanna climbed in with me and Marie and we headed back to camp.

Marie, stimulated by this new and captive audience, began a gossipy recital about working conditions, personality clashes, epidemics—and finally got around to her favorite subject without missing a beat or taking a breath. "We have this driver, Joanna, who wears a cowboy hat and has two nice motherless children. He says that our camp needs about forty loose women, ha-ha . . . he says the waitresses won't give because they're too well taken care of at home, ha-ha . . . and we have a third assistant whose girl friend was murdered by her husband when he caught them together, and . . . "

Joanna cut in sharply. "My God, Harry, I'm glad you came along on this location."

"So am I, Ducky, so am I." And Harry cornered the conversation for the rest of the trip. Marie subsided and sulked.

Harold stopped me as I passed his cutting room. "I'm so tired of mess-tent food," he said. "Let's go into Page, have a good dinner, and shoot some pool. I have to run dailies with Stevens first. He wants me to *see* the film but won't let me touch it. When I'm through I'll come around and pick you up at your new cabin. They moved me too, y'know. I'm only a couple of doors away from you in E-5."

I typed the log identifying the takes with the reel numbers, then trotted across the compound to my new castle, now glittering in the floodlights. Inside, taking his ease at the table, was Vandraegen.

"I see that you and the camp are all in one piece," he said, shaking my hand. "After flying up here with Mr. Army Archerd of *Variety*, I was prepared to find the desert in a state of disarray."

"You just spoiled my day," I said. "My opinion of Army Archerd promotes acute indigestion."

"I'm in concurrence. My wife reads his column on a rare occasion, but as a steady diet we prefer English to Americanese."

"How *is* your wife?"

"Well, last night she developed a temperature of one hundred and three, and I doubted if I could make the trip. But when she awoke this morning, her fever was almost normal. We have a nurse for her, the doctor looks in twice a day, and I shall keep close touch with her by phone." He opened a notebook. "This is irrelevant, but interesting, and I want to try it out on you. How do you pronounce (he spelled it) the name S-A-L-O-M-E?"

"Most of my intellectual friends correct me every time I use that name," I said, "but I still pronounce it Suh-lō'-mi."

"That's correct. You may thumb your nose at all your intellectual friends. How would you pronounce T-H-A-D-D-E-U-S?"

"Thă'-di-us," I answered quickly, sure of this one.

"Wrong." He grimaced. "It's Thu-dee'-us. And here's another. S-E-P-P-H-O-R-I-S."

"Sounds like it might be a venereal disease."

"Come, now. It was a major city of Israel, captured by Rome, its people sold into slavery, and finally destroyed completely, only to be rebuilt again. I'm vexed because none of the dictionaries deign to give it pronunciation."

"I'm vexed too," I said. "I never even heard of it, and I thought I knew most of the place-names in the Bible."

"Oh, it's not in the Bible."

"Then what is it doing in this picture?"

He laughed. "There are many things in this film, including the language, that are not in the Bible, as when Jesus says, 'Fasten your belts, be vigilant, with lamps alight'."

I chuckled. "Sounds like an airline stewardess I know. I give up, how *do* you pronounce it?"

"I think it's Sif-fore'-iss, but that's only an educated guess. I'll ask Tony Van Renterghem, he knows everything." Then, abruptly: "How are things here in camp?"

I started to tell him about Ed Wynn's arrival, the heckling I was getting from Vellani, the meeting with Joanna Dunham, but paused. His eyes were as glassy as his spectacles; he was simply not listening. When I cleared my throat, he gave a little hitch in his chair.

"That's fine," he said. "Now I must go see dailies," and promptly fitted action to the words, wearing his parka.

Mary's bottle of vodka was still on my bedroom shelf. I mixed it with a little water, on the rocks, and it felt good going down. It softened the edges of my shell, and I began to see—through the thinning barrier—my lonely inner self peering out speculatively at me. Together we examined the data of recent experiences, explored the solemn, virus-laden, antisocial activity of a man married solely to his work.

"Why are you such a lone wolf?" it asked. "What error in character makes it so difficult for you to indulge yourself in the interpersonal relationships of social intercourse? Why so protective—afraid you'll catch the clap? Ha! Why don't you cut loose and get in trouble? What the hell are you so afraid of—being discovered?"

"That's it," I answered. "I'm afraid of being apprehended as a fraud. I don't want to admit that, not even to myself."

"Who says you're a fraud?" came the question.

"I do," I retorted. "Now *you* answer a few questions. Am I a truly qualified musician? Do I know the mass of academic knowledge, the works, the men, the methods, of the art I practice? Am I really good at my job? Do I have a selective file tucked away in my memory filled with accurate facts, or just half-assed guesses? I know who I am, and I know that I love life, but what the hell am I doing with it?"

"Well, right now you're doing a lot of mental masturbation. What the hell do you *want* to do with it?"

"I know this much," I snapped. "In this more than lovely miracle of creation, I want to do just one thing better than anybody else—just *one thing*. And over that one ability I want to be recognized as the undisputed master."

"What for? To get your picture on the cover of *Time?*"

"Hmmn, maybe," I answered thoughtfully.

"You're an idiot! A champion imbecile!" it barked. "All you'd have to do for that quick notoriety is to assassinate a world figure, and destruction is not what you want at all. You want to be the master of something. How about mastery over *yourself?*"

The glass was empty. My accusing visitor-self had retreated behind the thickening wall. I just sat there twisting the last question around, looking at it from all sides, till my stomach began clanging loudly for attention. And abruptly, I remembered Harold and our dinner date in Page.

He wasn't in his cabin, so I pinned a note on his door and went to the mess tent—and there he was, worriedly eating at a table with Eric Stacey, Frank Davis, Ray Gosnell, Bill Hay, and George Stevens. It was so obviously a power huddle that I sat at a table in the rear where Frank O'Neill found me.

I said, "What's the pow-wow?"

"They ran the dailies till eight-fifteen, then they had an argument just outside the cutting room. Seems the daily flights to and from L. A. are breaking the transportation budget, Stevens is playing house with operation costs, for every day they've been shooting on this location they've *lost* a day, putting the company more than two months behind schedule, and they've just discovered that Joanna Dunham is three-months pregnant. On top of that, I'm a little bit tight."

He rubbed his hands together gleefully, anticipating my shocked reaction. I let him down.

"None of this surprises me very much, Frank, not even Miss Dunham's pregnancy. Stevens is famous for over-shooting, scrapping schedules, and squandering money. There's a true story about him sitting in a projection room with composer Dimitri Tiomkin, ostensibly to spot music in the picture *Giant*, and for three solid hours the only thing appearing on the screen were cattle galloping past the camera. Finally, Tiomkin turned to George and said, 'Good sound effects, poor story, no music necessary. You waiting for one of those cows to wink at you?' But who remembers those bad things? *Giant* was a blockbuster of a film. In ten years this one may be equally great—or it may be a washout like this desert will be when the dam is finished— Joanna's offspring will be nine years old, and we'll be remembering experiences made here that nobody will ever have again. How about some food?"

"You're a point killer and a big damn bore, Darby." He turned to the waitress. "Gimme the meatballs."

We ate in silence. The meatballs were tasty, but the pasta had the flaccid consistency of cheap knitting yarn. The main title of

Shane drifted in from the tent next door, but there was standing room only. It was a Stevens picture.

I went on into the recreation tent and saddled one of the galloping pinball machines with Clint Althouse and Tony Van Renterghem. We were having a fine time lighting up all the pink, gold, orange, and yellow lights when Vandraegen came in.

"Oh-ho! I have found you out. 'The gods are just, and of our pleasant vices make instruments to plague us.'"

"*King Lear*, Act Five, Scene Three," said Van Renterghem.

"Check. Just testing, Tony. Little did I imagine that you big brains were pinball addicts."

"The world has room for a number of things," I said, "and this instrument of vice is quite a remarkable adding machine." I pushed in a quarter and grinned at him. "Here, be my guest and witness what man hath wrought for the young at heart."

"You dog," he muttered, "you have trapped me with those last three words."

Clint and Tony maneuvered him into position, and soon he was throwing body-English into every bounce of the little iron balls with all the concentration of a pro.

"Now we have something on *you*," I said. "But whatsoever else shall happen tonight, we will understand, but give no tongue."

"A misquote from *Hamlet*, Act One, Scene Two," said Tony.

"Oh, shut up!" I laughed with the others. "Don't always be so damned right."

"I can't help it," Tony said dolefully.

Vandraegen put in, "I told you he had a brain like a big computer. Tony, how do you pronounce S-E-P-P-H-O-R-I-S?"

"With difficulty. But if I did, it would be right."

"How do you stand a person like that?" I asked.

"We don't. We walk away and leave him. Come on, Ken."

Vandraegen and I walked back to the bungalow together. He wanted to talk about the picture, but I steered him into a more personal area—a subject he would like equally well—himself and his work. "Your life at the university must be very gregarious."

"It is, if I were to attend all the functions. We have friends in nearly every department: Philosophy, Psychology, Theater Arts,

Anthropology, Chemistry, and two of our dearest friends are mathematicians."

"What about Education?"

"You have just put into my ear an offensive word, Mr. Darby, unconsciously touching upon a sore nerve and a pet peeve. I have a serious quarrel with that department. The professors are invariably 'Holier than thou,' and their tenet of operating is, in a compound word, mass-production. They level the potentialities of the students to the common denominator of mediocrity. They work with the whole, not the individual. No specialization is permitted. The Education Department paints them with surface information, stamps them with a teacher's credential and tosses them into a common pot from which they can be plucked for *any* job in *any* department of *any* grade school, like a string of identical sausages.

"You see the picture? A young woman, for example, who could have been a great professor of languages, ends up as an unhappy teacher of fourth-grade English. If she desires to enhance her academic status, she must start over again, swimming back upstream to find training in the one specialty for which she was initially best suited. This specialization could be accomplished much quicker, easier, and with less cost *if* the Education Department supplied the opportunity in the first place. It's a terrible waste. The department needs an overhaul. And the English Department is little better, though technically, I am *in* that department. It was only by the greatest pressure— most rigorously applied from higher up—that I was allowed, yes, grudgingly *permitted*, mind you, to work outside the university for Warner Brothers, and here for Stevens. The English Department frowns darkly on extracurricular income for its professors, although all other departments take pride in their industry-endowed faculty members, some of whom have been retained by giant corporate colossi at salaries above those of their superiors—to everybody's benefit."

We entered the cabin and took chairs around the table.

"By and large," he continued, "the university considers a professor to be the sole property of the college during every waking hour of his career, whether in the lecture hall, at home, or in the shower. Furthermore, if he awakens in the middle of the night—as I most always do—any product of his mind belongs to the university." He adjusted his glasses.

"It's like this: a teacher and a career educator are poles apart. The first is accredited and does as he is told, while the second is specialized—and does the telling."

I started to give him an example from my own experience wherein my friend, Nado Shutt, a fine pianist, took his degree in Education and ended up teaching second grade arithmetic in the grammar school in Topanga Canyon, but I didn't bother to finish the story. There were enormous eyelids behind his glasses. He was sound asleep.

"Well," I said in a loud voice, "it's been a long day."

He started up. "Yes. Yes it has. I've been up since five this morning." He unbuckled his belt as he rose from his chair, revealing a pair of boxer shorts with crimson hearts lavishly splashed on a field of flying arrows, and shuffled, laughing, into the bathroom.

"A valentine gift from my wife," he said, "last year."

I read until I was sure he was asleep, then turned out my light, thinking how strong becomes the man who thoroughly knows his calling, and conquers it. Such a man attains mastery—even over himself.

SEVENTEEN

"Gad, I wish I had your ability to sleep for eight hours. I'm lucky to get five."

This is Sunday, I thought, and that's Vandraegen.

"I was too hungry to wait for you to wake up," he went on, "so I have already surrounded a sumptuous breakfast."

I looked at my watch and yawned. It was eight-thirty. "Didn't you sleep well?"

"Very well for about four hours. Then I read myself to sleep for another hour. After that I *had* to get up, and I didn't see any point in going back to bed."

"Did I keep you awake snoring?" I asked.

"You did not." He was emphatic. "You were as quiet as though absent."

"Do you have any special drill for this lovely Sunday?"

"Yes. Eight disciples, then Von Sydow—beginning now."

He left, and I performed the morning's ablutions and functions, afterward hurrying to the mess tent for bacon, eggs, and hotcakes. The Inbal men were engaged in a game of soccer, peeled down to pants and shoes by the warm, oblique sunlight. Robert Bush sat in the doorway of his cabin watching them, but I could see that he was meditating on the sweetmeats of memory. The dunes spread invitingly, and I started walking. With every step, the monstrous tower hovering over the gravel quarry grew ominously nearer and higher, its long tentacular conveyor arms reaching out on three sides to the gray piles of rocky exudate it had spawned, the gnashing crusher quiet and unmoving. The haul road was Sunday silent, glazed to a shiny black and hypnotically straight, narrowing and disappearing into a wilderness of sunburned desert.

I soaked it all in, remembering the soft voice of my old friend, J. Farrell MacDonald, as we had stood together on a lofty peak overlooking Lone Pine, California, years before.

"The container is always greater than the contents," he had said. "The more you contain, the bigger you become, so take it all in, son—all you can hold."

"Ya lookin' fer somebody, Bub?"

I wheeled around and almost bumped into the side of a black and white patrol car.

"Ain't nobody allowed up here," declared the driver. "Gu-v'ment prope'ty. You from the moshin' pitcher comp'ny?"

I told him I was.

"My wife's gonna be one-a them extries you fellas hire. She signed up on a piece-a-paper tacked up in the Glen Canyon Mo-tell. She's a good looker with nice wide hips an' legs like Betty Grable. Maybe she'll get a good part. Name's Cord."

"I hope she gets it—and I'm sorry to be trespassing. You have a nice quiet weekend." And I left abruptly before he could get me in a verbal clinch about what I should do to promote his actress wife. And he let me go.

Walking back, I was glad for the whispering stillness, the wide scene, the quenching air and the clear, dry sunlight. I scuffed the sand, looking for arrowheads, and noted that other feet had walked this way. Big feet, bigger than mine—a heavier man with outward splaying toes. And then I saw the smaller, daintier footprints beside his, and I became curious, following them a long way over a far-rising dune and down the other side to a small protected dell surrounded by boulders and sandhills. There, in that shadowy place, the prints came to a stop, but I could read the story of a swift physical clamor in the scattered marks upon the soft earth, a slow searching struggle that ended in the sharp imprints of small heels set wide apart, dug deeply into the sand.

I turned away, almost guiltily, as though I had been a peeping Tom, and walked the long slow distance back to camp feeling like an alien on a strange planet. The earth turned, and nearby mountains flung their jagged shadows out to meet me, then over me, and then on toward the horizon to meet the sky of evening, and it was dark when I arrived back in camp.

The plane had departed at six, and with it Vandraegen. I was about to enter the mess tent when out stumbled Mary Bash, practically into my arms, and I remembered with horror that I had promised her a trip to the Mormon ruins this Sunday.

"I'm tight," she warbled giddily. "Somebody stood me up today, and I got very verrry tight. Th' sumabitch!"

"My God, Mary, who would do a thing like that to you? Come on! Let's get you a cup of coffee and something to eat."

She struggled blindly, got herself upright and pushed me away. "I jus' ate. Now I'm gonna go in an' throw it aaaaall up!" She marched off vigorously, defying the force of gravity, and slammed the door of her cabin. So much for Mormon ruins, I thought. How could I have forgotten? Would she remember?

At the executive dining table, all were present except George Stevens. Off to one side I saw David Sheiner with Jamie Farr and I joined them. Immediately they baritoned their way into the 136th Psalm, David apparently having learned it from Jamie. I said, "What? An apple for teacher? Dismissed!"

"I am now James the Elder," David announced, pulling a long face. "They accepted me because of my outstanding ability and good looks"

"I know," I interrupted. "You told me before. And I've been removed from my bungalow on the grounds that I am not fit to dwell under the same roof with so important a James."

"Oh, but they threw *me* out too. Ed Wynn has our old C-3 cabin. I am sharing a similar hut with my long-nosed friend—as you can see by his long nose."

"I thought Jamie was in the same cabin with Bob Blake."

"I was," Jamie said, "but Bob's such a goof that I got him a transfer—finagled him out, so to speak, into residence with Michael Anderson Junior, where those two kooks can raise all the hell they want to without destroying the morals of the rest of the chosen people. They deserve each other."

"Smart work," I said. "I give you the order of the Psalm."

"Oy!" shouted David. "He's one of us."

Over David's shoulder, I saw Joanna Dunham and husband Harry come into the tent. They looked around, saw us laughing, and came to our table. David and Jamie were instantly cordial, and I recognized the easy social intercourse that operates among actors. It was less than three minutes before Joanna announced her pregnancy, and we all offered our congratulations at once.

"Thank you," Harry said. "We are quite pleased to be pregnant, even though it has created rather a nasty furor in the halls of the mighty."

"Isn't it dodgie," she said. "Mr. Davis told me that I will be informed shortly if they decide to cancel my contract. It *would* be a bit risque photographing a Magdalene visibly large with child."

"The obvious rotundity would easily have been circumvented if the shooting 'shedyul' had been on target," Harry put in, "but filming has been so delayed at this point that the camera may well see a bit of our prenatal offspring before Joanna's work is completed. However, on the practical side, Mr. Stevens gets two actors for the price of one."

"It isn't really Mr. Stevens or Mr. Davis," sighed Joanna, "it's the insurance company. The underwriters will not insure a pregnant woman on the set. She could easily halt production in any number of ways, and I have that pregnancy clause in my contract. They have the right to cancel me if they wish."

"They cannot cancel *you*, my dear, without canceling our child, and that I will not permit." Harry chortled over his bit of humor, and we joined politely.

At that moment, David Hedison and Peter Mann bustled in, back from a weekend trip to Las Vegas. Joanna pulled them over and introduced them to Harry, then said, "Guess what, David? We're going to have a baby."

David registered shock. "We *are?* So *soon?* I only just got here. When did we . . . ?"

Harry grabbed a dinner fork and made a playful swipe, and during the ensuing badinage, Sheiner, Jamie Farr, and I excused ourselves and headed for bed.

There was a slice of new moon hanging above the recreation tent that followed me all the way across the compound to E-7. The cabin was warm and still, and very shortly thereafter, so was I.

EIGHTEEN

I opened one eye for a quick look at the weather. Not a ray of sunlight. It would be another frustrating day for photography on the set. It was chilly in the room. I turned up the furnace before showering. As I dressed, I could hear distant motors coughing and rumbling from the car pool. Extras, actors and technicians hurried by toward the waiting buses, their voices brittle and sharp on the frosty air. I had heard it all before, but never with such startling presence.

My slacks were not quite zipped up when the door flew open, and in charged the maid of this particular cellblock. She marched forward with determination, ignoring my zippering efforts, whipped the sheets off my bed and started out.

"Laundry day," she announced. "I'll be back later to clean house."

I noticed that she was wearing a hearing aid and raised my voice. "I'll be out of here right away."

"No need to shout. And no hurry either. I have other cabins to do."

I put away a good breakfast in the company of the child bride of one of the Inbal Dancers. She was a Presbyterian, Iowa-born slip of a girl who had spent her married life moving from one city to another with the troupe. The symptoms of her early disillusionment were unpleasantly evident. Without any questions from me she let it be known that she was fed up with the gregarious, nomadic life, and that she was going to leave her husband and his troupe the minute their work on the picture was finished. "They're so all-the-time Jewish," she concluded. "I feel like I'm in a foreign country."

Hal Weinberger's voice was paging me on the compound horns, and Tony Van Renterghem was waiting for me at Operations.

"We have the projection room. Charlie McCleod has your ten reels of film. We can start listening. Vellani can't be with us."

"Buddha make—a *miracle*," I said.

Tony squinted. "Tuptim's big line from *The King and I.* Right?"

"As usual, Tony. And I ought to know. Let's go."

The projection room was warm and comfortable. We threw off our parkas, and I switched on the intercom between our control panel and the machine room.

"Reel One, Charlie. Whenever you're ready, roll it."

As I made my selections, I discussed them with Tony so he could later report to Vellani that I had done so. None of his "perambulating microphone" experiments were remotely useable, and I eliminated all of them. Van Renterghem concurred—almost too heartily. He was attentive, discriminating, and very pleasant. We put in several hours together culling, thinning, and selecting. It was arduous and wearying.

When we finished, I went directly back into the cutting room, where Harold and Frank were both winding film, and spent the rest of the day discarding the rejected material, editing pieces from several of the questionable takes, realigning and renumbering the reels, and making sure all splices were tight.

Frank took the seven edited reels into Charlie's machine room for me while I typed a new rough draft of their contents. When I finished the log, I took it over to Mary—in the office—and she wore her fingers out copying it in triplicate for Mr. Stevens' arrival. It was still long; more cutting was needed.

Tony Vellani found me there in the office and started to open his mouth, but before he could say anything I startled him by shouting, "It's ready!"

"Good!" He paused a moment, looking embarrassed. "Mr. Stevens won't be able to hear those recordings tonight, but I will. In fact, I'll listen to them right now if, as you say, they're ready."

"Charlie has the first reel on the machine," I said.

Van Renterghem passed us as we walked to the theater, and on a kind of hunch I grabbed his arm and pulled him with us.

We listened to the new reels, playing the volume up and down at Vellani's request, finding an optimum level for each successive performance. In the middle of the 22nd Psalm, I heard the theater door open and looked around. It was Stevens. He stood there with his head cocked to one side, his hand behind his back, smacking his lips. I motioned a greeting, half invitation, half salutation, and turned back to the controls. When I heard the door close, I presumed he had taken a seat.

The moment we finished running, Vellani began launching a program. "Ken, you said you wanted to combine some of these recorded tracks. We ought to do that before Mr. Stevens hears them. You have my authority to start."

I looked around to see if Tony was grandstanding for Stevens, but George was not there. Vellani continued; "We should mix these right away, since the composite result is what we're after. What's the best way to do it?"

"The best way," I said distinctly, "is to take the tracks back to MGM, get a good dubbing mixer like Bill Steinkamp, and balance them to the best effect. It's very simple when the right equipment is available.

"Haven't we got enough equipment here?"

I stared at him in disbelief. "Not this side of Phoenix, and I doubt whether . . . "

Van Renterghem interrupted, and I sensed a welcome ally. "What are you trying to do, Tony, mix a playback?"

"Well . . . no—not a playback?"

"Then what's the point? We don't have stereo either, so why bother?"

"Because," Vellani said evenly, "I want Mr. Stevens to hear these tracks the way I know they can sound. I want him to get a picture of my thinking. Now, tell me how we can mix them right here on location. There must be a way."

The two of us just looked at him.

Tony was stumped. "I can't go to the expense of flying people and cans of film to MGM and back. Why can't we mix a few of these tracks on the Lease Breaker?"

"No way!" Van Renterghem said. "That machine can only transfer disc to tape, or copy one tape to another."

I stood up, reaching for my parka. "Stevens is not an imbecile, Tony. He can apply as much imagination as *we* can to these recordings, and probably with superior intelligence. Furthermore, the discussion with him will be of greater value if there is something left to discuss. You know that."

Tony was exasperated. He pulled at his lip, looked from me to Van Renterghem, and sighed. "I suppose you're both right. We'll just have to leave everything as is."

At that moment, the door opened and Charlie McCleod came in, his face the color of rice pudding.

"Jeeze!" he said in a hoarse whisper. "When Stevens walked out on you he came up into the booth with me and he stayed there—with a glass of Beefeaters, havin' a nip—and your intercom mike was open out here on the panel. We heard every damn word you said, and he wouldn't let me turn off my speaker. I was sure you'd pop off and get him sore."

Van Renterghem grinned. "Relax, Charlie. When did he leave the booth?"

"Right after Darby said Stevens wasn't an imbecile. He just laughed, picked up his glass and beat it."

Tony Vellani was red in the face—and still determined. "Tell me the truth, McCleod. Can we mix those tracks here?"

Charlie didn't equivocate. "Hell no! It takes a four channel dubbing panel at least . . . and a good mixer."

That ended the session, and I was glad to escape.

Outside, leaning on the tall pole that supported the big loudspeakers, was Harold Kress. Behind him, partially hidden from view, was George Stevens. Abruptly, the speakers burst into sound. "BOB BAYLIS. BOB BAYLIS, PLEASE COME TO OPERATIONS. YOU HAVE A LONG DISTANCE TELEPHONE CALL, MR. BAYLIS."

During this stunning recital, Stevens stuck one finger in his ear, half doubled himself over, and hopped around the pole like a plump Navajo doing a rain dance. When the horns fell silent, he pulled his finger from his ear and said, "By damn! What a racket!" Then he saw me and winked. "Everything all right?" He grabbed my arm to steady himself.

"Fine," I said, "but I apologize for being such a poor projection-room host. As you heard, we were holding a wake in there, and I forgot to bring a suitable bottle."

He showed his fine even teeth. "I didn't forget." He produced a half-filled tumbler of gin from under his coat. "You're ready for me now, aren't you?"

"Yes, sir. Some of the sounds are interesting. You must judge for yourself how well they will accommodate the scenes in the film."

"I'll hear them, but I can't tonight." Hiding the glass, he headed for his cabin. "Maybe tomorrow night. Take care."

Harold and I walked to the mess tent, amused by Stevens' futile bid to have a quiet cocktail before dinner. We dined on a menu that would have excited Vandraegen to poesy: soup, salad, top sirloin steak, string beans, baked potato, and tart cherry pie a la mode.

Afterward, I left Harold for an hour with the pinball machine, then trekked to my haloed haven under the new moon. There were several differences between this cabin and my other abode. The carpet here was all the same color; in C-3 it had been a job of leftovers. There were extra nails here for odd garments, a cabinet for linens in the bathroom, and two beds in each bedroom instead of a single. One thing was the same: the distant slash and hum of the trucks along the haul road. They sizzled past with the same monotonous regularity, interminable in their haste to complete the Glen Canyon dam.

I lit a pipe, and read the *New York Times* that Perris delivered every morning to the V.I.P. cabins, noticing that Wall Street was calling it a "flagpole market"—all straight up. My pipe tasted rich again, my interior was pleased with itself, and my breathing apparatus was clear. Now, if only I could trap Stevens into listening to my recordings soon, *maybe* I could get home before Christmas.

In a dream I was climbing an enormous fir tree laden with glittering ornaments. As I reached the top, a shining angel embraced me, whispering, "Hello Ken. My name is Maybe."

NINETEEN

Tuesday, December 7, 1962, entered the world as a clean spring-like day with the bluest sky ever painted on a limitless backdrop. Temporary Tuesday, always dragging some Wednesday by the hand, forever jostling old Monday out of the way in a feverish rush to become yesterday. Wouldn't it be wonderful, I thought, if Tuesday (just for once) refused to be in such a hurry and decided to drop anchor in the *Now* for a decade or two? A few children would be born, not many though, and a few old people would die, but peacefully and far between—and those in bed with a warm and diligent companion could join the immortals of Pierre Louis' nirvana: "unendurable pleasure indefinitely prolonged." Did the men at Pearl Harbor look upon a day as beautiful as this before the bombs began to fall?

I kept waiting for Vellani's knuckles to shatter the spell. The longer I waited, the happier with Tuesday I became. Perhaps this was Tonyless Tuesday. I tiptoed out of bed to spy on the world through my louvre windows. All was quiet except for a solitary truck lazily dragging a huge raft of planks—piled high with granite boulders—around the compound, flattening and smearing away all tracks of Monday, leaving it as clean as a harvester's dinner plate. Nothing else moved.

I spent the morning bending over the cutting bench, revising, cutting, and reassembling the reels. When I had them in order, my log looked like this:

I.   The Infant Massacre—7 takes in varying perspectives
    A.   Women mourning for their dead children
II.   Instrumental and Vocal Experiments
    A.   Shepherd's Flute; Three Themes
    B.   Psalm 22 in Hebrew by a Congregation

C. Psalm 22 with Cantor and Group Responses
III. Mixed Voices Mourning the Death of Lazarus
IV. Lamentations from Job and Jeremiah
    A. Hebrew Version with Mixed Voices
    B. English Version with Men Only

Now I was satisfied. Each idea was complete and of itself, and all of them were in four reels instead of seven. I had cut over six thousand feet!

Lunch was buffet style, and the main course was the most tenderly delicious pot roast I had ever tasted. I relished every morsel, went back for more, and tried to store the memory of its texture and flavor for some time in the future when I'd be forced to eat crow. On an impulse, I went back into the kitchen to congratulate the chef. My mind wasn't prepared for the shock it got when he turned to face me, offering a deformed hand, but I introduced myself and expressed my admiration for his culinary artistry.

He had been horribly burned in a flash fire years ago. His face and hands had been knitted together with skin grafts. The mottled patchwork of gray, white, pink, and mauve maculations with their dividing ligatures of scar tissue gave an alien, other-worldly expression to the inflexible face which hung, as though suspended, between the towering chef's hat on his brow and the white scarf around his throat. Only his eyes were alive; they gleamed in acknowledgment of my compliment.

"Thank you," he said in a cultured voice. "I am deeply pleased and grateful. A chef needs applause, too, Mr. Darby."

When I left him, I felt as though I had been knighted.

At two-thirty, I rounded up my disciples and herded them into the theater. When I dismissed them an hour and a half later, they could sing Psalm 136 in their sleep and synchronize their lips to the playback. Most satisfactory.

I left the theater with them, and walked away from camp toward the mesas. The afternoon was strangely aglow, and far across the valley the buttes and devil's chimneys appeared flat and two-dimensional, as though painted on blue cardboard. I circled slowly out into the desert, taking in the grandeur and the fresh air until I overflowed with physical and mental serenity. Tonight, I thought, I'll have a triumphant session with Stevens;

tomorrow—home and family. Yet, even as I anticipated leaving this place, I knew that some part of me would dwell forever here—even beneath the waters of Lake Powell—drowned in memories of a primordial wilderness as beautiful as any imagined heaven. I found the footprints I had made on Sunday and wondered about the lovers who had made *their* short memories among the dunes. Had they seen the beauty? Were they counting the days?

Then, as with all others, Tuesday withdrew over the rim of the mesa, wearing a bright cerise tiara in her altocumulus coiffure. The lights of the company's motor caravan came curving through the valley, returning from the set, and I started back to the cutting room, arriving there just as Mr. Stevens' car drove up. He walked off hurriedly to the office trailer with Stacey, Davis, Florence, and Vellani.

I waited.

Frank O'Neill poured three ounces of bourbon, tasted it, and remarked, "I have a nice capacity for this stuff—but only before dinner. My dad and granddad were both boozers—real souses—so I guess I inherited the stomach for it, but I saw too much of drunks when I was a kid ever to be one. I can take it or leave it alone. When I get too tight—like the other night—I just go home and go to bed."

"You're lucky," I said, peering out of the window. "I get a hangover ten minutes after I take a drink."

There was a bustle of activity outside, and a parade of heavy feet crossed the wooden porch and went into the theater.

I waited.

Frank swallowed and sighed, then poured another big shot.

"Funny thing," he said. "Some people can drink and some can't. The ones who can't drink wish they could and the ones who drink too much wish they could stop. Doesn't make sense."

"Alcohol gives me a headache," I said absently, wishing he'd shut up and read his magazine.

He heaved another big sigh, sat down and picked up his magazine. "Booze and philosophy will never replace sex."

I let that remark pass . . . and waited.

Somebody opened the projection room door, and then there were footsteps on the porch. I picked up my hat, ready to go, and Charlie McCleod came in.

"Are they ready for me?"

"Hell no," he said. "They've just started a summit meeting in there, and they asked me to leave the booth. From the way it looks, they may lock themselves up till morning—or the second coming—whichever comes first."

He pulled a chair over near the door, opened it a crack, and sat down. "When I left, they were talking about making a ten percent cut."

"That's silly," Frank said. "They can't cut union scale by even one percent, let alone ten."

"Not money, you dope—*people*," Charlie said sharply. "They've got over four hundred people up here. What they're talking about is sending forty-five of them home . . . for keeps." He put his eye to the crack, the fur cap with the turned-up earflaps making his head look like an anemic egg in an inverted fur nest. I threw my hat on the bench and sat down in Harold's director chair. Frank poured more bourbon.

I waited.

Charlie said, "Damn! Here comes Florence." He disappeared through the crack, letting in a puff of polar air, and returned in a moment grumbling. "She wanted me to take a note in to Stevens. I told her to take it in herself. Who the hell does she think I am, her private messenger boy? I'm not going back in there until Stevens sends for me personally!" He restationed himself at the door.

Everybody is afraid of George Stevens, I thought. All except Wally Wallace, who has a cattle ranch and an income and doesn't give a damn whether he works or not. *All* of them. Then I began to wonder if *I* was afraid of Stevens. I decided not. At the moment I felt bored, let down, pushed aside, but not afraid. I looked at Charlie sitting anxiously on the edge of his chair, eye glued to the crack lest he miss some signal from the theater, and I let go of my own anxiety. An anxious man is a frightened man.

I waited.

Frank reached behind his bench, pulled a new bottle from a film carton, opened it and poured another three ounces.

"By the way, Frank," I said, "did you ever tell Charlie about those two miserable characters in your cabin who've been making your life hell for the past three weeks?"

Frank choked and sprayed good bourbon all over the floor. The strangling spasm produced a blueish tinge around his chin. When he could get his breath, he fired an unexpected broadside.

"McCleod's *one* of them." he spluttered. "He's the *worst* one, always egging that other chowderhead into a fight with me."

"Now wait a goddam minute," Charlie exploded. "This screwloose bastard came into camp and right away wanted to change everything around to suit himself."

"I only wanted a little fresh air," yelled Frank. "You jerks always keep it so stinkin' hot in there."

"It stinks worse since *you* moved in, little man! You weren't satisfied to be accepted as a guest, you wanted to be Cabin Manager, Boss of the Windows, Custodian of the Head, and Commander of the Furnace—always going around turning off the heat and opening all the windows in the middle of the night and making a goddam pest of yourself."

"You cocksuckers were trying to suffocate me."

"You've just given me a terrific idea," Charlie bawled. "That's exactly what we'll do—with a pillow over your head—the next time you sneak up and open the windows from *outside* the cabin . . . ."

"No, sir! I never did—I *never* did!" shouted Frank. "And what about *you*, McCleod? Tellin' your buddy to mark his liquor bottle and hide his Scotch tape and lock his pushpins in his dresser drawer, like I was some kind of a . . . a *thief!*" He got unsteadily to his feet. "And who was it said he was going to throw me out of the cabin in my pajamas and lock the door? All I gotta say is he better not try!"

"Oh, he could do it all right," Charlie snapped. "My roommate may be short on brains, but he's strong as a bull—and all *your* muscles are in your ass!"

"Yuh see how it is?" Frank screamed in my ear. "He keeps his goddam needle in me all the goddam time, and he won't let up. Why don't you fuck off, McCleod, and let me alone?"

"Why should I?" Charlie was on *his* feet now. "You never leave *us* alone, not for a minute. Three of us had been livin' in that cabin for five weeks before you ever showed your ugly puss, and nobody made any trouble. Then you showed up and we ain't had a minute's peace since. We *asked* you to move out, even went to Jack Lacey and had him offer you two or three other places to live. You wouldn't go. So, you made your own choice. Now, either stop being a prick or take the goddam consequences!"

Frank was weaving dangerously, and almost on the edge of weeping. "Helluva choice I had. What I wanted was a bedroom to myself, and when Lacey couldn't find me one, I said why bother to move at all. One bunch of shit-heels is as bad as another."

"You had a bedroom to yourself just the other night, right here in the cutting room. I hope you froze your balls."

"I did," Frank said. "I literally froze my balls."

"And you been comfortable since then?" Charlie was being suddenly very solicitous.

"Yeah, I've been comfortable."

"Well just remember that the next time you start screwin' around with the goddam windows," Charlie bellowed. "Because if you ever touch 'em again, we're gonna throw your ass the hell out in the ditch and lock the goddam door on you!"

I thought Frank was going to throw his glass at Charlie, but there was still some bourbon in it. He swallowed the whiskey instead. I started to laugh.

"Fuck you, too!" he said. "Everybody thinks it's so goddam funny. Fuck *all* of yuh!"

The door opened just then, and in walked Vellani, looking guilty and disappointed and apologetic. I knew what was coming even before he spoke.

"We'll have to put off our meeting with Mr. Stevens till tomorrow, Ken. Can you stay over just one more day?" It was a plea.

"What would you like me to say, Tony? Yes?"

"Yes."

"Then I'll stay, but I must call home and alter some plans." I thought, if he says "good" I'll break down and weep tears.

"Good," he said. "I'll tell Mr. Stevens."

After he was gone I said—to no one in particular—"just another runaround." And quite suddenly I knew why. Tony Vellani was an ambulatory checklist. He kept reminding Stevens of *this*, and calling attention to *that* as persistently as a nagging wife. And, like anyone who is badgered too much, Stevens was now reacting to Vellani's reminders by rejecting them. All Tony had to say was, "Remember, you wanted to hear Ken's music tracks tonight," and immediately Stevens *wouldn't* want to hear them. Alfred was so right. All these eager satellites, in their mad orbits about Stevens, were not only neophytes—they were sycophants. He had them on the run.

Charlie had gone next door. I left Frank nursing a few of his maudlin wounds and walked into the projection booth.

"Charlie," I said, "I didn't know you were in the same cabin with Frank or I would never have unzippered my big flannel mouth. I hope your fracas tonight cleared the air a bit, but it taught me one thing about Frank: he can't drink."

"Two," corrected Charlie. "He can't drink and he can't take any ribbing. None at all. We'll have to stop heckling the poor guy." He gave me a thin smile. "And he's so damned easy to heckle."

"He was made to order," I said. "Maybe you three can work it out. I hope so." And I shoved myself out against a tide of cold, cold air.

The food at dinner took its place high in the realm of fine arts. Bill Hay and I dined and *dined*. We sent a note to the chef. Then we skipped the showing of *Seven Brides For Seven Brothers* in favor of the favorite Inbal pinball machine. Our seance with the mechanical marvel was interrupted by the arrival of four Inbal experts who also had deserted the movie, and I kept hearing the words "Babalu, Babalu" until I asked Bill what they were talking about. He explained.

"The boys put boards under the front legs of the machine, raising it almost to the 'Tilt' position. Then, if they get the ball to roll slowly enough through that upper left-hand slot, it sometimes gets hung up on the wire trigger and the machine starts running wild, adding up the maximum score. The higher the score, the more free games. It's unethical, but what the hell. They've won as many as twenty free games. The limit is twenty-six, and when that happens, they call it 'Babalu.' All they need is the money to start it going."

"Let's give it a whirl, boys," I said. "Here's nine, no ten quarters. Make it Babalu."

They attacked the problem seriously and scientifically. Each young man was a well-coordinated, compact specimen, and each one slapped and pounded the machine until it was firmly planted on the boards just short of "Tilt." Then they all were silent, holding their breaths, as the champion aimed and fired the first steel ball up the track. Half an hour later they were disgusted—and bankrupt. Three of them walked away muttering epithets of some kind, but the fourth coaxed Bill into investing a quarter, and none of their shots started a chain reaction.

"Step aside, novices," I said, "and watch a master."

I slipped in my last quarter, pressed the button to release the first ball, took careful aim with the spring-loaded plunger. The ball glided up the chute, arched around the top of the board, struck the bumper, and bounced back gently, almost in slow motion. Hypnotically, we watched it teeter on the lip of the magic slot, then ease down along the rail, coming to lovely rest against the wire trigger, and remain there!

The machine seemed to suck in a deep breath, then bells rang, lights flashed, horns honked, and the seven counters revolved in whirling frenzy. Everybody in the tent stopped, afraid that any movement might influence the shaking machine into jumping off of its boards and yelling "Tilt." Then the word flew around the tent like a syllabic humming bird:

"Babalu! Babalu! Babalu! Babalu!"

When the counter registered 9,999,999, and the scoring meter lit up with the figure "26," the Inbals shook the machine until the "Tilt" sign winked on, cutting off all the power, and our mechanical friend became quiet.

"Meestair Kan Dahbee! New Babalu Chahm-peeone," shouted my Inbal companion, and they all applauded. Inside of me, the small boy laughed delightedly.

The boards were kicked out from under the front legs, and we settled down to dispatch the free games. Everybody took a turn. At eleven-thirty, they were still shouting and banging on the busy box when I said goodnight. They stopped just long enough to give me a goodnight cheer as I left the tent, then went back to shouting and banging. I walked to the bungalow feeling fine and young.

Very satisfactory, I decided. Disciples rehearsed, the recordings completed, the soundtracks edited and ready for the man, the bug in my chest subjugated, and now—Babalu champion. Fine, young—and very satisfactory. Or just plain childish.

I goosed the furnace, closed the windows, stripped off my clothes and stepped into the tin sarcophagus of my shower, shampooing, soaping, and scrubbing, drying my hair in front of the warm blast of air, leaving it uncombed and flying, exactly like Stokowski. Then I set everything right for the night and slid into bed with an old Ellery Queen, but my eyes were too heavy with the sheer weight of my accomplishments.

I dropped the little book on the floor and rolled over. Damn Tuesday, I thought. It was such a fine, satisfying day. Why couldn't it have stuck around for a decade or so?

"That's ridiculous," said my drowsing subconscious. "If Tuesday hung around for a decade, you'd be stuck here in the desert with Tony Vellani and you'd *never* get to see Stevens."

I shuddered.

TWENTY

I was struggling to cross an endless purple desert, but with every step my feet sank into pools of glistening silver dust—a dust so fine that it swirled in clouds about my face, blinding me. I tried to brush it away, but my hands were bound by gossamer strands against which muscles were helpless. A tight band was being spun around my throat, and every gasp sucked the stifling dust into my lungs. I knew I was strangling, and I fought in breathless panic to end the nightmare.

Sunlight was streaming in on me. A tumult of gray hair was down over my eyes. There was a revitalized tiger in my chest, gnawing ferociously at my windpipe.

"What the hell is *this*?" I croaked, and was immediately wracked by a spasm of coughing.

With concentrated effort I rolled out of bed and dragged unbending, aching legs into the bathroom. The mirror sent back a frightful parody, looking at me with swollen eyes, its mouth hanging open, its chest heaving, and its outrageous bush of hair waving like animated cilia.

"Medusa!" the mouth said. And I began laughing, choking and swearing all at the same time.

After a long while I was able to shave the beard and comb the hair and dress the body. The trachea was raw meat; glottis and uvula were tender and turgid with irritation. As I was gargling, something my loving old grandmother was fond of repeating slipped out of a slot in my memory: "Don't bathe with a cold when the frost is hoar; you'll catch more cold than you had before."

"And how!" I appended, and threw open the door.

Shocking radiance burst into the room. Dancing in every beam of sunlight was a glittering mote of silica dust, spawned in

116

billions by the truck outside as it pulled the drag-raft around the compound. Silica—and what else? I wondered.

I sank down in a chair by the table, letting the December sun play over my back, and tried to take stock of myself and this discouraging relapse. I had had pneumonia in 1942, I remembered, and this feels much the same. I don't want to be hospitalized in Kanab or Page; they don't even have radio commercials. What can I do to startle George Stevens into seeing me before this revolting development knocks me flat?

I pulled a tablet of paper toward me, unlimbered my pen, and sat quietly trying to think my way through to some kind of sane and logical disposition of my problems.

"Dear Mr. Stevens:" I wrote. "A grave personal matter has arisen that requires my immediate presence and attention. I regret having to depart without a further conference with you, but the following report will perhaps serve to sum up my activities thus far."

I wrote—and rewrote—until twelve-thirty. Then I spent a listless hour over a lunch which I could neither smell nor taste and went back to writing, finally completing a full-scale detailed report by three p.m. Mary was in the trailer, and I asked her to make me an original and five copies. She gave me a hard look—then a second one of concern—and said, "They'll be ready. You look awful. Go lie down somewhere."

Frank Davis was sitting in Stevens' private office at the end of the trailer. I walked in and rasped, "Frank, I've got a serious problem—one I must take care of in person—so, with or without a final meeting with Mr. Stevens tonight, I'm leaving on the plane for Los Angeles at six."

"Sounds like an ultimatum," he said, puffing smoke. "As soon as I receive the telephone call I'm waiting for, I'll go out to the set with you and we'll talk it over with Stevens. If he knows you *must* leave, perhaps he'll listen to your recordings early enough so you can catch the DC-3. If not, can you leave later on Bonanza Airlines at nine?"

"Just as long as I can get out of here tonight and be home tomorrow." I was relieved to learn that there was more than one avenue of escape for me.

"I'll order a car and meet you at Operations," Frank said.

The infirmary was close by, so I went in and sat down, feeling flushed and disconnected. Jerry Parker walked over, stuck a thermometer in my mouth and took my pulse.

"You've got a fever of a hundred and three. Get your ass into bed." He handed me a paper cup full of pills.

"No time for bed, Jerry. I'm going home right after I see Stevens—and I don't want your damn pills."

"You take 'em," he commanded. "They'll see you get home in one piece." And he brought me a cup of water.

Hal Weinberger paged me on the loudspeakers, and I went plodding over to Operations.

"Davis just called," Hal told me, "and he can't go with you to the set. You're to go on and see Stevens without him."

I looked in on Mary, saw that she was on page three and still going strong, then eased myself into the car and the driver bounced me through the ruts to the Lazarus set. The trip was part vivid reality and part hallucination.

The sun had lowered beyond the mountain of rock behind Lazarus' house; the tombs, high above the garden, were locked in deep shadow. As I approached the front gate, lifting each leg as I had in my nightmare, I saw the bustling motions inside the walls. Floodlights suddenly bathed away the darkness around the tombs and the white-robed figures of another age moved and poised in long-forgotten attitudes. Stevens came through the gate with a group of clerics. One of them swung around for a last tender look at the reincarnation of his Saviour and crossed himself. They murmured their thanks to Mr. Stevens for his hospitality, and Tony Vellani faded in nearby to escort them from the set. Stevens seemed to be looking at me, and he took a step closer.

"Something I can do for you, Ken?"

"Yes, George, there is. I must return home tonight—an important family crisis has arisen—and I was in hopes that you and I could have our meeting before I go."

My voice wasn't sounding like me; it was telling strange orange-colored fever-branded lies all by itself.

"I'm sorry you have a problem. Is there anything I can do? Would it be best to forego the meeting?"

"Yes to the first question—no to the second. I ask you to give me thirty minutes of your time before dinner this evening to hear the recordings I have made, and provide some answers that will help Alfred."

Vellani had dissolved in beside me and was listening.

"It's done," Stevens said. "Tony, we'll hear music as soon as we break from the set."

I saw his smile, and then it seemed to move, as though trying to trickle off his face. Vellani looked opalescent—a heat-wave image of himself painted on a rippling sheet of canvas. He was nodding, then speaking, and his funny cap with its silly bill was doing a reverse echo of his chin, and both were aimed at Stevens.

"If you go im-med-i-ately from the set to the the-a-ter at fiive-thirty, Ken could c-a-t-c-h- the cc-oo-mm-pp-aa-ny plane a-a-a-at s-i-i-x fi-ft-e-e-e-e-n . . . ."

I knew the words couldn't be coming out like that, in slow motion. It was all a mistake. Vellani wasn't supposed to be helping. It was something sick inside altering my perception. I held tight to my drifting faculties and squinted at Stevens. He was leaning over Vellani—a great hawk descending upon a rabbit! Illusion, I thought . . . and impossible. Both men are the same height.

"That I cannot do, Tony." There was impatience and a rebuke in his voice. "You *know* I must rehearse the scenes for tomorrow. With the lights on I could stay out here until six-fifteen myself. I've already told Ken I will hear music before dinner."

Then he turned and looked at me, and I could see him weighing Tony's eagerness against my problem, reacting to the mobile checklist that was Vellani. He might even react so violently that he would put me off again. It was prescience.

"Maybe it isn't really necessary for me to hear those recordings just yet. I could listen to them later—without you, Ken, and report directly to Al."

I had come this far; I would go down swinging. No more runarounds. I cleared my throat and spoke much too loudly. "I prefer that we run the tracks together. Then I'll know where we are and where we're going. Bonanza has a later plane to Los Angeles. I'll take that if you'll give me a half hour."

"It's done!" he repeated firmly, and walked back through the gate into the walled garden.

Those two words were terribly and awesomely final. God must have used them in just that terminal way at the end of the sixth day.

Everything around me was rotating slowly, tipping ever so slightly sideways, circling slowly around me like a stealthy predator. I stood on the axis of this weaving vertigo and decided I'd better walk. Then I was moving within movement toward a bright, out-of-focus coffee urn, sitting like a metal gnome on a wooden bench, and I was pouring myself a cup of hot coffee. It burned wonderfully going down, only it wasn't coffee but hot chocolate, and I was drinking a second cup when the trees, rocks, garden wall, and the bench I sat on ground to a rumbling halt, and Tony Perris was standing before me.

"Come on, Ken. I've got a car. Let's go back to camp."

I don't remember the return trip.

Mary had finished my report. I gave Perris three copies: one to be delivered to Harold Kress, one to Vellani, and one to be placed conspicuously on the control desk in the theater. I earmarked one for Alfred, put one in an envelope addressed to Eric Stacey, and locked the remaining one in my folder.

The production office was open, and Lee Lukather phoned in my reservation to Bonanza Airlines.

"You know about the layover in Phoenix, don't you?"

"No," I said, "tell me about it."

He pushed his head up close to mine and squinted into my face. "You're not hitting on all your cylinders, Darby. Go see Doc Parker before you leave."

"I've seen all I want to of Doc Parker. He's a quack."

"Granted. Forget I mentioned it. Now, you'll arrive at Phoenix about midnight and take off by Western's new jet at eight o'clock tomorrow morning. You'll arrive in Los Angeles at seven fifty-eight, two minutes before you took off from Phoenix. How about that?"

"A Time machine? Somebody ought to tell Ray Bradbury."

"Pay attention. You've got a reservation at the Sky Rider's Hotel right near the Phoenix airport. Understand?"

"Yes, sir. And thanks, Lee. You'll never regret it."

"You're cuckoo, Darby. Go to bed."

I walked back to the cabin and began to pack, but even that small effort was too much. I flopped. The bed enfolded me and

I sank into a big hole of nothingness, coming awake thirty minutes later a bit refreshed and able to navigate.

The sun had dropped out of its short December day, and the first cars began arriving from the set. I swallowed a few of Parker's pills, put on my wools, and shuffled across the compound to the theater. Charlie McCleod met me at the door of the projection room.

"Harold has a reel of dailies," he said. "I'm setting up to run his stuff first, then yours. Y'know, I'm sorry you're leaving." His voice rose a perfect second on the last word, but it wasn't a question.

"Thanks, Charlie. You'll be seeing me later, unless we drop dead. I'm on for the run of the picture. So far, I've met only two difficult people, and it may be that *I'm* their difficulty." I managed to grin.

Charlie grinned back. "Name dropper. Vellani and O'Neill you said, didn't you? *You're* not their difficulty, *they* are."

"Mind reader. Are my reels in there?"

"All set. Just press the button."

"Okay. I'll wait in the cutting room where it's warm."

Frank was sitting at his bench winding film. He didn't say anything, so I sat down in Harold's chair—the one given to him by Greer Garson—and leaned my head back on the film rack. One part of me became detached and looked around the room with clear eyes.

"This is your interim nightmare," it said. "You've been doing something like this all of your life—sitting and waiting on someone—concocting arrangements of other people's songs, revising bad lyrics, making other composers' music sound better. What have you done for yourself? What music is *your* music? What songs are *your* songs? Damned few! And here you sit, sick and futile, like an old Narcissus afraid to go near the water; going to pot, growing old, waiting—waiting—waiting . . . while all around you events are spinning and whirring with ideas from somebody else's brain, in a speeded-up world where they're just catching up to ideas you threw away twenty years ago. That big fiery hoop is still hanging up there in front of you, and you're sitting here waiting for the fire to go out before you'll take a half-assed run at it. What good will it do to gather your old bones together and take a flying leap through that hoop after the fire has gone out? You are fast declining into an opinionated old poop, insulting the present by living in the past, an obsolete Narcissus who may finally look in the water—too late—and end up a senile old reed, whistling in yesterday's wind."

I felt a breath of wind on my face and opened my eyes. Vellani was standing in the open doorway. I had lived through this scene before. I knew what he was going to say, but this time he fooled me.

"Mr. Stevens wants you to come in and see the dailies with us, Ken. Are you okay?" Was he actually solicitous?

I pulled myself back together and followed him into the theater. Stevens was warming his generous back side at the wall furnace. He motioned for me to sit in the front row, and Vellani took the chair right behind me. I looked down the row: Mellor, Paul, Mo Rosenberg—all camera men—Frank Davis, Eliot Elisofon, Harold Kress, and Van Renterghem. Stevens was talking about lights and angles; I heard him through a soft cloud. In the back row with Vellani were Robert Bush, Bill Hay, Ray Gosnell, Saul Wurtzel, Florence, Novarese—all highly talented people. I didn't have time to inspect the third row; Stevens rubbed his bottom and said in a silky voice, "Okay, Charlie, we may as well have a look."

Instantly the lights went out and the screen began to glow. "Focus, Charlie." Stevens walked through the shaft of light and sat down at the control desk.

"Look at that shot!" someone exclaimed.

There were seven figures on the screen, perfectly composed: Peter, John the Beloved, Thaddeus, Little James, Nathanael, Thomas, and Jesus. They were standing on a round dome of blue-white rock, shading their eyes with upraised arms and looking into the distance. John was the first to speak.

"What a mighty fortress! I've never seen a city that looked so powerful."

"The city is given over to wickedness," said James.

Peter's nasal jigsaw voice cut across the screen. "You have spent a lot of time in Jerusalem, have you?"

"No, Peter, I have never been in the city myself."

"Then how do you know all this wickedness?"

Little James lowered his head. "My brother told me."

An off-screen voice said, "She that was great among nations has lost all her glory. Now she stretches out her hand, but there is no one to comfort her."

"There will come a time to enter," Jesus said. "Oh, Jerusalem, Jerusalem! The city that murders the prophets and stones those who are sent to her. How I long to gather your children as a hen gathers her brood under her wings. But you shall never see me until the time when you say, 'Blessings on him who comes in the name of the Lord.' "

There was a long, long, long close-up of Jesus, shading his eyes and gazing lovingly at the far-off city, during which I almost strangled trying to abort a coughing spell. Stevens was saying, "Haven't we got another take of this close shot? What? Well, why wasn't it printed? Order one right away! In *this* one the ragged end of Christ's sleeve is in terrible juxtaposition with his beard. One looks like the reflection of the other. Damn!"

Then Jesus was saying, "We must go on. Our work will begin in Galilee." And the disciples followed him down a long narrow path at the base of the mountain toward the home of Lazarus. That was all.

The lights came up and everyone began talking in low conversational voices. Stevens looked over at me and picked up my envelope from the desk.

"Anyone who wants to may go to dinner," he said. "I'm going to remain here and listen to a musical concert. Those of you who like music may stay."

Nobody moved except me. I stood up carefully. "It's hardly music, and hardly a concert. Actually, it's more like an ancient wake."

Still nobody moved.

Stevens said, "Come over here next to me, Ken. You, too, Vellani. Let's put our heads together on this."

I moved over while he tore open the envelope. He read all three pages of my letter in total silence, going Mmmm, and Hmmmm, several times. No one else spoke. Finally he patted my arm. "Damned good report. As we listen to these sound-tracks, make notes on the ones I like, and remind me where they appear in this letter. That way, when I refer to these notes later, I can rehear the sounds they describe."

I took out my pen and cleared my throat. "Is the first reel ready, Charlie?"

"Yes, sir," answered the little speaker on the desk.

"Okay, then; and leave the lights on."

I held up my schedule so Stevens could see it and he read it aloud: "The Infant Massacre."

From the screen, "as upon the wind," came the sounds of grief-stricken, weeping women. Stevens leaned back in his chair, just as he had in the bungalow—was it a year ago?—and closed his eyes. He listened; I moved the volume control slowly down and down, fading the sounds, then bringing them closer—to the end.

"This is a frightening experience," he whispered. "Truly a marvelous sound, better than I could have imagined possible. Those women are really in terrible anguish."

"They were wonderful," I said. "They wept real tears during the recording."

"Sorrow comes so naturally to those little people," he observed. "They have suffered so long it has become a racial memory. The recording is exactly right for the scene, don't you think?" He had turned on the last three words, and I saw heads nodding in quiet agreement.

The room swam, and the sounds went on. I heard them, I heard the comments, and I made the replies, but not in any sense of reality—except when my pen touched the paper to put a check after the takes he especially liked: check, check, check . . . and the half hour was abruptly over. Stevens was clapping me on the back and squeezing my hand. Eliot Elisofon had tears in his eyes—or were they in mine—and Bill Hay went, "Babalu, Mr. D!"

They had heard it all: the mourning for Lazarus, the temple prayers, the Hebrew psalms, the English lament, and the misty shepherd's flute. They had finally heard it all.

"Now," Stevens said, "the items in Reel Three and Reel Four must be ready to play on the set tomorrow morning."

Vellani gave me a look that plainly said "I told you so." "We can't," he said flatly. "All this tape is thirty-five millimeter mag stock.* It runs at ninety feet per minute, and our truck can only play seventeen millimeter tape at forty-five feet per minute."

---

*magnetic film

Something inside me clicked and I was thinking clearly. Tony was quoting *me*, but in reverse. "Wait a minute," I said. "You *can* play these tracks from the sound truck, but we need Wally Wallace to make it work."

"Get Wallace over here," Stevens ordered quietly, and Tony Perris literally ran through the wall in his haste.

Stevens' face underwent a subtle alternation. "Tony Vellani, did you make notes?"

Vellani looked bewildered, and I intercepted the pass.

"I have the notes here, Mr. Stevens. I'll transfer them to Tony's schedule—and also to yours—before I leave." I turned to the rows of faces. "While you're all here—and I have the floor—I want to thank everybody: Tony Van Renterghem, Mary, the sound crew, Harold, Charlie, and all of you, but most especially Wally Wallace and Tony Vellani. I am very grateful."

There was applause, and I was conscious of Vellani's pleasure. The murmur of conversation was halted by the fast entrance of Wallace. Saul Wurtzel started to tell him what was required, became confused, and there was a babble of interlocking chatter.

"That's an awful lot of talk for such a little project," Stevens said, getting to his feet. "Can we or can't we play these tapes tomorrow on the set?"

Wally was typically fearless and emphatic. "We sure as hell can't play thirty-five millimeter tape from the sound truck, and I'd like to know who said we could!"

Stevens turned to me, and Vellani looked triumphant.

"Bring over your truck," I said to Wally, "and connect a line from the output of the projection machine amplifier to the input of your recorder in the truck . . . "

Wally grinned and took it from there, " . . . and transfer from ninety FPM mag film to forty-five FPM tape everything you need for the set tomorrow. Sure! *That* we can do. And we can play it back anytime and anywhere anybody wants to hear it. Very simple, Darby."

"Well, then," smiled Stevens, "send for your truck. You have done miracles before. This one should be easy to knock off before dinner—say half an hour?"

"Right!" Wally said, and disappeared.

Stevens turned to me. "You've done a good job of capturing sounds no audience has ever heard before. Say hello to Pappy Newman. Tell him that Salome's Court Dance is just what I wanted. Play these tapes for him to show what our Inbal Dancers can do beside dance, and tell him I'm looking forward to his score for this picture. It should be his best." He lowered his voice. "If this film doesn't inspire him, I'll eat labels off my next case of Beefeaters. Good luck . . . and thanks. I'll see you in Culver City."

I mumbled something huskily; he hugged me around the shoulders, gave me all thirty-two teeth and said, "Wonderful."

I moved outside with the others. Charlie pulled me into the booth. "Jeeze, what a session! Smooth, man. Here's the tape, all packaged. I hope we'll be seeing each other again."

"We will . . . and thanks, Charlie."

Harold Kress had a hold of my arm. "All those hours in the cutting room paid off. Nice editing, and thanks for the complete notes. I know Stevens will try to catch me up on some of this stuff, but I'll be ahead of him. Hey! You don't look good at all."

"I'm not *any* good, Harold. I think I'm going to be as sick as you were—was it a hundred years ago? And thank you."

I walked uncertainly to my tin temple and changed clothes, putting on my civvies and adding two cashmere sweaters, an overcoat, muffler and gloves—enough wrapping to smother a mummy—but tonight I'd need it all. Outside, it was below freezing. Everything was packed, except Mary's bottle of vodka. I put it on her desk in the trailer, arranged to have my bags picked up, and checked in at Transportation.

"We'll have a car ready to take you to the airport at nine-fifteen. It's only eight-thirty now. Why don't you get a bite of dinner? You look like you could use some ballast."

"Dinner?" I was croaking now. "Why, yes. Thanks, Lee."

"Don't be late," he warned. "Nine-fifteen."

I walked stubbornly toward the mess tent, but it kept moving away from me. Miles later, I managed to reach it. Hal Weinberger was eating alone. I slumped down across from him, and Frank O'Neill saw me. I motioned him over and told him how sorry I was for igniting the furor between him and Charlie McCleod.

"Forget it," he said. "It really did both of us a lot of good. Things are going to be all okay between us from now on."

I heard part of the conversation, made answers, ate a few bites of something, but my memory mechanism was dislocated and I remembered only one thing. I asked Hal, "Are you any relation to the Weinberger who composed the great variations on 'Under the Spreading Chestnut Tree?' "

"You mean Jaromir Weinberger? No, I'm not."

A few minutes later I remembered thinking what a funny thing it was that I, an alleged musician, could not recall the composer's given name, but Hal—chief of Operations—*he* could!

And then it was ten minutes after nine. I picked up my overcoat and walked over to the executive table. Stevens and Bill Hay both scraped their chairs and stood up.

"Please don't," I said. "Let me say thanks again, and goodbye for now. God willing, we'll meet again."

My hand was gripped, and words were said. My shoulder was patted, and Vellani followed me to the exit.

"I had a feeling this would happen. Just when we come to the moment of truth, you won't be here."

"Tony, Tony!" I husked. "The real moment of truth comes later—in the dubbing room."

I walked away from the mess tent for the last time, trying not to offend my twice-insulted lungs by breathing the icy air too deeply. It was all over—finished. True, there would be a long extended coda somewhere in the future, perhaps next year—or the year after—but I would not see this place again. As once before, I stood in the center of the compound, turning a complete circle, taking in the curving rows of aluminum huts coldly reflecting the December moonlight; noticing that the infirmary sign was visibly whimpering, its neon gas stricken with some aeriform virus. I stepped through the shadows of the triple loudspeakers, now frozen dumb, and touched briefly the silver-tipped branches of the giant Christmas tree, symbol of Christ's birth—borrowed from pagan folklore—and wondered if he could fathom the busy conspiracies that buzzed in the minds of men. Or was it really George Stevens who was God, preparing another crucifixion out here in His American Galilee, creating Christmas trees before the fact, producing lunches of cold manna, Kosher food for the chosen people, dictating the hours of each day, commanding the sunrise and the sunset, and whirling above His creation in a winged chariot?

This is the Gospel according to Stevens, I thought. He is creating a new life of Christ. But is he so omniscient and discriminating? Is he trying to render simplicity out of chaos, or is he making chaos out of simplicity? And these people who do his bidding—are they disciples and believers? I thought of Van Renterghem: scholarly—and obsequious. Bill Hay: very capable—but haltered. Chico Day: energetic—and wary. Saul Wurtzel: experienced—and frustrated. Vellani, the perfect disciple: adoring—and whipped.

I thought about them as the company car fled through the desert darkness toward the airport. All of them were afraid. But of what? Of being found out, like me? Of having Stevens find the chink in their life's armor and bore a hole through it to the quick? Would *I* have cringed and become one of them if he had turned his auger on my work back there in the theater instead of larding me with flattery and praise?

I waited a long time in the overheated little trailer that was headquarters for Bonanza Airlines on the edge of a landing strip near what? Arizona or Utah? Tiny-shiny febrile rotifers swam busily in my peripheral vision. They formed the shapes of glowing faces—a swarming of noses, chins, mouths, ears and eyes—buzzing in bee formation . . . disciples, Navajos, Inbal dancers, multitudes, actors . . . and the funny-beautiful mug of Jamie Farr. Windblown sparks, they flickered in swift cyclonic frenzy about the brightest spark of all: Stevens! As I watched, he metamorphosed into rapidly shifting patterns: disarming, charming, raptorial, brilliant, flattering, commanding, and—engulfing. A man like other men? No! What other man had the stupendous power to bless, to reward, to bestow grace, to bait, to indict and judge, to condemn and punish, to paint a living landscape, populate it with thousands, and create his own holyland? He beamed there in my dozing vision, the smiling orifice of a radiant funnel. All the rest of us were twinkling grains of sand . . . pouring through *him*. He was *Director!* All the rest of us know our secret inadequacies. Ah . . . but *he* knew them, too! Was it possible that Stevens had no inadequacies? Was he really superhuman? Did he never make mistakes? I wondered idly if

Alfred and I would one day be engulfed and overwhelmed by his punitive power—consigned to some Georgian purgatory. Thankfully, I was not clairvoyant.

The Fairchild prop-jet swung firmly into the cold sky and circled the gash of light illuminating the stealthy ponderous growth of the Glen Canyon dam. On the next upward sweeping turn, the silver rooftops of Stevens' earthly tabernacle lay crisply revealed, strung out in twin configurations, gleaming parentheses planted on the desert floor. I watched them grow smaller, smaller, then disappear. The contour seat cupped my heavy weariness and I sank deeper and deeper. How many years left for me, Lord? And when they are over and done will anybody know I've been here . . . or care?

A ghostly Vandraegen was bending over me, his face dark with concern. In a voice that blended with the engines, he rumbled, "I go to rehearse Jesus. Be not afraid."

That's the key, I thought dreamily: be not afraid. No more practice runs at life, no more casual rehearsals. Just once, before the fire dies out, I must take that flying leap through temerity's hoop.

The drone of the engines faded to a soft murmur, and the murmuring became syllables, then words. They fell into the cadence of a cantus firmus, spoken by many voices, hushed and reverent, and I heard my own voice among them . . . whispering . . . chanting . . . questioning . . . questioning:

> Will Time write up my final scene
> With love and praise from devotees,
> Or give me two parentheses
> With *nothing* written in between?

"Of course," Vandraegen thundered gently. "Everyone wants to achieve *something* between birth and death."

The stewardess was shaking me. "Wake up, sir. Wake up. We're about to land."

"Oh? Yes! Saint George told me we'd stop over . . . in . . . in . . . parentheses?"

I heard her call: "Joe! Come help me. We've got to get this man off the plane. He's sick!"

The rainbow arch of the bridge over Glen Canyon from the Arizona side. The peak at left is split to make room for the road bed. Indians said that many evil spirits were released when the dark mountain was broken apart.

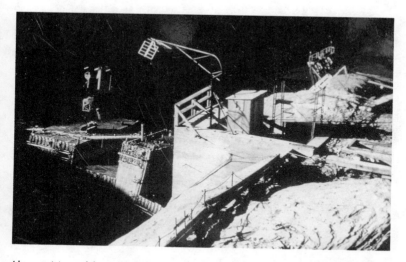

Above: Moveable cable cranes mark the construction site of Glen Canyon Dam (Nov. 17, 1962). *Below:* The last rays of sunlight illuminate two crenelations of the dam. Cables lower concrete and steel to a swarm of antlike workers atop each monolithic tower (Nov. 17, 1962).

My first earth-bound glimpse of Stevens' city: a silver streak on the desert floor. "Welcome to Galvanized Galilee," Kress said. 11/17/62

Above: Utah Location: George Stevens Production Camp, *The Greatest Story Ever Told.* "Aluminum City," now under Lake Powell near Page, Arizona. *Below:* Operations! Bulletin board, Payroll and post offices. First point of entry for cast. 1962

Tin temple C-3, my first abode in Hollywood Holyland. I shared this cabin first with Daniel Vandraegen, then with David Sheiner (1962).

Above: Official greeter and film editor, Harold Kress; the rooms for editing and projection are behind him (Utah, Nov. 17, 1962). *Below:* Recreation, rehearsal, and mess tents on a cold windy morning.

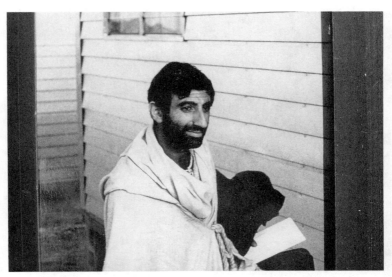

Above: Jack Lacey's "Girl Friday" hauling linen to bungalows. Standing behind and to the right is Max von Sydow, made up and ready for the set. *Below:* Jamie Farr in his role as Thaddeus.

Michael Tolan in his role as Lazarus.

Above: The operations offices contain phone booths and restrooms and support omnidirectional radio antennae connecting this hub of activity to all surrounding locations miles away. The bus is waiting to take the Inbal Dancers to a distant set. *Below:* Wardrobe and make-up tents.

Jack Lacey, cabin master and logistics magician, with wardrobe mistress at the Operations Shack.

Above: Self-portrait taken in a make-up mirror. *Below:* I walk into the desert, following a path toward the ravenous rock crusher and its huge piles of stony exudation.

Above: The Haul Road, straight as a rifle shot from crusher to dam. The truck and trailer are accelerating to 85 mph. *Below:* A mountain of wind-sculpted faces gave me the uneasy feeling that I was being watched.

Above: The Inbal men play soccer on Sunday afternoon. The foreground is red-brown, hills tan, sky deep deep blue. *Below:* Stevens' jet helicopter. This machine, having no pistons, made very little noise and was as steady as a rock in the air.

Above: Stevens taking off to the distant set in his French jet helicopter. It was so steady in flight that he used it on several occasions as a camera boom.
Below: The shadow of the flagpole points to my new cabin, Number E-7, where pneumonia almost caught me! (Utah, 1962).

Harold Kress with Ed Wynn outside the door of Harold's cutting room, taking the sun (1962).

Above: Dr. Daniel Vandraegen, Frank O'Neill, Charlie McCleod, and Harold Kress share a rare peaceful moment (1962). *Below:* Harold Kress surreptitiously splicing "dailies" in his Utah desert cutting room, a task *verboten* by George Stevens (1962).

Robert Bush, dialog director and actor, sitting in his doorway contemplating the universe. 1962

Above: Leach field for Tin City's sewage system. In far distance, at base of mountain at right, is the set of Jerusalem Walls. *Below:* A quiet Sunday for the rock crusher and the haul road. Glen Canyon Dam required mountains of gravel and sand (1962).

The Lazarus-House set built beneath a towering mountain. Two visitors stroll in foreground. Three tombs are visible just above the pillared portico. Every blade of grass, bush, and tendril of ivy was imported and kept green with paint (1962).

Closer view of the three tombs. All greenery is false.

Above: Lazarus' house rests upon a great rolling wave of solid, wind-and-rain-eroded rock. *Below:* Christmas comes to Tin City. The cabin behind the woman in the white sweater is Kress's cutting room attached to the taller theater. The motor home at next right is the Business Office, and to the right of that is Stevens' personal cabin (Dec. 1962).

Above: Navaho Indians trained by a Marine sergeant to be Roman Legionnaires! (Utah desert, 1962). *Below:* The Inbal Dance Group poses for my camera while waiting to be called to the set. The woman in black (*standing, second from right*) is Madam Sarah. *Standing, third from right:* Ovadia Tuvia, the musical director and interpreter of the troupe (Utah 1962).

The Walls of Jerusalem: Returning from Lazarus' House at twilight, I walked
among the shadows toward an opening gate in the Walls of Jerusalem. There
are few things as lonely and obsolete as a set which has performed its duty;
deserted and abandoned, the scene which saw so much energetic action still
seemed haunted by ghosts of extras, actors, technicians, and crew.

INTERLUDE, by Fred Steiner

It was sometime near the end of October 1964—after almost three months of virtually continuous activity, scoring television programs for CBS and 20th Century-Fox—I found myself, as we Hollywoodians euphemistically say, "in between." I was just beginning to enjoy the welcome respite (while wondering where the next job was coming from) when my agent, Marc Newman, called me to proffer a most unusual undertaking. He told me that his brother Alfred, also his client at the time, was in serious trouble; the picture he had been working on for almost a year was being extensively cut and re-edited, which meant that much of the music already completed would have to be redone.

At that time, I was at about the midpoint of what, in retrospect, has been a busy, varied, and mostly satisfying forty-year career as composer and conductor in radio, TV, movies, and whatnot (recently as film music historian), and the prospect of collaborating on a film score with another composer held little appeal for me. On a few previous occasions, when close colleagues of mine had gotten into similar tight spots, I did (and still will) help them out. But doing that sort of thing usually entails the obligation to develop or arrange someone else's musical ideas, almost always without screen credit (this being an unwritten rule or gentleman's agreement, especially between friends) and, under most such circumstances, with much less remuneration than similar labor would earn when one works alone.

This, however, was no ordinary request. True, Alfred Newman was not a close colleague or even an acquaintance, but to me—indeed, to most screen composers of that day—his name was a magic one. He represented the very pinnacle of achievement in the world of music for the movies, and even today stands

153

as a symbol of the Golden Age of film music. Newman was a pioneer who arrived in Hollywood in the earliest days of the talkies and remained to compose some of the most famous motion picture music of all time, to win nine Academy Awards, and to become the most powerful and perhaps the most influential music man in the film-making capital during the Forties and Fifties.

I had met Alfred Newman only once before, when he was still heading the music department at 20th Century-Fox, and even though several years had passed, I could still remember clearly the impression made on me by the forceful personality of that small but dynamic man. When Marc Newman told me that his brother had chosen me to work with him on *The Greatest Story Ever Told*, I was extremely flattered, but—I must confess—not a little puzzled. After all, there were many reputable, experienced composers and arrangers to choose from, most of them older and much better known to Newman than I was. Yet, from what little he could have heard of my music, he apparently regarded me as trustworthy enough to help him out of his difficulty. Additionally, as it turned out, the pay was very good—in fact, almost as much as I would have been able to command for a picture of my own in those days.

My pleasure and excitement at such an extraordinary opportunity increased considerably when I learned that the only other composer Alfred had selected to assist him was the gifted and highly respected veteran, Hugo Friedhofer. David Raksin, himself one of filmdom's most distinguished composers, once said that Friedhofer was the most learned, best schooled, and often the most subtle of film composers; and even to this day, many of our confreres regard him as the master of us all.

My appointment book for 1964 shows that my first conference with Alfred Newman took place at his home in Pacific Palisades on a November afternoon. I was shown into the composer's studio by the Newmans' houseboy, Ronnie. Alfred was seated at his Steinway grand, the ever-present cigarette dangling from his lips. There was another person in the room, a tall, distinguished-looking man, whose warm handshake and friendly grin did much to assuage the nervousness and anxiety I felt in the presence of the world-famous screen composer who was about to entrust me with his music. Although I can not remember if I had met Ken Darby before that moment, I certainly knew who he was. Having worked for years in radio, recordings, films, and television, Ken already had a firmly established reputation as one of the most talented, active, and eminent members of the Hollywood music colony.

Until that meeting, however, I had not been aware of Ken Darby's close association with Alfred Newman, an association that had begun at 20th Century-Fox sixteen years earlier, and whose depth and significance became more and more evident to me during the weeks and years that followed. Obviously, this is not the place for a technical explanation of how motion pictures are scored, but I must advise the reader that sitting down and composing music is only one part of the process. There are many other essential, ancillary operations which, under most circumstances, are handled entirely by the studio music department. In this case, however, Alfred Newman was functioning more or less on his own—working out of his house, so to speak. In fact, United Artists no longer had its own music department. Thus it was absolutely necessary for him to have someone like Ken Darby by his side to take charge of all those other operations.

To suppose that Ken Darby merely functioned as Alfred Newman's aide-de-camp would be way off the mark. It was not long before I began to realize that he was Newman's partner and co-worker in almost every way (as the composer himself was often to state). Ken attended spotting sessions and sat in on the conferences with George Stevens. He also scheduled meetings with the composer for Hugo and me, for the orchestrators, Leo Shuken and Jack Hayes, and for the music editor, George Brand. He saw to it that photocopies of the music were made and turned over to those who needed them. He ensured that orchestrations were delivered to the copyists. He conferred with the orchestra contractor, Bobby Helfer, and the sound department at MGM about setting up recording schedules. In addition to fulfilling these and other responsibilities, Ken served as Newman's choral director, made all of the vocal arrangements, and I seem to recall that he even found time to adapt two long cues himself.

Hugo and I screened the rough cut (i.e., without sound effects or music) of *The Greatest Story Ever Told*. It took two days, and we began to understand Alfred's dilemma. Mr. Stevens' Biblical epic seemed ponderous and interminable, especially without music. Our reactions were mixed.

During the next ten weeks or so, I worked with great intensity and as much speed as possible. For the most part, my task (and Hugo's) was to recompose or rearrange cues already completed by Newman for sequences that George Stevens had subsequently re-edited. There were also a few sequences that Newman could not finish in time; for those I composed entirely new cues, always utilizing his thematic material. The routine was simple: following a conference with Newman, I would take the revised timing sheets and a stack of already completed cues home with me, and return a few days later with a completely detailed sketch. Then, after going through it thoroughly with the composer and getting his approval, or incorporating any changes he might request, I gave the sketch to Ken, who would see that it was turned over to the orchestrators. (Because of the urgency of the situation and the constantly pressing recording deadlines, neither Hugo nor I had time to do our own orchestrating.)

The fate that befell Alfred Newman's score for *The Greatest Story Ever Told* has become a sort of legend in the movie music lore (David Raksin calls it "The Saddest Story Ever Told"). In these pages, Ken Darby retells it for the general public, adding many details hitherto known only to a few people closely connected with the project. Having no wish to disclose the ending of his story, all I can say here is that I can still remember my feelings of shock and disbelief when the news of what had happened reached me, for I sincerely felt (and still feel) that the music he wrote for this film was some of Alfred Newman's finest work.

Several years passed without further contact with Alfred Newman or Ken Darby. Then, in 1969, Hugo Friedhofer and I were both summoned to help Newman again, this time under circumstances much sadder than those surrounding *The Greatest Story Ever Told*. Now we were needed because the composer had become seriously ill while working on what was to be his last score, for Universal's *Airport*.

At that point I had no way of knowing the gravity of Newman's condition—I only knew that I was pleased and privileged that he had chosen me again to help him in an hour of need. For Hugo and me, the task was much the same as it had been on *The Greatest Story*: to compose or arrange cues, utilizing Newman's melodic or rhythmic material. Again I met Ken Darby, saw that he was at the composer's side, sharing the work as before and handling, always with his customary efficiency, the multitude of daily recurring essential tasks that normally would have been left to a studio music department. But this time it was plain to see that Ken had more responsibilities than ever. Because of his weakened condition, Newman was reluctant to drive, so Ken chauffered him to and from the recording sessions at Universal. There were times when Newman was unable to attend the dubbing, and Ken was entrusted with monitoring that phase of picture completion.

Work on *Airport* occupied me for about a month, and then I returned to the hectic world of TV scoring with which I was involved during the Sixties. The last time I ever saw Alfred Newman was when I said goodbye to him at one of the *Airport* recording sessions; a few months later came the shocking news that he had succumbed to his illness. I don't remember if I had a chance to say goodbye to Ken at that last session. Perhaps it is because he may have been much too busy to give me anything more than a quick wave of his hand as I was leaving the recording stage. In any case, neither one of us would have had the slightest notion at that time that our association with Alfred Newman would bring us together again a few years afterward, and that this time we would become the best of friends, bound by our mutual admiration for the man who did so much to shape the growth of that peculiarly twentieth-century art form: music for the movies.

Now, in the parlance of the film editor, the scene dissolves to the University of Southern California in August of 1975. After four years of classes, lectures, seminars, term papers and other scholarly endeavors, I had passed my qualifying examinations for a doctorate in musicology at that venerable institution. Some of my professors had been urging me to select a topic in film music for my dissertation, and I considered several possibilities. But when I learned that Alfred Newman's widow, the present Mrs. Martha Newman Ragland, had donated his music, records and other effects to USC and established a memorial library there, my choice became clear. And when I began my research into the life and music of Alfred Newman, the subject for my first interview obviously had to be Ken Darby, who had already assembled, sorted and cataloged most of the material that Mrs. Ragland had given to the Alfred Newman Memorial Library at USC.

It was during that first interview that Ken told me he was writing a book, "complete with pictures," about his involvement in the filming of *The Greatest Story Ever Told*. When I commented that such a book might be an eye opener, Ken agreed, but added firmly that he did not want anybody to see his manuscript until, as he put it, time would allow him to edit "anything that might offend surviving relatives of George Stevens"—this despite his conviction that what he had written about the director was not unkind, but simply honest. Nevertheless, regardless of his reservations, Ken let me satisfy my curiosity by allowing me to take his manuscript home with me.

From the very first page, I found myself utterly enthralled—captivated as much by Ken's engaging and witty prose style as by his vivid descriptions of the often strange, sometimes downright bizarre goings-on connected with the location filming of *The Greatest Story Ever Told*. I urged Ken to finish the manuscript and seek a publisher, but he still seemed to feel uneasy about disclosing his story to the public at that time. For my own part, I could find very little in his writings to cause much trouble, but it was evident that Ken, aside from his previously stated concerns, was also uneasy about the possible effect his words might have on some of the other people who figured—not always in the most favorable light—in the book. Although I ventured the opinion that telling the truth could do no harm in the long run, I did not press the matter further.

For the next four years, my Newman dissertation progressed by fits and starts, while I continued to work part time at my profession. Then followed two more years, during which I had to forgo almost all scoring assignments in order to complete the dissertation before the deadline fixed by the USC Graduate School (which had already given me an extension of time). One unfortunate cause of delay was the appalling discovery that I would have to reconstruct, almost from scratch, the story of Alfred Newman's early years, because everything about his youth that had appeared in print to that time was full of errors and contradictions. Correcting the record cost me much more time than I had contemplated, but to have allowed it to stand as it was—perhaps simply to start my treatise with Newman's arrival in Hollywood, leaving the responsibility for the rest to some other researcher—was unacceptable to me.

Throughout those years of searching, probing, gathering and evaluating data, examining and appraising hours of music, writing and rewriting, years beset with constantly recurring doubts and fears—doubts if I should be doing what I was doing, and fears about potential damage to my career—my most ardent and enthusiastic supporter was Ken Darby. He heartened me by his own faith in the value of what I was trying to accomplish and with his continuous offers of help. To recount only a few of the things he did to ease the burden of my research: providing me with my own set of keys for the Alfred Newman Memorial Library at USC, furnishing duplicates of the catalogs and other volumes of Newmaniana he had lovingly and painstakingly compiled for the library, photographing and photocopying documents, pictures, and other items from the archive and his own collection when I needed them, and then, at the end, allowing me to meet my deadline by typing the final draft of my dissertation (all 464 pages of it), and doing as perfect a job as any professional typist.

At long last my doctoral work was finished, and I was entitled to put the coveted "Ph.D." after my name. (I still have trouble whenever someone calls me "Doctor"!) A short time later, I was delighted to learn from Ken that he had completed his memoir about *The Greatest Story Ever Told* and was seriously considering the possibility of publication. His first book, *The Brownstone House of Nero Wolfe*, had just been published by Little, Brown & Co., and he now seemed to feel confident and at ease about disclosing to the reading public his behind-the-scenes account of George Stevens' religious epic. When Ken asked me if I would like to look over his manuscript again, I jumped at the chance. Despite the fact that I had already learned more details of the *TGSET* saga in the course of my research, I found this chronicle even more absorbing and enjoyable than before.

By this time it must be obvious to the reader that I, like Wally Sterling, am a Ken Darby fan and have much of the same difficulty as Wally in trying to be objective about this man. Nevertheless, I honestly believe that had I never met Ken nor been personally involved with some of the events in *Hollywood Holyland*, I would still take pleasure in this book and esteem it as a valuable contribution to the literature of the cinema. Why did I find it so special? And why am I grateful that Ken is allowing it to be published? To begin with, I am not only a film composer but a student and devotee of the history and art of motion pictures, and this book offers me and my fellow movie enthusiasts a rich, colorful picture of a facet of film making heretofore little known to us: what it is like to live and work on location under difficult conditions during the making of a giant Hollywood spectacular. Secondly, I find myself gripped—at times deeply moved—by Ken's candid exposures of what I know to be some other, less attractive aspects of movie making, ones which have rarely been discussed in print and are therefore little understood by the movie-going public: the personality conflicts, insecurities, frustrations, disappointments, and heartbreak that can result when it becomes apparent that a huge, costly project—one that shows high promise—is going to turn out badly.

Finally, and maybe most meaningfully, from these pages emerges a portrait of Ken Darby the human being, the man of compassion and humanity his friends and family know. Ken holds up for scrutiny and sheds light on the two opposing yet interconnected aspects of the art and business called the cinema—the positive and the negative aspects, or the "Bad and the Beautiful"—writing about them vividly, honestly, wittily, often with mordant humor, but never with bitterness or rancor. On the contrary, he writes with tolerance, understanding, and sometimes sympathy even for those who, the passage of time has shown, made lamentable errors of judgment regarding Alfred Newman's music for *TGSET*.

If the book has any flaw, it may be this: that Ken Darby has been too modest, tending to underplay his own contributions to the production of the score for *TGSET*, contributions whose significance was acknowledged publicly and privately by Newman himself. Readers like me, who frequently grow weary and impatient with too-often-encountered books about movies that are full of Hollywood "hype," self-serving puffery, and sometimes downright ignorance, should welcome with pleasure *Hol-*

lywood Holyland, a view of film making which is more than
different—it is unique.

                                   Fred Steiner
                                   Encino, California
                                   February 1987

BOOK TWO

TO THE NEWMAN FAMILY
WITH LOVE

To have been intimately involved in the preparation and recording of musical salutes to greet the natal days of Lucy, Fred, David, Thomas, and Maria provides me with a special joy.
I love them all.
kd

SCENE I

The Thirty-Sixth Annual Academy Awards Presentation was televised on the night of April 13, 1964, from the stage of the Santa Monica Civic Auditorium. At six-thirty that evening I was driving our freshly-waxed Black Beauty toward that exciting destination. No nominee is blasé on Oscar Night.

The weather at the beach was damp and cold. Vera huddled next to me bundled in her mink stole. Martha Newman, equally fur clad, sat shivering behind me while Alfred—warmed from within by preparatory, well-timed shots of 13-year-old Jameson's Irish whiskey—rode comfortably in the right rear seat with his window wide open, impervious to the biting chill of ocean air. He was cheerful and complimentary.

" . . . so when Ken is behind the wheel I feel as safe as I do in my own bed. And isn't this a beautiful car, Martha? If you weren't forever having to fetch and carry all the kids in Pacific Palisades, we could own a luxurious Continental like this instead of that big Ford station wagon."

During this I surreptitiously turned on the heater and began nudging the switch that controlled the right rear window, inching it upward every time he turned toward Martha, on the off chance that I could close it before we contracted pneumonia. Suddenly, he patted his pockets, muttered a familiar expletive, leaned forward urgently and tapped me on the back.

"That was my last cigarette. Ronnie forgot to put a new package in my tux."*

"No problem, we can both smoke mine." I passed a fresh pack of Salems over my shoulder while slyly closing his window. "Light one for me, too, please."

---

*Ronnie Felchon, the Newman chef, housekeeper, babysitter.

Martha said, "You both smoke too much. But I suppose tonight isn't the time to talk about it."

Pap's lighter flared, and a moment later a cigarette was placed carefully between my upthrust V-formed fingers. He fumbled at his armrest for a moment, found the control and down came the window—wide open again. I turned up the heat.

"Is this our fourth or fifth trip together?"

"Fourth," I said.

He blew smoke. "It should have been our sixth. I wanted your name with mine on *With a Song In My Heart* and *Call Me Madam*, but I was negligent. Your credit was sent in too late for the lab to get it on the title cards. You were already listed as Vocal Supervisor, but that wasn't enough. I've always been sorry . . ."

"Don't ever be—not ever!" I cut in. "That was years and thirty pictures ago. It was worth *twenty* Oscars just being on the team, working with you and those great casts—and especially with our beloved Walter Lang. Walter deserved Oscars for both of those films. He's been shamefully neglected by the Academy."

"It's a sorry fact that not everyone who *deserves* an award wins one. But win or lose tonight, Ken, I count the time we spent together scoring *How the West Was Won* as the most enjoyable professional experience of my life."

"Right," I said. "I feel exactly the same. It was pure pleasure and joy all the way, except for that first day on the MGM sound stage when we recorded the Main Title before we knew where their engineers had placed the microphones."

Alfred chuckled, and I raised his window another four inches.

"Where *were* the microphones?" Martha asked.

"Thirty feet up in the air hanging from the ceiling in a cluster like a bunch of grapes." Pappy opened the window wide again, flicking ashes. "They could just as well have been hung in the toilet. Ken rushed into the monitor room and dragged Frank Milton on stage. I dismissed the orchestra for half an hour and we finally persuaded Frank to hang the mikes where they belonged: five of them spread low over the sections of the orchestra, and the sixth one off at the far end of the stage for the long-shot pickup. Then we made one more take and played them both back in the theater."

"What happened?" Vera asked.

"End of argument," Pap said. "You'd have thought our names were Edison and Bell. The brass crackled, the strings had resin on the bows, and the woodwinds sparkled—in *stereo*."

He took a drag on his cigarette, and I concluded the story. "Sound engineers appeared from everywhere rubbing their gooseflesh, surprised and delighted that MGM could produce such a rich sound."

"After that it was smooth going," Alfred said. "It's a great sound crew, and they gave us their best. It was a wonderful job from start to finish. I'm glad we'll be recording there again."

"Speaking of which," I said, "I went by there yesterday with the tentative outline of our recording needs for *The Greatest Story Ever Told*, and guess what: they've made up a long white pole, about the diameter of a broomstick, with a red band painted around it exactly six feet seven inches from the floor. Clipped to it is a metal tag embossed with the words: *Set mikes at red line for Alfred Newman*." I heard Pap snort and stifle a cough, and added, "Jimmy told me that *all* the conductors have been using 'The Newman Pole' ever since they heard the sound we got on *How the West Was Won*. When we start recording on *Greatest Story* we won't have to go through *that* hassle again."

"Microphone placement will be the least of our hassles on *The Greatest Story*. Did I tell you that Stevens has asked me to *audition* my score for him—on the piano?"

"That's insulting," Vera blurted.

"And preposterous!" I said, guiding the car into the lane marked off for the nominees.

"You aren't going to do it, are you?" Martha asked.

"Stevens is the Director. He commands, everybody obeys."

"But how can you possibly convey an orchestral score on the piano?" Vera objected.

"Obviously, that's impossible," Alfred said. "I can play the themes for him, but they won't tell him anything without the sonorities of the instrumentation. I suppose that Ken—or I—will be forced to prepare a descriptive commentary . . . ."

Vera was fuming. "But *why*? After all the superb music you have composed for films, and the tremendous reputation you have earned, why should George Stevens insult you by asking for a demonstration—as though you were some green newcomer—and hadn't just scored *The Diary of Anne Frank*—for *him*? I don't like him. He should be ashamed of himself!"

I braked sharply to avoid colliding with a high-rumped Flying Cloud that came bulldozing into the space between me and the car ahead. Alfred reacted violently.

"Look out! *Look out!* Give him the horn. Better yet, go ahead and hit the irresponsible bastard!"

We all laughed at his vehemence. Not a fender was scraped. The face peering out of the high rear window mouthing "Thank you" was not one I'd ever choose for myself, although it had done pretty well for its owner, having won for him an unbelievably exquisite woman. "It's Tony Martin," I said. "Does that explain anything?"

"That explains everything," Pappy growled. "Tony Martin is a rude, raw ego encased in a bag of attractive skin tied at the top with sterling silver vocal cords. And as astonishing as it may seem, his bad manners are so contagious that he's actually infected his Rolls Royce."

I blew two beeps of forgiveness on the horn, mainly to cover our laughter.

The area in front of the auditorium was awash with light and paved with red carpet. On each side of the entry promenade, crowded bleachers exploded with frenetic fans cheering their favorite stars: Sophia Loren, Gregory Peck, Patricia Neal, Rex Harrison, going wild over Paul Newman, making obscene gestures at Kirk Douglas. We unrecognizables ran their gauntlet virtually unnoticed.

Once inside we were handed programs and escorted to our seats on the aisle in the fourth and fifth rows from the stage. The cover of the program was white-flocked paper that looked and felt like doeskin suede. I fondled it for a moment, then looked inside. *How the West Was Won* had received nine nominations. From every page its title jumped out at me like the repetitious flash of neon lights. I saw my name beside Alfred's and paused to relish the flush of warm satisfaction. We had become more than two men working in music, more than members of a musical team combining our efforts on a commercial project—more even than good friends. We had grown to be interdependent, honoring each other's talents, seeking each other's advice, criticism, and counsel, and sharing that inexplicable intellectual affection that goes far deeper than ordinary professional partnership. Impulsively, I reached around, took Martha's hand and planted a big flourishing kiss on it, then did the same with Vera's.

"What's that for?" they asked, almost in unison.

"That's for sheer love. This is the 13th, my lucky day, and my lucky number. I love everybody!"

Pappy patted me on the shoulder and I turned half around in my seat, watching him as he spoke. "It's good to love, but not *everybody*, and luck hasn't anything to do with tonight—neither has your superstition. The votes are already in and counted. Somebody's already won. We *are* lucky to be nominated. From here to the stage is only a few steps, but for the losers it might as well be a thousand miles. For some it's twenty or more years, and for many—it's never. That's our lucky number."

I started to reply, but applause broke in as our old friend, Hal Kanter, walked on stage and began his warm-up.

Looking back from a lonely room in 1990, I see all too clearly how precious were the hours we shared. Alfred and I won simply by being alive and working together. Our exploits were exciting, surprising, discouraging, even disappointing, but, as I look back, all were precious in every detail, as life is precious—as time is precious.

The Oscar for Best Achievement in Sound went to Franklin Milton, MGM Sound Department for *How the West Was Won*, and Pap poked me between the shoulder blades, going "HA!"

The next award went to Harold Kress—Best Achievement in Film Editing—for *How the West Was Won*, and Alfred's punch nearly knocked me out of my seat. I turned and gave him a look of mock irritation. "Two wins do not a landslide make," I hissed. And he batted a paw at me.

But I was right. The next four nominations for which *HT-WWW* was in contention: Costume Design, Color Cinematography, Art Direction, and Set Decoration, all went to 20th Century-Fox for *Cleopatra*.

Then came the paralyzing moment. Sammy Davis, Jr. trotted on stage, made a fast-running series of remarks which I didn't hear (nominees go numb at moments like this), and, taking his cue from idiot cards, read the nominees.

"For Best Music Score, adaptation or treatment: John Green for *Bye Bye Birdie*; Andre Previn for *Irma La Douce*; Leith Stevens for *A New Kind of Love* . . . " And at this point I was hearing him loud and clear. I hurriedly opened my program and discovered that the continuity was all wrong. He should have been reading the nominees for Best Music Score, substantially original. Somebody had loused up the cue cards. ". . . Maurice Jarre for *Sundays and Cybele*," Sammy went on, and I half turned, but Alfred was already at my ear.

"They've screwed up the order. If Sammy has the right envelope it'll be all right. If not!"

" . . . and George Bruns for *The Sword in the Stone*. May I have the envelope, please?" Sammy fussed with it, drew out the card, and read it without thinking. "And the winner is—John Addison, for *Tom Jones!*"

There was a gasp from the audience. Sammy stiffened and put his reaction into immediate words. "Wrong envelope? Or wrong cue cards? Just wait until the N-double-A-C-P hears about *this!*"

The general laughter covered up the error long enough for him to scramble for the right envelope and announce, "The winner is Andre Previn for *Irma La Douce*."

And that was it. Alfred was back at my ear again. "We lucked out. Shot down without a fight. We might as well relax and enjoy the rest of the show."

Sammy's next announcement had no suspense at all—and no punch line. "For the record," he said, "the nominees for Best Music Score, substantially original, are Alex North for *Cleopatra*; Dimitri Tiomkin for *55 Days at Peking*; Alfred Newman and Ken Darby for *How the West Was Won*: Ernest Gold for *It's a Mad, Mad, Mad, Mad World*, and John Addison for *Tom Jones.*" John Addison wasn't there to receive the Oscar.

How the West Was Won took another award. It went to John R. Webb for Best Story and Screenplay Written Directly for the Screen. Best Picture of the Year award went to *Tom Jones*.

The rest of the evening was a montage of faces and old friends. When we congratulated Harold Kress he remarked, "You were cheated." Frank Milton generously conceded that "It was all your fault that I won—you and your mike setup—and you both deserved to win." The Beverly Hilton was glamour town. Our table was assaulted by well-wishers mourning our loss. The music of Manny Harmon had the dance floor jammed. We saw it all and dined extravagantly, fending off waiters. I looked up from dessert to see Elaine Thompson, our good secretary-psychiatrist-indispensable-girl-Friday, struggling through a press of bodies, and I got up to run interference and give her my chair. She greeted Vera and Martha, then spoke pertly to her bosses.

"Tomorrow's a working day, you two. You're having lunch with Mr. Stevens at noon in his private dining room on the old Selznick lot, and, oh—incidentally—you should both call your insurance agents. You were robbed tonight."

Alfred touched her arm. "Forget the burglary. We'll be in the office by eleven-thirty. Don't bother to come in till one o'clock. We want you to get your beauty sleep."

"Let her stay up all night," Vera said, smiling.

"Yes," Martha added. "She's got more beauty than she needs right now. You look out for these men, Elaine."

Elaine laughed her throaty, feminine yet hearty laugh, infectious and merry. She was a perfect catalyst for good humor. A good organizer, competent worker, and, most importantly, she loved working for *us*. She leaned toward Vera and Martha. "They really deserved to win, you know, and there are a lot of people who think so." Then she turned brightly to Pap and me. "Goodnight, you two. See you tomorrow."

Tomorrow, I thought. The day after 468 yesterdays. Now comes the moment of truth, Mr. Vellani.

I left Pap's window down all the way home; the cool air felt fresh and comforting. We hadn't won the Oscar, but we were on our way to another one someday. If we could survive *The Greatest Story Ever Told* .

SCENE II

Rising from the wide expanse of lawn fronting the old Selznick International Studio on Washington Boulevard in Culver City, a freshly painted sign announced in elegant script that here was now the home of George Stevens Productions, Inc. The semi-circular driveway leading up to—and away from—the dignified colonial entrance of the main building was liberally embellished with smaller signs: "No Parking at Any Time" and "Reserved for Mr. Stevens." In defiance, a string of luxury vehicles jammed the drive. There was one space left, and I occupied it without compunction.

"Nicely done, but aren't you risking perdition?" Alfred questioned as we stepped out onto the lawn.

"Probably, but it's a very long walk from the official parking lot out back, and I want to use the time to show you what Elaine and I have been doing this past week in preparation for your arrival. We still have thirty minutes before we meet Stevens for lunch."

"Show me," he said, and started off toward the main entry.

I caught his arm. "This way, Pappy. I bribed the keeper of the grounds to give us a key to our own private gate."

I led him across a short space of lawn to a lattice fence, put my hands through, manipulated a padlock, and swung open a three-foot section. We entered a breezeway between the west end of the main building and our rambling white bungalow. The bungalow itself was adorned with twin porticos, flowering hedges, cement walkways and ornamental shade trees. The new inscribed plaque attached to the wall next to the screen door announced that this was

MUSIC DEPARTMENT
ALFRED NEWMAN & KEN DARBY

"Some department," Pap said. "All chiefs and no Indians."

"Pocahontas here." Elaine opened the door, laughing. "Welcome to the catacombs, our new sanctuary. I came early because I wanted to see your first reaction. You'll just have time for the deluxe tour before Mr. Stevens feeds the lions."

"All Christians, I presume," he said. "Lead on."

We entered the main hall. The first door on the left opened into our utility room. There was a wide desk, now serving as kitchen, with a grill for sandwich making, a percolator, bread drawer, and two other drawers for utensils. Beside it was a supply cabinet with storage space for spirits, canned food, paper goods, glassware, dishes—and books. Next to that was our refrigerator, well stocked with mixes, cold cuts, and cheeses. The other wall was occupied by a duplicating machine for copying manuscripts, with reams of paper stored on the shelf above.

Straight ahead, at the end of the hall, was a large bathroom. The door on the right led into a living room. It was crowded with furniture: chairs, end tables, lamps, a big leather divan, and a coffee table. Alfred stood in the center, pursing his lips and counting the doors.

"Whoever designed this shanty must have been in a hurry to get out. *Four* doors? They must be props."

Elaine laughed. "Two of them go into *my* office, don't ask me why. One of them is blocked off because I needed the wall space. Then my office has a third door into the hall, and a fourth one into a lavatory." She turned. "This one is the entrance to your studio."

Alfred walked in, noting the placement of the desk, the chairs, the cabinet stocked with pads of his monogrammed manuscript paper—and the Steinway grand. He lifted the keyboard cover and struck a few chords.

"Fine," he said. "It will take me a week or so to learn my way around. I'll probably meet myself coming out of one of these funhouse doors, and some one will have to guide me to the john for a few days, but it's fine. We're all together again, and I like that." He walked back into the living room, paused, and sniffed the air. "That's not Elaine's perfume, unless Helena Rubinstein has developed an Eau de Mildew. What is that? Smells terrible."

"We're only using the front end of this bungalow," I explained. "In the back, beyond the hall bathroom, there is another hodgepodge of rooms filled with all kinds of props, furniture, and junk. One of them was used as a rehearsal hall for dancers. The tumbling pads, drapes—and even the woodwork—are objectionably raunchy. I'll have the rooms sealed off and sprayed with Lysol."

Alfred sank into a deep leather chair. "You're right, Elaine. This will be our catacomb sanctuary, dank smells and all, but let's ask the art department for some pictures to put up on these bare walls."

"Already requisitioned," Elaine said, smiling. "They're being painted to order by Mr. Woolworth."

"No Biblical scenes," Pap warned, "or you get baptized."

"Right. No Bible scenes."

Alfred sighed. "I can only hope we'll have as much real pleasure doing this film as we had on *How the West Was Won*. I was sorry to see that assignment come to an end. Every time we wrap up and finish a picture—it's like a little death." He paused and looked around. "I'm already anticipating some relaxing end-of-day sessions here. I want us particularly to invite our Executive Producer, Frank Davis, over for cocktails as soon as we're settled in, so he can see for himself that we are spending our own money as lavishly as we will soon be spending his. By the way, did George Brand report in?"

Elaine nodded. "He'll be with you for lunch, and at the screening that follows. He seems like a very nice man."

"I hope he works out. We've never used him before, but from the scuttlebutt out of Paramount, he seems to be one of the finest music editors around. On this picture we'll need the very best. Now, show me the way out. It's time for lunch."

Alfred and I crossed the breezeway and entered the west end of the main building, walking the long hall toward the central foyer, passing the offices of Frank Davis, Tony Vellani, Tony Van Renterghem, Nino Novarese, and Richard Day. We stopped a moment in the foyer to admire the beautiful black-and-white stills: memorable scenes from *Shane*, *The Diary of Anne Frank*, and *Giant*, all recently installed among a gallery of other photos drawn from the filmography of Samuel Goldwyn, many of which Stevens had directed.

We ascended the wide staircase and followed the second-floor hall back the way we had come to an open door. Stevens' secretary rose to meet us and led the way into a massive room, easily thirty-by-thirty feet square, with high ceiling and lofty windows. It was occupied by tables, maps, models, books, paintings, books, photographs, books, an enormous desk, and—George Stevens. He was jovial and hearty.

"Wonderful to see you again, Al, Ken. I hope you're as hungry as I am. I'll show you around this office later. Come, it's this way. We have a wonderful chef, and we're right on time. Watch your head, Ken. This door was never made for tall men."

I ducked my head, as directed, and stepped through the door after George and Alfred. When I straightened up I could almost feel the swell of ocean waves. We were standing in a perfect replica of a ship's dining salon—a very small English ship, with dark oaken beams pressing down close overhead. A central service aisle was interrupted here and there by sham vertical posts; richly upholstered benches lined each wall, and the oak tables were sanded and waxed to a silky patina. Three centrally hung hurricane lanterns—plus a candle on each table—provided only enough light for the eye to discern deep browns, sullen reds, dark green table linens, and sparkling crystal. A very fussy connoisseur, this Stevens.

George worked his bulk around the edge of his table and sat on a bench against the wall. Tony Vellani took a seat beside him, and Frank Davis stood to introduce us to the young man in the captain's chair opposite.

"This is our music editor, George Brand. George, meet Alfred Newman and Ken Darby."

My first reaction to George Brand was one of disbelief. He presented the same reed-like one-dimensional aspect whether viewed from the front or in profile. In the shadowy light he gave the appearance of a starving man. Alfred and I were to discover—over the next forty-odd weeks of lunches with him—that he ate like one! His contact lenses were new and not at all comfortable. His voice was as smooth and well-modulated as a singer's, and his hair was clipped exactly one thirty-second of an inch from his scalp, which partially disguised that fact that its recession gave him a forehead spanning the remarkable distance from eyebrows all the way back to the coronal suture. Immediately, I liked him, and Alfred—who always reserved an opinion until after second impressions—enthusiastically took the captain's chair next to him, leaving me to sit between him and Stevens.

Lunch was a splendid masterpiece from start to finish. Almost before we had unfolded our napkins, cups of rich lentil soup were set before us. The salad was served on chilled plates. The forks and the romaine were frosty cold, and the fine herb dressing gave the crisp lettuce a flavor of mountain springs and fresh clover. The main dish was a tour-de-force Marco Polo: white meat of hot turkey with tender slices of Virginia ham on toasted buttery English muffin topped by broccoli spears, the whole smothered in a perfect Hollandaise. Dessert was blackberry ice, an exotic wafer, and coffee. Our enjoyment of the food was heightened by the obvious gustatory delight George Brand took in dispatching each part of the meal. And he consumed slice after slice of the delicious homemade bread.

There was random small talk bordering on business: the state of the economy, the film itself, and one Winston Churchill brandy story told by Stevens, but most of the conversation revolved about the immediate pleasures—the food and service. Stevens asked our waiter to bring the chef, and when she appeared—in a black dress with white apron and cap—our group awarded her a cordial ovation.

And so began another series of days, weeks, and months in what was to become the longest scoring assignment of our lives, initiated by a quite spectacular luncheon in the company of men who were to lead us—and themselves—into episodes of pain and attrition which Alfred was later to term "The via doloroso to our American Golgotha."

Behind the main building and attached to it was a long veranda-like open-air colonnade that ran the full length and faced the back lot. Our music bungalow was at one end, the projection room was at the other. I dashed to fetch Elaine and caught up with Stevens and his well-fed group as he led them through the colonnade and into the barn-like theater. It was equipped with rows of comfortable seats at one end and an enormous Cinerama screen at the other. I waved at Tony Perris.

He was standing at the back wall beside Stevens' big Lease Breaker, and I had the sinking feeling that he had already scored the picture with quarter-inch tape.

George Brand, Elaine, Alfred, and I were directed to sit with Stevens in the front row. The lights dimmed, and I felt—rather than saw—many other people taking seats behind us.

That afternoon we viewed the first half of the picture: three solid hours of film! It was beautifully photographed, loosely edited, and some of the sound was bad, but it was a very vital piece of work. The illusion of antiquity became so strong at times that I was drawn into an emotional experience, only to be jerked back to reality whenever the too-well-known movie-star faces intruded to rob the cast of its authenticity. I resented this cavalcade of Hollywood actors for destroying my personal involvement. By the time dear old Ed Wynn ran ecstatically into Jerusalem, his robes flapping around his bony knees, and the milky white contact lenses glittering in his eyes, I no longer cared who the actors were, having taken refuge (along with Alfred) in the enthralling color cinematography of Mellor and Griggs, the marvelous costumes designed by Novarese, and the extraordinary concinnity of Elisofon's hues and patterns.

The rudest shock of all was hearing Alfred's music from *The Robe*, injected at high volume, accompanying the ending of Act One, played by Tony Perris—at a wave of Stevens' hand—on the Lease Breaker which had been fed into the speakers behind the screen.

When the lights came up after the long fade-out, there were several moments of silence. George Stevens looked at each face, then spoke in his soothing drawl. "That's all for today, Charlie, thank you."

Charlie McCleod's familiar voice came from the desk. "Same time tomorrow, Mr. Stevens?"

"No. Nine-thirty, Charlie. We'll start with reel one. Florence, I'll want you, Vellani, Perris, Van Renterghem, and Kress with me. Tomorrow we start tightening." He stood up, stretched and turned. "For those of you who have never met him, this is our composer, Al Newman. Al, meet Tony Perris, Tony Van Renterghem, Florence Williamson, Dick Day, Eliot Elisofon, Harold Hourihan—our paymaster—and, coming in the door, our projectionist Charlie McCleod."

Alfred acknowledged the introductions and said, "This is our music editor, George Brand, and our department secretary, Elaine Thompson. You've met Ken before."

I turned and acknowledged the greetings, seeing them for the first time without their parkas and fur hats—away from the tents and tin huts of the desert—noting the alterations which the intervening months had wrought on their faces. I saw weariness and preoccupation; Charlie was thinner, Stevens had put on weight; Florence's nose was still pink.

Stevens was talking with Alfred. "I'm sorry I didn't have the film ready nine weeks ago when your contract began, but Ken tells me you have developed some very beautiful music just from reading the script. If you feel that your approach is right—after seeing the film today—when might I hear it?"

Alfred gave me a warning eye, meaning, "Keep your mouth shut," thought a few moments before answering, then said, "This is Wednesday. Give Ken and me the rest of this week to print copies of the manuscript, prepare piano parts, and complete the principal theme." He looked at me and added, "I'm sure we can be ready by Monday afternoon."

Stevens put his big hand on Pap's shoulder. "Fine. Next Monday then. Would one-thirty be a good hour?"

Alfred nodded, and Elaine made notes. So—the audition rumor was now a fact. George Brand gave me a questioning look that said as plainly as though he had uttered the words, "Is he kidding?"

I answered him sotto voce: "You can turn the pages."

SCENE III

Thursday I picked up Alfred's original manuscripts at his home in Pacific Palisades and brought them to the studio for duplication. Elaine took the holographic pages to Frank Davis, there being a "clause for hire" in Alfred's contract stipulating that they were henceforth the property of George Stevens, as though he had composed the music himself.

I spent three hours making piano parts, reducing them from Pap's sketches, in preparation for the Monday audition. Friday was a musical repeat of Thursday. In addition, Elaine and I helped George Brand organize his cutting room. It was a narrow rectangular space in a separate one-story building about a hundred yards from our bungalow. To reach the one from the other we had to skirt a long-unused swimming pool, its water a pristine blue. When we finished moving the necessary furniture, there was a Moviola, a large desk, two bins for loose film, a rack for film cans, a typewriter on a stand, and two chairs: one for Elaine and one for George. It would be his job to time the scenes Alfred would score with music, and Elaine's job to take his dictation of the action portrayed in those scenes, then type the breakdown so Alfred's composition would conform exactly to the footage of the scene. It was a process requiring great patience and constant attention.

"Now," George said, "we're ready to start whenever Mr. Stevens and Mr. Newman decide where they want score—and can give me the film. I've got a feeling this picture is going to have wall-to-wall music."

Elaine and I had to agree.

On Saturday afternoon I arrived at Alfred's home, opened his study door—and stopped short. The floor was a blizzard of manuscript paper.

"Come in, come in. I'm glad you're here," he exclaimed, throwing down his pencil on the card table beside his piano chair. "I've been beating my brain. Drag up a chair and let's talk—no, no—don't bother to pick up all that paper, it's junk, nothing but fits and starts. I've been looking for a new way to say what I have said often before. I may be running dry. This is my tenth confrontation with a religious subject of one kind or another, some pagan, some Christian, from Aton to Joseph Smith!* What I need now is a long melody line, one that doesn't just ramble. One that will have substance, dignity, and, of course, modality. And I haven't come up with a thing for the flesh and blood Jesus."

"You've already written it," I said, my arms full of paper. "It was right here on the floor." I dumped the scraps on the couch, picked up the three pages I had been reading while he was talking, and put them in front of him on his piano desk.

"Junk!" he snorted. "That's only a six-bar phrase."

"But look what you started to do with it on this second page. You repeated it a flatted seventh higher, and the continuation on page three is a natural development leading back." I stopped talking because he had put down his cigarette and was playing. The pieces went together so logically that when he reached the end of the third page we just looked at each other without comment for a full half minute.

"You really like it that much?" he asked.

I nodded, not trusting my voice.

"Then so be it. I couldn't write anything better today anyway." His pencil scrawled "Jesus of Nazareth, April 1964, A.N." Then he turned to the third page. "I'm not very happy with these ascending and descending triads at the end. They sound contrived. I'll write an alternate ending."

He played the phrase, quickly simplifying it, writing in the alteration on the staves below. "There, that's better." He played the revision and stapled the three sheets together. "Here, have fun tomorrow. Just make a simple piano part, none of those fat chords you like so much that require fourteen fingers to play."

---

*A Man Called Peter, Brigham Young, Cardinal Richelieu, Come to the Stable (Theme Song), David and Bathsheba, The Egyptian (with Bernard Herrmann), The Keys of the Kingdom, The Robe, The Song of Bernadette.

He handed me the manuscript, turned his chair to the card table, stubbed out his cigarette and added, "I honestly would have thrown all that stuff away."

"Then I'm glad I came before you tore it all up."

"Let's save being glad until Stevens puts his stamp of approval on it." He picked up a dozen pages of manuscript from the table. "Come look at this. I need your opinion."

I gathered all the discarded pages from the couch and stored them endwise in his big brass waste basket. Now I was behind him looking over his shoulder at a manuscript entitled "Christ the Lord (Adonai): Rough Preliminary Sketch." He began to play—and since all of his sketches bore explicit indications of the instrumentation—I was able to hear above the tone of the piano the choirs of horns, woodwinds, brass, and strings notated on the pages.

It was a majestic musical statement of strength and solemnity. It moved from cadence to cadence with a sense of tonal inevitability. The harmony flowed from modes of antiquity to dissonances unfamiliar to the ear—blending past with future—and its architecture seemed to fill the room with reverential awe. I stood entranced.

Here was this man—slight in physical stature, with unruly hair and a stubborn prognathous jaw—creating ineffable beauty. Born in 1900 of Jewish parents in New Haven, Connecticut, he had fought his battles in the show-business jungles of New York City with only his talent, pugnacity, and guts for weapons, had won that war before he was twenty (with the help of his mother), had helped all his siblings through school, then waged another successful campaign in Hollywood against all odds! In a world of "me first" he was an unbelievably generous man, yet strict in principle, totally intolerant of intolerance, often cruel and unbending in his criticism of himself and of those who failed to live up to his expectations (or to their own potential—or who fell short of the dedication commensurate with their talents); here he sat, the acknowledged master of his art form, the most honored film composer of the century, constantly voicing his plaint: "I'm running dry," yet pouring out greater music than ever before, creating this inspired musical impression of Christ, the Lord—even though he was admittedly an agnostic!

I leaned over and kissed him on the cheek.

He was pleased. "I hoped you would like this. Is there a false note anywhere?"

"Not one!"

"Have I cannibalized myself too much?"

"You've quoted yourself in the horn figures—going from minor to major—but how can one plagiarize oneself?"

"Easily!" He laughed. "I do it all the time, sometimes unconsciously, sometimes willfully . . . "

"Then so did Mozart," I interrupted. "And *anything* by Beethoven could only be Beethoven."

He held up a hand. "I'm not a Beethoven, worse luck—and comparisons are odious."

"That's a cliché," I retorted, "and I'll bet my right arm that neither Mozart nor Beethoven could score a film with . . . "

"Here!" He stopped me short, handing me the manuscript. "Duplicate this on Monday. I'll refine it when George Brand gives me the timing breakdown. Right now, I'm concerned about Monday's audition." He lit a cigarette. "But to hell with it!" He looked at his watch. "Sit down, don't leave me. Good, it's that time again." He stood, stretched, walked into the bathroom to a little cupboard we both knew about and returned with the familiar bottle of Jameson's and a shot glass. "You know you're a disappointment to me in only one way—you don't drink."

"Tonight I do! Just to celebrate."

"Well, well, I'll make a heathen out of you yet." He got another shot glass from the bathroom, sat and poured an ounce in each. "Here's to us."

"God bless," I said.

We touched glasses. The first sip spread out over my insides like a flaming oil slick, and it was in my bloodstream before the fiery core had reached my recoiling duodenum. He watched the tears well up in my eyes and laughed.

"The first one is a scorcher. You won't feel the second."

And he was right. Two ounces and forty minutes later I was feeling no pain anywhere—never would again—and was full of exhilaration. A joyous, juvenile geyser of well-being was spouting inside me.

"Drive carefully," he cautioned. "And put one of these Sen-Sen under your tongue so you won't smell like an Irishman. I'll be ready by ten o'clock Monday morning, but come a little early if you can. We'll plan our attack on the way into the studio." He handed me four pages of lined yellow paper, well covered with his distinctive handwriting—in pencil. "Here's a tentative routine of what we should play. If you want to mull it over tomorrow and change the order, go ahead."

"Okay," I said. "If we're going to run competition to Ferrante and Teicher as the newest piano team, we should have a couple of hours to practice before we show off for Stevens."

"I dread it," he said. "But, as my dear mother used to say—God rest her soul—'If you're going to hang by one foot you might as well hang by the other.'"

SCENE IV

It was a nervous Monday for me. By 9:30 all of the music was ready, I had phoned Elaine, she and George Brand were busy arranging the seating in our piano room at the studio . . . and I was pulling into Alfred's driveway. Then, for an hour, we went over the material together. He approved my piano part of "Jesus of Nazareth" (I would play it for Stevens), and we rehearsed the sequences on which four hands would be necessary; the rest he would play himself.

I loaded the car with books, metronome, stop watches, and music. Martha kissed us both for good luck and waved as we drove out. Pap fretted all the way to Culver City.

"The worst difficulty today will be one of communication. I think in musical terms, and they can be confusing to George, so if you see him beginning to act mystified, don't hesitate to break in and translate. And do the same for me, because he frequently talks in circles."

"Or in parables," I interposed. "Wouldn't it be nice if he'd carve out something on stone tablets today? We'd have a permanent record and he wouldn't be able to change his mind.

"He'd simply inscribe new ones."

Elaine and George Brand were ready for us. While I ran off copies of the piano parts, they showed Alfred the seating. Stevens would be in the first chair at the treble end of the piano, Vellani and Van Renterghem would share the love seat at Stevens' right, and Frank Davis would have his chair at the foot of the piano. My spot was at the desk behind Alfred, in position to turn pages and slip onto the piano bench for the bass parts, and we decided to leave all eight doors open for ventilation.

Pap thought he was too nervous to eat lunch until Elaine and George started talking about "the marvelous delicatessen just across the street," and he gave in. It turned out to be a happy hour. George ordered *two* beef dip sandwiches—on a pair of French rolls as thick as his arm—and calmly disposed of them along with a quarter of a pound of French fries, regaling us between bites with bright studio scuttlebutt, and Elaine's laughter eased all the anxieties. By coffee time, we had all but forgotten the ordeal ahead. I scrambled and outmaneuvered Pappy with the check, and shortly after 1:15 p.m. we were back in the bungalow, fortified, unified, and ready.

Ten minutes later the phone rang. Elaine said, "Music Department: Mr. Newman and Mr. Darby." (pause) "Yes, we're expecting you." "In five minutes? Fine, thank you." She hung up, saw the frown on Pappy's face and said, "Cheer up. I have a cold bottle of Dom Perignon waiting in the refrigerator to be consumed by the four of us after the departure of the audition committee."

Alfred relaxed and smiled. "You've thought of everything, my girl, except how to project us from *now* to *then.*"

George laughed. "Just think about cold Beluga caviar with lots of chopped eggs and onions on water wafers."

"You think about that," Pap countered drily. "Food is your department. I'll think about the Dom Perignon."

There was a heavy knock on the front door. Elaine brushed past, placed a hand momentarily on Pappy's arm and whispered, "This, too, shall pass."

"Diarrhea passes also," he shot back.

Elaine was merry when she opened the door, and our small bungalow was abruptly full of bodies.

For the next three hours we were on trial. The old bromidic assertion: "I don't know anything about music, but I know what I like" was the central premise of Stevens' authority. I mused that if such a jury had presided over the new works of Beethoven, at least half of his work would never have been written, and men like Debussy, Stravinsky, Bloch, and Schoenberg would have had to join civil service and deliver mail.

Alfred began by explaining his musical approach—that there would be two fundamental themes: one for Christ the Divine, and another for Jesus the man. Eventually these two would converge into a triumphant "March of the Spirit."

"Very pretty," Stevens said, "but how does it sound?"

Alfred started to explain his explanation, but I slid onto the piano bench and said, "This is the music for Jesus of Nazareth, the child born of Mary, the man of flesh and blood." And I played it through without interruption.

Stevens was nodding, Vellani was nodding; Van Renterghem and Frank Davis tipped their pipes up and down. Unanimous nodders, I thought. The rest had to be imitating Stevens. And it was he who spoke first. "I want to open the picture with this music. It's perfectly beautiful, Al, and quite inspiring. For my own identification purposes, however, I'm going to call it 'Meditations.'" He turned to Vellani. "Make a note of that, Tony. Now, how about the music you've composed for Christ the Divine?"

Alfred said, "Voices will be used with the instruments in parts of this; they will be altos in a low register mingled with double woodwinds."

"I don't want a lot of low heavy notes in this score." Stevens was frowning. "They tend to make everything somber."

"I'll keep that in mind, George." And Alfred started to play without further comment.

I divided my attention between the substance of the music and the reactions of our jury. Stevens put his head back and closed his eyes. Vellani looked at the ceiling. Van Renterghem bowed his head. Davis refilled his pipe, eyes down. I found myself humming the vocal line softly against the theme, and then it didn't seem to matter much anymore what *they* were thinking. Alfred seemed to catch the same mood. He played it superbly, and when it ended he turned to me with a look of complete confidence. Stevens roused himself and applauded. The others followed his lead.

"Wonderful, Al! Just wonderful."

But all of it didn't receive the same accolade. The music for "Three Magi" was objected to as being "too oriental and too sprightly in tempo." Alfred said, "If your Magi are *not* from the Orient, I'll remodel this piece to fit them when I see the final cut."

Several other themes were questioned—explanations were required—but in general the score was approved, subject to eventual tailoring, and they departed pleasantly at 4:45 p.m.

Alfred went immediately to the john, flushed the toilet, ran water noisily in the basin, and came out toweling his hands. "I feel like Pontius Pilate," he said. "My motif for the Redeemer has just been turned over to the executioners."

George Brand was twisting the wire on the champagne bottle. He said, "We overheard the remark about the Magi music being too oriental. I had to clap my hand over Elaine's mouth to keep her from exploding."

The ejected cork punctuated on cue. Pappy tossed the paper towel into a waste basket and slumped into a chair by the coffee table. "I'm so glad that's over and done with that I don't care if Stevens brings Magi from the Bronx."

"The Medes and the Persians have no monopoly on Magi," George observed as he poured the champagne.

"We could get some from Memphis," I put in, "and score the scene with 'The Tennessee Waltz.' "

"Post-audition brain damage, Ken," Pap said. "Cheers!"

Elaine's laughter infected us with gaiety, and so did the Dom Perignon. We consumed it slowly with appreciation. The caviar was cold and George was hungry, and a ritual was established in our sanctuary—an end-of-the-day ritual that we would all come to look forward to and enjoy.

Presently the phone rang. It was Stevens' secretary. Elaine listened, said yes a couple of times, hung up and happily announced, "We are *all* invited to lunch at the Captain's Table tomorrow noon. Then, beginning at 1:30, we will view the second half of the picture. And are you ready for this? Reels one and two will be ready for music spotting on Thursday, and Mr. Stevens wants to be with you when you make your decisions where music will start and stop."

"Naturally," Pap said. There was a long pause. Then he turned down his empty glass, and an expression I had seen often spread over his face. It was the look of a seer, gazing into an unforeseeable future. "This is the end of April. I want to go on record with you three, here in this room, that *The Greatest Story Ever Told* will not be ready for scoring *before* the first of October.* Goodnight, my dear friends. Come on, Ken, let's go home."

---

*Alfred's prediction fell *short* by six weeks. The first scoring date on the picture was November 16, 1964.

SCENE V

Following our April audition, May rushed us into a hot summer. We sat for hours in the projection room with Stevens, George Brand, Elaine—sometimes Tony Van Renterghem—and invariably with Tony Vellani, who sat behind us beside the big Lease Breaker with Tony Perris. We viewed the film on a reversible projector—forward, backward, and forward again—to plot the structure of the score. Alfred unerringly found the places where music would give importance and tempo to a slow-moving scene, or where it would raise a particularly dramatic moment to even greater emotional heights, but he chafed under the pressure of Stevens' constant questioning.

It was over the non-use of music that their most heated clashes arose. When Stevens insisted on having music in a scene where Alfred's intuition—supported by experience—told him that music would be intrusive and distracting, Stevens demanded to know why, and a debate ensued, Frequently, when these disagreements occurred, there would be a breakdown in communication and I would become involved.

Stevens called me aside after one such session and asked me to explain in layman's terms what Alfred was saying. Fortunately, I was able to do it, and the point in contention was resolved in Alfred's favor, but at other times Stevens merely issued a decree: "I want that scene to have music. If it doesn't work I can always yank it out or have it rewritten, but *I want music in that scene.*"

Ultimately, because of these directorial edicts, thirty minutes of unnecessary music was composed and recorded for the picture, and all of it was "yanked" before the film was released.

Alfred had a silent weapon. Those who knew him well, and especially those who had been its victims, called it the Newman

death ray. When someone around Alfred overstepped the
bounds of decency, blurted an opinionated or bigoted statement
of bald stupidity, or perpetrated a witless and insulting act, the
blistering gaze Alfred turned on that guilty individual was crushing. It was a look of scathing revulsion, so loaded with raptorial
ferocity that it could set fire to a wet cat.

He had an occasion to use this formidable weapon one day
in the projection room when Tony Vellani suggested to Stevens,
in an elevated tone of voice, that it would be effective to score
Jesus' return to Capernaum with a Bach Toccata. Alfred turned
his head, took aim, and fired. Tony's face turned tomato red,
and I swear that smoke came out of his ears. He never got over
it. "I was joking," he said, "just joking."

With the onset of hot weather, Elaine requisitioned the
impossible—and got it: air conditioning for the bungalow. We
were enjoying it one afternoon when Harold Kress came into
our living room. "Hey, it's cool in here. Show me to my room,
I'm moving in."

George said, "There's a film can under your arm. Does it
mean anything special, or are you just crazy about movies?"

"That," said Harold smugly, "is the first reel of music dupe*
turned over by Stevens for you to start breaking down. He has
put his final okay on it, and I quote: 'There will be no further
changes in this reel.' End quote."

"Have you actually cut negative?" George asked.

"Oh, no. That will come later."

"Then Stevens can still make changes in it," I said. "But
anyway, we can go to work."

Harold sipped the Scotch and soda Elaine had served. "There
will be another reel coming tomorrow. You're going to be busy
all right—from now on."

He was right. As the days passed and the reels came in I bent
more and more over the copy machine, George Brand pored
over his Moviola, and Elaine typed her fingers numb. On my
daily trips to Alfred's home I carried the results of our labor:
moment-to-moment accounts of each scene where music had

---

*A music dupe is a black-and-white copy of edited film which is used by the music cutter
to time the scenes to be scored with music.

been decided upon, and Alfred began fitting his thematic material to the timings indicated.

Then came the day when three of those "finally edited" reels were hauled back into the projection room—and *recut!* All the previous work had to be repeated: new breakdowns timed by George, new pages typed by Elaine, new copies made by me, and the music rewritten—foreshortened or elongated—to fit the new length of each scene.

Our frequent command parades to the projection room became known as "that last mile again." Only the vivacity of Elaine and the witty optimism of George Brand kept Alfred and me from frustration. We traveled that colonnade through fog and sweltering heat, smog and drizzling mist. Once in an unexpected downpour I drove Alfred in through the back gate of the studio and right up to the theater door, ignoring the rain-slickered guard who angrily motioned for me to stop—and parked the car right next to Stevens', practically on top of a fire hydrant. When Alfred objected, I said, "So who could need it on a day so wet? In this weather even a clever arsonist couldn't burn down this joint—dammit!"

One cheery soul who gave us moral support was Charlie McCleod. His little yaps of chirpy conversation through the squawk box from the projection booth were always pleasant. Harold Kress, however, began to wear an ever-increasing look of worry on his now doleful countenance, and he often sought comfort in our bungalow after a particularly tempestuous day. His complaint was always the same: "Stevens won't let me do my job."

One day he said to me, "Suppose a producer engaged you to compose music for a film, gave you a nice salary and a good room with a piano in it, then walked in and made you watch while *he* wrote all the music. How would you feel?"

"That depends," I said. "If I needed the money, I'd take it quietly and let him do the work. If I didn't need the dough, and felt demeaned and unhappy about it, I'd get the hell out and go home."

"That's no answer," Harold said. "A man is hired to do his job, and he should be permitted to do it—not become a pariah, or a . . . a sycophant."

"For Lord's sake, Harold, you're neither one! You've just rammed head-on into George Stevens, who is producer, director, script writer, editor, and god on this film. Both he and Sam Goldwyn think they're the greatest editors in Hollywood. They both love to cut what they shoot. You wait. I know you'll get your chance when Stevens tires out."

Between trips to the projection room, Alfred stayed at home to work at his piano. I went around each day to see how he was progressing, taking with me click track sheets, bar breakdowns, sequence timings, and general information gleaned from Elaine, George Brand, Vellani, Harold Kress, and Davis. We'd chew over procedures and plot schedules and compare notes for a couple of hours, and I would leave his study with one, sometimes two, original manuscripts of music tailored to the film. His system of identification left no chance for doubt—e.g., Act I—Reel 1, Part 1 & 2. Overture—Main Title, ("Meditations"—"Jesus of Nazareth"). I would take these to my copy machine for six prints, and turn the originals over to Frank Davis. The operation became routine.

Since we could never be absolutely sure that Stevens was through editing a given scene, we had to gamble in order to be ready for recording. That required gambling with our principal orchestrators, Leo Shuken and Jack Hayes, who came to the house or to the studio whenever the music was ready for orchestration. I was usually in on all the sessions with them. Alfred went over every bar, making sure that they understood all of his written instructions, asking them to make their own notations when in doubt, and giving each one a copy of the music he was to orchestrate.

Years before, Leo and Jack had called me aside to say, "This is crazy, man. Al's sketches are so complete, and annotated so precisely, that a *copyist* could lay them out on the score paper. What do you need orchestrators for?"

I answered them a bit impatiently. "You dopes! A copyist would put it down exactly as it is. Both of you have seen the film. You know the substance of the scene and the intent of the composer. If either one of you ever has the faintest feeling in the seat of your pants that Pappy's choice of instruments is in some subtle way wrong, or could be improved by the addition of another instrument—or placed in another octave—and *don't follow that hunch*, then you're making no contribution at all, and sooner than later he'll catch up on it and raise hell. That's why he loves you guys. You're great orchestrators, *not* copyists. So—go orchestrate!"

Some of their subsequent suggestions were brilliant. But others were summarily snowed under by Pap's better judgment.

One night in mid-July, Alfred greeted me as I entered his study with "Say, aren't you supposed to go to the Bohemian Grove next week? Don't you and Wally Sterling* have a show to put on up there?"

"Normally yes, Pappy. But this is no normal year. I couldn't leave, even for a weekend, and keep up with the work we have on hand."

He sighed. "I was hoping you'd say that, because as much as I'd like to sneak you off for a few days of rest and fun, I'm afraid I'd be in such a flap when you returned that I'd never catch up with myself. What will you say to Wally?"

"I'll just tell him the truth: that we're both boxed in with too much work. I'll send him a quick musical format for the show and let the other two King's Men carry the ball. While I'm writing him, I think I'll invite him down to have lunch with us as we did during the scoring of *How the West Was Won*. If he sees how busy we are, he'll *know* I was telling the truth."

"That's fine. I'd like very much to see him again. He's a great man and I have a deep regard for him and what he stands for. Tell him to make it soon—and give him my best regards."

I wrote the invitation, and the following correspondence ensued:

Letter from Wally Sterling, 21 July 1964 (longhand)

Dear Ken:
    Whatever it is that obliges you to take a sabbatical from the Grove *must* be important. But I'm burning a set of candles in the hope that you may yet make it for the Sunday Night Program.
    Thank Alfred for his greetings and good wishes, and tell him that I look forward to a stirrup cup in the studio to

---

*J. E. Wallace Sterling, then President of Stanford University, later to become Chancellor.

celebrate the successful completion of The Greatest Story. If given due notice, I can arrange to be as thirsty as the occasion requires and/or permits. Frank Denke is alerted and ready to take your place at the piano. Even so, I've told him that there is a chance you may be present on Sunday.

All the best,
Wally

Letter from Wally Sterling, 3 August 1964 (typed)

Dear Ken:

Oh brother, did I miss you! Everyone present was wonderful, but it just ain't the same without you on board. Until late Sunday I waited, wondered and wandered, clinging to the hope that you'd show up. And as I waited and wondered, I thought of you and Alfred sweating it out, and I'm here to tell you that the score of The Greatest Story had better be good because I now have a blood investment in it even if the investment is vicarious. I hope you're not killing yourselves. I shall keep you posted as to when I shall be in Southern California this autumn with some free time.

All the best,
Wally

Letter to J. E. Wallace Sterling, 8 August 1964 (KD/et)

Dear Wally:

Your letter laid a fitting blanket of semantic roses on the tomb of my lost July weekend. Alfred saw it lying on my desk, said: "May I?" and read it with mixed emotions—mixed because he relished the note but regretted that I couldn't share the Sunday Show with you. His remark about you is worth recording: "Here's one great human worthy of the race God intended. Give him my profound respect and tell him to take it easy. The world needs him."

Message delivered.

Please don't fail to let us know when you come this way. We have a convivial setup just north of the Mount of Olives into which we will be delighted to initiate you. Meanwhile, honor thy departed ileum and make haste slowly through the fall responsibilities. I vow not to kill myself with work if you will make the same promise.

Always, with affectionate regards,
Ken

Letter from Wally Sterling, 26 August 1964 (typed)

Dear Ken:

I'm delighted to know about the convivial setup which you and Alfred have established just north of the Mount of Olives, and I hope one day to visit you there. But, if I may make a point: I should like you to know that, despite its location, with its suggestion of gin, I still prefer Scotch and water. Shall I bring my own?

All the best,
Wally

Letter to J. E. Wallace Sterling, 30 August 1964 (KD/et)

Dear Wally:

Your letter was read aloud to a group of our good friends, many of whom you met in our MGM office during the scoring of HTWWW. They were volubly appreciative, and made certain suggestions, most of them improper.

I must explain, at the behest of those present, that our situation here on the Jordan is both fluid and diversified. Our ambry contains "water-turned-to-wine," the Celtic potion of no small power which is your favorite, and a New World product rendered from corn, a good portion of which you and I have been passing back and forth between us recently. The soda springs are bubbling and Elaine keeps a pot of hot coffee in synchronous alignment. Three times a day, John the Baptist (a local chiropractor) makes his rounds, so sin and sacrums are well under control. It remains for you to show your rugged map in our holy of holies and we shall rend the veil. Please remain well. Bye and bye we shall gather at the river? Yes!

Fondly,
Ken

The show Wally Sterling and I were putting on at the Bohemian Grove really has no place in this chronicle, but it does have a fascinating history, and I include the following at the suggestion of my friend and fellow musician, Fred Steiner, Ph.D.

John Charles Thomas initiated an evening program around a campfire in the Bohemian Grove in the mid-thirties, during which he sang several solos, and a choir of forty men performed hymns and folksongs. He dubbed the program "Preachers' Son's

Night," he being the son of a preacher, and when he was dying of cancer in 1960, he bequeathed the program to another minister's son, Wally Sterling, urging me to take charge of music.

Thus, for 24 years, Wally and I hurtled correspondence at one another until Wally fell ill and died on July 1, 1985. He asked me to be his surrogate at the podium, marking what would have been his 25th year as Sire, and to take the lectern on the 1986 program, which we had already written, and which commemorated the 50th anniversary of John Charles' first show.

I, in turn, found a perfect heir to the pulpit in Thomas Hudnut, who was definitely overqualified for the job. His father, grandfather, and two uncles were all preachers! The show did go on—and it still does—every July in the redwoods.

Alfred's admiration and affection for Wally were very great. Pappy was a self-taught intellectual, and his almost wistful regard for such a superbly educated man was not only personal, but an expression of his love of learning.

Wally, being an amateur pianist, held the same regard for Alfred's accomplishments; their meetings were invariably exciting and stimulating, witty and jovial: good friends!

Wally and Alfred were linked by another circumstance: Their careers had been distinguished by a vast multiplicity of honors, each—in his unique field of endeavor—being recognized for extraordinarily high achievement.

In our wacky storm of filmic fantasy, Wally represented a serene port of sanity, and we frequently dropped anchor in confidential communications with him. Hence the letters.

SCENE VI

All through August and September our work progressed by jerks: one step backward for every three steps forward. Stevens continued to re-edit, revise, and recut film that had previously been declared "final" and had been timed. Alfred was "chained to his piano" (his phrase)—stopwatch in hand, metronome clicking—revising music already once revised, or rewriting it altogether.

One evening in early October, Alfred put down his pencil as I walked into his study and said, "Frank Davis just called. United Artists is pushing to release the picture before the end of the year—for the usual tax reasons.* According to the schedule he laid out for me, we would have to be recording the score and dubbing the final soundtrack at the same time. I pointed out to Frank that it was impossible to do this at MGM because they only have one six-track dubbing room, and *it* is also used for recording orchestra and chorus. He said I must be mistaken. He would check and call me back. I'm a liar. So—here we go again; the pressure is on. Stevens is still cutting and playing with the film, U.A. is demanding an early completion, and we're caught in the middle—as usual."

I pulled up a chair. "Harold Kress brought us similar news at the studio. Elaine and I spent most of the afternoon working up a chart, trying to schedule some recording dates for the scenes that are now orchestrated and ready to go. It looks like this." I handed him a big sheet of paper.

---

*Expenses incurred in the production of a motion picture are not deductible until the year in which the product is released to the public. Hence, a significant tax credit is realized if the picture can be released near the end of the year and not carried over into the next.

Pappy picked up his desk calendar and began checking my schedule against it. Then he gave me a startled look and said, "This is fine—for *us*—but you've scheduled our final recording dates in January of next year!"

"I know. But I discussed it with Frank Milton and the crew of the sound department today, and they agreed it was the *only* way it would work. Then Milton got on the phone with Davis and told him so."

"But that doesn't give United Artists the finished picture until sometime in February. They want it before Christmas."

I grinned at him. "That's Stevens' battle. And don't bet any money on United Artists. I think he will have his own way with them, and that will relieve *our* situation. Now, I have something to show you."

I spread before him on the piano rack the final sketch I had developed from the Adonai theme, designed for sixty mixed voices and symphony orchestra. It was complete, with text and instrumentation, and timed to fit the scene beginning with the raising of Lazarus and ending with the final curtain of Act I. I played the rapidly moving bass line while he handled the treble clef, and I could feel his growing enthusiasm.

We played it through to the end, and he punctuated the last chord by slapping me on the arm. "Marth and your mother will love this," he exclaimed. It's exciting and jubilant—and at the same time reverent. Best of all, it still retains an aura of a modal antiquity. I wonder if it will work as the finale of Act II?"

"It won't," I said, reaching for my bag. "But *this* will." I pulled out five pounds of manuscript paper and handed it to him. The title page announced "Resurrection and Ascension."

"Oh, yes. This starts on that marvelous sunrise shot, with just a scrim of high strings, and I see you've started the voices very softly. Good."

He didn't play it, just read it through, noting the quickening tempo and the crescendo where the action became hurried as Mary Magdalene ran to the tomb. Then, under the dialog and narration, the slower movement based on the vowels "ah-lay-loo-yah," leading at last to the restatement of the principal motif: "And of His kingdom there shall be no end; He is risen, He is risen; Hallelujah—Amen."

He put his hands on the manuscript and looked at me.

"Let's record these two sequences together on the same day. Allowing time for orchestration, we could do it about December 29th, right after Christmas. I want Stevens, Vellani and his jury, Frank Davis, and everybody at MGM invited to this recording session. And get the best singers in town."

The loud demands made by United Artists for a speedy conclusion to the picture were silenced and overpowered by George Stevens. He would move as fast as he could, he said, but "the miraculous" was not in his repertoire. However, in quieting United Artists, he had wrought a much more profound miracle than he knew. The pressure on music scoring was still great, but it was acceptable. The chart I had made of our recording schedule became firm, and on the 16th day of November, 1964, we recorded ten minutes of music: "The Nativity" and "The Last Supper." And we recorded again on the 17th, the 19th, the 20th, the 23rd, and the 24th.

Stevens attended part of every recording session. Some of his reactions were interesting: "I don't recall that tune. It didn't sound that way when you played it on the piano. Are you sure it's the same melody?"

"Can you transpose this music a little higher? Those low notes give me a feeling of menace."

"Could the music for this scene be played slower? It seems to be rushed."

"Beautiful, Al. Just lovely. Could it move a bit faster?"

It was a brutal six days, but when they were over, George Brand had enough music to cut into the first four reels, and dubbing began the day we left the recording stage.

The members of the dubbing crew now entered their own Gethsemane. Every reel had to be rehearsed and criticized. Sound effects were altered, dialog was equalized—or moved a frame or two (sometimes six sprocket holes) to synchronize with the actor's lips. Music was made louder, softer, removed, reinstated; all the elements were considered, changed, replaced, until everybody was satisfied that everything blended. Only then, after hours of laborious attention to every detail, did the recorders roll. The first reel of master soundtrack took four takes—and four hours to reach general approval.

During the early dubbing sessions, Alfred and I were on hand to coach our veteran music-mixer friend, Bill Steinkamp, in the treatment of the score. Stevens always appeared at the critical time to put his "OK" on the final take.

More recording dates were drawing near, and as the time grew less so did Alfred's stamina. One day when I walked into his home studio, he was sitting dejectedly in his piano chair, both hands flat on the card table next to the keyboard, his head bowed. When he looked up at me I could see resignation and defeat in his eyes. Without a greeting he began talking.

"I'm not going to make it by myself. There are too many revisions and alterations coming in, too many notes to write. Marc has called Hugo Friedhofer and Fred Steiner to help me. Both of them are coming this afternoon. There's no other way I can finish this one! Please—don't leave me."

I stayed with him that afternoon—and met Fred Steiner for the first time. I had known Hugo for many years, but the future was to hold a deeper friendship for Fred and me. Together, Hugo and Fred performed a series of dramatically impossible musical rescues—some to no avail!

Alfred was not only spending too many hours at his piano, he was smoking too many cigarettes. He had developed a nagging cough and was certainly not up to physical par when we again found ourselves on the recording stage with a big orchestra and twenty women singers. On December 3rd and 4th we recorded six hours each day, then rested two days, and continued on the 7th, 8th, and 9th.

George Brand and his new assistant, Milton Lustig, worked through the weekend (the 5th and 6th) cutting music into the reels and the dubbing crew went to work immediately on the 10th. Alfred didn't come in that day. He was bone weary and ill. I arrived late, after the crew had gone to lunch, to find George Brand and Elaine sitting in the darkened theater consoling each other over sandwiches and coffee.

"Any progress?" I asked.

"None." George dropped his coffee cup into a waste basket. "What we accomplished this morning you could stick in a gnat's eye and he wouldn't even blink. Mr. Vellani didn't like the sound effects, and new ones are being found or made."

Elaine wadded up her paper napkin, handed it to George, looked up at me and said, "I think it's time for you to get this past week off your chest. How about me taking dictation?"

I agreed.

Letter to J. E. Wallace Sterling, 10 December 1964 (KD/et)

Dear Wally:
   We have just finished five days of recording that are probably not as earthshaking as they seem at the moment. The immensity of this project has drawn both Alfred and me to the tips of our toes, from which lofty pinnacle we have collapsed. Now that the pressure is off (at least for ten days or so) the balance between agony and ecstasy is all askew.
   Self doubt is a miserable companion. I always review what I have done with the stubborn suspicion that I could have done it better. But—good or bad—we record again on the 21st through the 23rd hoping, but not really expecting, to complete the score.
   The amazing circumstance is that tickets are now being sold in all the cities for a February opening, and George Stevens is still editing the film. Until he tidies up, we cannot even put the music on paper.
   If you can get down for our next session, we'll have a studio car pick you up. Can we expect you?
   Affectionately, but with some weariness. . . .
   Ken

By the 14th, Frank Milton's energetic sound department had satisfactorily completed two more reels, which left only *twenty-seven* to go. Alfred had come in, feeling fairly fit again though still coughing, and Elaine handed him an envelope addressed to both of us. During a lull in the preparation of a reel in the dubbing room, he opened and read the enclosure.

Letter from Wally Sterling, 13 December 1964 (typed)

Dear Ken and Alfred:
   I can't possibly make it on December 21–23. I shall then be in the throes of luring an Harvardian to Stanford. And all in the alleged spirit of Christmas. More later, but I thought I should dispatch this (for me) disappointing news post haste.

At this moment I'm about to take off for lunch with a
British Chemist-Nobel-Laureate, Lord Todd. Which
brings to mind:

> It does seem to me very odd
> That a scholar who calls himself Todd
> Should spell, if you please,
> His name with two d's,
> When one is sufficient for God.

Merry Christmas to you all,
Wally

Our recordings of December 21st, 22nd, and 23rd were very
difficult and lengthy. Exhausted at the end of the third day, we
sought the quiet refuge of our MGM apartment near the recording stage, a suite recently vacated by Elvis Presley. We
found that Elaine had decorated a Christmas tree, and with the
help of George Brand, was serving to a small group of our closest
on-the-lot friends and associates. In this glowing and festive
group our energies revived, and when everyone had gone except
Elaine—gifts magically appeared. I gave Pappy an electronic
clock for his study—"to mark your happiest hours"—and he
gave me a gold extensible pencil that opened into a twelve-inch
rule engraved "To Ken—love always, Pappy." We each had gifts
for Elaine, which were opened with laughter and one small tear.
Then the three of us sat, contemplative and still, staring at the
lights blinking on the tiny tree. Pap broke the silence. "Merry
Christmas and happy birthday, Lord Jesus. Please smile on our
little triumvirate."

And we drank a toast to each other.

SCENE VII

At nine o'clock on the morning of December 29th, I was in the rehearsal hall at MGM with sixty of my singers. Among them were many old friends, mixed with new discoveries, all of whose vocal abilities and musicianship were above the level of mere excellence. Some had been the Munchkin voices in *The Wizard of Oz* twenty-five years before, and several would go on to become recognized artists in the world of opera.

Working with singers was always a very special time for me: teaching, drilling, conducting, while bringing to life the hundreds of notes I had written, hearing them soar off the page; seeing the lyrics turn mouths into vowel shapes. Even more exhilarating than standing before a great orchestra was this electric response from the faces, their eyes wide, their voices raised, their animation keyed to mine. And—we worked well together.

I led this select group through Alfred's music carefully, taking it apart, letting one section hear what the other was doing, putting the dynamics into their minds, restraining them as one would hold tight reins on Pegasus, then letting them go, watching as they caught the inner spirit of the music—until they sang for the sheer joy of singing. I loved them!

While I was busy with my chorus, Alfred was on the recording stage with his orchestra rehearsing the accompaniment, feeling as elated from the rapport with his musicians as I was with mine. And so the morning passed swiftly.

At noon, I ushered my singers into the recording stage, grouping them twenty feet behind Alfred, facing the orchestra. George Stevens, the three Tonys, Harold Kress, and Florence Williamson stood off to one side between the groups where they could see and hear both orchestra and chorus. Bobby Armbruster, then head of the MGM Music Department, had brought a dozen of his people, and Frank Milton's Sound Department was represented in depth—right through to the secretaries.

Pappy greeted the singers, smiled at Stevens, and gave me a questioning look. I nodded confidently; he turned to the orchestra, raised his baton, and no more thrilling performance ever took place on that stage. It was magnificent. The choir was inspired, and the orchestra members were awed.

As the final "Amen" echoed into silence, there was a moment of absolute quiet. Then Louis Kaufmann, the concert master, began tapping the back of his violin with his bow. It set off an explosion of applause from everyone on stage. I bowed to my singers, shook hands with Pappy, and Stevens shook hands with himself, like a prize fighter, arms raised.

Over lunch, Pap and I discussed—and agreed upon—two or three lyric changes. George Brand told us that the film was already in the projection booth, both sequences punched and streamered with Newman Leader.* Elaine said, "Everybody is talking about your 'Hallelujah.' There's an excited expectancy going around, as though a royal baby had been born, or a new Pope was about to be chosen, and a lot of studio people are asking if they can sit on stage while you record."

"Keep them out," Pap said. "If they want to go sit in the theater, fine, but I don't want anyone on the stage who is not directly involved with the recording. Check?"

"Check!" we agreed.

So, beginning at 1:30, Alfred recorded the orchestral accompaniments to "The Raising of Lazarus" and "The Resurrection

---

*Newman Leader was an invention of Alfred's, devised to help guide him in conducting what he called "fluid music in a frozen medium." It consisted of a wide line scraped in the film from left to right over a six-foot (or greater) length, called a streamer. This was followed by a punch, so named because the film was literally punched full of holes: one hole every other frame for sixteen or more frames. These visible streamers and punches matched broad lines and X's drawn on his conductor parts in bright red ink. The system allowed him to be at an exact point in the music precisely at the proper point in the action on the screen, but permitted greater flexibility than a click track, which he disliked, or a stopwatch, which he detested. These coinciding marks appeared every eight bars, more or less, giving him great latitude for expression, a freedom he considered absolutely essential to the art of conducting, an art of which he was conceded to be the undisputed master.

and Ascension," fitting the music to the film, which he could see projected on a screen above and behind the orchestra. While he was busy recording, I worked with the chorus again in the rehearsal hall, sharpening the dynamics and the diction.

The orchestra finished at 3 p.m. and was dismissed. By 3:30, my singers were seated on stage before the microphones, each wearing a single earphone to hear the orchestra track. Pappy sat in the theater with the recording engineer, Lysle Burbridge, with George Brand and Elaine nearby, hearing our performance mixed with the orchestra track through the big loudspeakers. We were keyed up together, alive with kinetic energy, and after two rehearsals—to let the singers adjust to the earphones and the tempo, and to give Lysle ample time to set his recording levels—we made an inspired take. As I gave the final cutoff, I clasped my hands together and bowed to my singers, waiting for the verdict from the theater.

"That was perfect," Alfred's voice boomed over the intercom. "Take a break and come listen."

The singers wanted to follow me into the theater, but I asked them to wait and relax. We still had the finale to do, and I didn't want to dilute their fervency by letting them listen to a "perfect" performance. It was a word Alfred used only as an expression of wishful thinking; perfection was something he strived for, but said he never attained. But on this performance he was happily accurate. It *was* perfect.

The music for "The Resurrection and Ascension" took more time, but we mastered it at last, and at 5:45 we were all in the theater: my singers, Stevens and his entire entourage, two dozen guests, and the personnel of half the studio. On the big screen came the beautiful color print of the picture, and from the speakers sounded the combined tracks of the orchestra and voices in six-track stereo. I sat at the mixing panel with Pappy beside me coaching Lysle, and the effect was an experience none of us would ever forget. Vision and sound blended into a fusion of glorious uplift, and when it was over many in the theater were unashamedly in tears. I walked down among my singers with Pappy, thanking them individually for their impressive performance. Stevens, at a distance, congratulated everyone in a stentorian voice, and they graciously applauded him. As the crowd broke up to leave, many stopped to shake his hand, commenting on the magnificence of his film and the beauty of the score. In our own adrenalin-charged enthusiasm we failed to notice that Tony Vellani was moody and quiet, preoccupied and withdrawn, remaining on the fringe of activity, expressing nothing. But Harold Kress noticed it and remarked later that Tony's reaction was cold, and that his attitude was enigmatic.

On the second day of January, 1965, Vellani's attitude was no longer an enigma. We were invited to walk the Last-Mile-Again to Stevens' projection room. We were not in any way prepared for the scene which took place.

The three Tonys—Perris, Van Renterghem, and Vellani— privately referred to by Alfred as Winken, Blinken, and Nod, were seated behind us and off to one side. Florence and Harold Kress were together at the editing desk in back. Elaine, Pappy, George Brand, and I sat with Stevens in the front row as we had for so many long hours during the preparation of the score.

Stevens started out gently. "I want to try an experiment, suggested by one of my staff, relative to the music at the end of Act One and Act Two." He pressed the button on his squawk box. "Roll the reel, Charlie."

The lights went out. On the screen appeared the sequence of Jesus raising Lazarus from the tomb. It was scored *not* by our recent recording, but by music Alfred had written twelve years before, in 1953, for the crucifixion scene in *The Robe*!

Stunned, we said nothing. Nor were we asked.

Stevens showed it again, this time accompanied by a very bad monaural dubdown of our December 29th choral performance, the one which had been so enthusiastically hailed and accepted by everyone. Everyone except Vellani.

We said nothing.

For a third time Stevens repeated the sequence, again using the music from *The Robe*. Halfway through he interrupted it with, "That's enough, Charlie. Now line up the other track." He turned to Alfred. "I want to use the music from *The Robe* for the raising of Lazarus instead of the new music you have written. Who owns the copyright?"

It was a blunt question, and Alfred answered it bluntly. "Twentieth Century Fox and the producer, Frank Ross."

Stevens then delivered the crowning insult. He turned to the Tonys and asked blandly, "Do you agree with me?"

There was a moment of shocked, breathless indecision. Then, in unison, they said, "Yes, sir."

I could see only Alfred's profile, but what I saw alarmed me. His face was drawn and his color was pasty.

"Fine," Stevens said. "Tony Vellani, you call Frank Davis and have him make the deal with Twentieth; I'll talk to Ross personally." Then, to Alfred—firm now, not gentle—he said, "In the scene where Old Aram starts to run toward Jerusalem, we will cross-fade from *The Robe* music into another piece I want to use. I'm going to rely on *you* to make it work. Roll it, Charlie."

The picture returned to the screen, but now from the speaker issued the "Hallelujah Chorus" from Handel's *Messiah*! Alfred and I sat transfixed to the end, not believing our ears. When the lights came on, Stevens started to speak, but Alfred was up and on his way out.

"I'll be back in a moment," he said.

Suddenly, I recalled that long-ago session in the mess tent out in the Utah desert when, by Vellani's orders, Tony Perris and I had transferred to tape the entire RCA Victor recording of *The Messiah* on the Lease Breaker. Tony had spent over a year inoculating Stevens with that damned phonograph needle. I looked over my shoulder straight into Vellani's face. He avoided my eyes, but the face was wearing a smug and triumphant expression. Beside him, Van Renterghem looked embarrassed. Stevens was now asking George Brand for an opinion.

"How would you like the idea of using Handel's "Hallelujah" at the end of the picture as a glorious finale?"

I started a spasm of coughing, excused myself, and went after Alfred. I found him just coming out of the men's room, his face flushed now, indignation having replaced shock.

"That's what is known as getting the shaft right up to the hilt," he muttered bitterly. "But, come on, we may as well get it over with right now."

We walked back in together. George Brand was saying—quite respectfully—" . . . so I think the decision, right or wrong, is entirely yours regardless of any layman's opinion, least of all mine. I'm not even an orthodox Jew, let alone a practicing Christian. Why not ask the best film composer in the business? He's right here."

I could have kissed him!

Stevens turned to Alfred. His tone was challenging. "Well, maestro, how do you feel about it?"

Alfred took his time, sat down, lit a cigarette, puffed, coughed, cleared his throat, and said, "I don't think it makes any difference what I think, George. You've already made up your mind—or your jury has." He gestured toward the Tonys. "But, since you have asked me, I'll put it this way: I do not now, nor will I ever presume to imply that my talent remotely compares with that of the great Handel. But in the context of this film, scored with antique modes from definite thematic sources, I think the use of the *Messiah* is vulgar and shocking, both stylistically and dramatically. It comes suddenly out of left field, totally major in mode, uprooting the audience's involvement with the film, and particularly so with the Christians—many of whom probably sang it in a Baptist church choir. My "Hallelujah" is made from the same cloth as "The Great Journey," which, in turn, was developed from the basic motif you liked so much in our April audition called "Christ, the Lord." He coughed away Stevens' attempted interjection. "That motif has been the genetic source of much of the score, and does not lead into anything as great as Handel's *Messiah*."

Pappy paused, puffed, coughed, and stubbed out his cigarette. Stevens was stonily silent for a moment. Then he spoke abruptly. "The very fact that church choirs sing it denotes public acceptance. And I want something acceptable and familiar here. You in the music department may go now. I want to run these two sequences several more times with *my* people and come to a final decision."

We left quickly and walked back to our bungalow, cold and despondent. Frank Davis was waiting for us. He motioned for Alfred to go with him into the piano room and closed the door behind him. George Brand, Elaine, and I sat dourly in the living room, hearing their voices but unable to distinguish the words. George said, "How can you possibly make the *Messiah* fit those two sequences—the finale of Act One and Act Two?"

"With scissors, a metronome, and a shoe horn," I growled. "We'll have to record both versions, and not only make them fit the scenes, but sound like the Mormon Tabernacle Choir. But first I have to find a score to cut. I don't know if there *is* a score in town with complete parts for full orchestra and chorus. Elaine, call Roger Wagner, he may have one."

Roger was in. He had the score and the parts, and I could pick them up at his Bel Air home anytime between seven and nine p.m.

"What's on the schedule for tomorrow?" I asked.

"Nothing tomorrow, but you record 'The Word is God' and 'The Three Magi' the day after."

"Then I'll stay home tomorrow and work on Handel." I looked at their woeful faces and had to chuckle. "A great way to start the New Year—with *two* big hallelujahs."

Elaine wadded up a piece of notepaper and threw it at me. "Dammit, dammit, dammit," she gritted, and added "Dammit, I'm going home."

Just then Davis and Alfred came out, and I knew the decisions had been made. Their relationship was strained; there were no invitations to join us for a cocktail, and Davis left with a curt "goodnight."

Pappy wanted to leave immediately, so we locked up the bungalow and said goodbye to George and Elaine. On the trip to the Palisades, Pappy kept chastising himself for having undertaken to score another picture for George Stevens.

"He has always been a good-to-great director, and he has always been adamant in his artistic convictions, but he has never before been rude and insulting—at least not to me. And he has never been so lacking in good taste. This disciple from the Italian cinema has mesmerized him."

We drove in silence through thickening traffic, and after a while he said, "Will you take over this business of the *Messiah* for me? I don't want to have anything to do with it—although *I'll* be the one who gets butchered by the critics for using it. You work it out with George Brand."

I stopped for a red light, and as I pulled away when it turned green he said, "I can't imagine what's gotten into Stevens. He's gone off his rocker."

SCENE VIII

Officially, we completed the scoring of *The Greatest Story Ever Told* on January 4, 1965, with a revised and watered-down version of "The Three Magi." Stevens was in a good humor, pleased that the oriental flavor had been removed from the music, but he was not amused when he heard me sing "We three kings of Orient are *not*" to Pappy as he left the podium. Pap thought my joke was ill-timed, but he was too tired to snap at me. Instead, he muttered, "Let's go home. There's nothing we can do here until George Brand cuts the remaining music tracks into the reels, and I'm not feeling right. Do you mind leaving now?"

As I went to get the car, my thoughts were sour. The constant attrition Saul Wurtzel had talked about in Utah was still operating in Stevens' behavioral repertoire. Pappy was very nearly stripped raw. Was there more to come?

All the way home, he talked of other matters: the five children, how they were progressing in school, would I help install an up-to-date stereo system in his study?—was I still enjoying my hide-away house on the shores of Lake Sherwood?—nothing about the picture. His mind was rejecting what his body had been forced to do—and vice versa.

I left him with Martha at the front door of his beautiful Lloyd Wright home, admonishing him to stay put for a few days. Martha said, "Don't worry. I'll see that he gets some rest."

I spent the next three days with Bill Steinkamp, running the tracks and setting their proper levels. Alfred, ill from exhaustion, stayed at home, but Stevens was constantly on the scene in the dubbing room. The three Tonys sat off to one side—always together—and Stevens conferred with them when a decision had to be made. Many times he returned from such a conference to request another take with less sound effects, or less music, or—"I can't hear the dialog. It's mushy."

On the third day, following several hours of aborted rehearsals on Reel Twelve, he became very upset with the way the film's many ingredients failed to gel, and he spoke sharply to Steinkamp. "You're crowding everything with too much music. The score isn't that important. Dig holes in it so we can hear what's being said on the screen. Run the reel again and I'll show you how to mix it."

When the reel was ready, he pushed Bill out of the way, took over the controls, and yanked the music down and up whenever the actors spoke a line, in the blatant style of the old Fox Movietone Newsreels. "Do it like that!" he ordered, and started out. "I'll be back when you can do it right. Send for me, Tony, when you think they've got it."

Bill Steinkamp watched him walking away, then called after him, "I don't think I can do it *exactly* like that, Mr. Stevens. You only gave me one lesson."

By the fourth day, everyone in the studio had heard that Handel's "Hallelujah Chorus" was to replace Alfred's. They learned it by many routes: the editorial staff heard it from Florence Williamson, Harold Kress, and Argyle Nelson; the music department heard it from the librarian who was helping copy the Handel versions; the sound crews learned of it from Elaine when she called to reserve the stage for the recording date. It was neither a secret nor a rumor. It was a fact according to Stevens, and everybody deplored it. But many refused to believe that Stevens would cling to such questionable taste, and the speculation grew that he would change his mind at the last minute and restore Alfred's music before the premiere.

Evidently, this speculative scuttlebutt got back to Tony Vellani, because at the end of a successful dubbing session on that fourth afternoon, Stevens stood up in the middle of the theater and proclaimed in a loud voice, "That's a print. Very good. Now, I want to settle something. All pay attention. I have learned from one of my staff that someone is spreading rumors about Al Newman's 'Hallelujah' being put back into the score. I want you to know that contrary to all such rumors, Newman's 'Hallelujah' will *not* be used in this picture."

He motioned for me to join him, and when I arrived at arm's length he jabbed his forefinger into my chest.

"I'm told that you, Darby, have been the agitator of all these disturbing contradictions. This is a warning. You are not to spread any more such rumors. the *Messiah* stays in the score! This picture will immortalize Handel."

There was a stunned silence. My mouth dropped open, then snapped shut. What could I say? I settled for saying nothing, just turned and started back toward the mixing panel.

"Wait a minute!" he called. "I have made several more changes in film that has already been scored. You will need these changes in writing when you take them to Al."

I motioned for Elaine to bring her pad and pencil, and she sat nearby while Stevens stood in the aisle consulting a scrap of paper. I remained a few rows back, listening as he dictated.

"Dear Al: Please adjust or compose new music for the following re-edited scenes: number one, The Flight into Egypt; number two, Matthew the Tax Collector; number three, Judas and Caiaphas; number four, Aram the First Witness. Please note that the press preview in New York will be one month from now in the middle of February. I know you can—no, make that I know you *will* be ready on time." He paused. "Sign it yours, G.S." He turned to the crew. "Start work on the next reel. I'll see you tomorrow at nine sharp."

So there it was: another layer stripped away. Darby on summary probation and Newman in purgatory. George Brand walked me to my car, and he was so dismayed by Stevens' twin proclamations that he wanted to laugh and cry at the same time.

"Four more scenes to retime and rewrite and record. I don't believe it! And did I actually hear him say that this picture would immortalize Handel?"

"Incredible, isn't it? Pappy won't believe it either."

And he didn't believe it. He thought Elaine was pulling a very unfunny gag on him when she phoned the news. Only after I delivered the new timings of the four altered scenes was he able to swallow the truth. Grimly then, he knuckled under and went to work. But he did not remain silent. He spent a lot of time on the telephone with Frank Davis, with Harold Kress, and with Elaine. He called his brother Marc, who acted as his agent, and had his attorney reread his contract with Stevens to see if there was any legal relief available.

Meanwhile, George Brand and I worked on timing the scenes for *The Robe* music and the *Messiah*. And in the midst of all this turmoil and push, Stevens sent all departments a long memo enumerating still more editing changes—fifteen to be exact—requiring twenty-five and a half minutes of new score! But none of these edicts were as horrifying as the musical viscerotomy that was ordered next.

George Brand, Elaine, and I were invited to make one more Last-mile-again visit to the projection room at the end of the Selznick studio arcade. Stevens sat with us in the front row, put his finger on the button of the intercom, and said, "Are you ready, Charlie?"

Charlie McLeod's voice didn't sound happy. "Yes, sir."

Stevens said, "Elaine, you and George take notes. Okay, Charlie, roll it."

On the screen appeared Christ's agonizing journey along the Via Dolorosa, accompanied by Alfred's beautifully tender recording of that scored sequence. Stevens raised his left arm, suddenly threw a salute at the screen, and said, "There! Stop the film, Charlie—back it up—hold it right there." He turned to me. "That's the place where I want you and Al to insert Verdi's *Requiem*. It will replace Al's music through the next four stations of the cross. I'll give you the exact cue when to take it out. Go ahead, Charlie."

The scene continued for two minutes and twenty seconds before Stevens again halted the projector. "That's where I want Verdi's *Requiem* to cross back into Al's score. Have you got those two spots?"

"Do we have any latitude at either end?" I asked. "If the two pieces of music won't cross-blend at those precise points we may have to make the change a bar or two later—or earlier."

"Then make the first one work. The crossover back into Al's music is flexible, but come as close as you can. That's all, Charlie." And he walked out, leaving us sitting there.

George Brand and Elaine had made odd-looking notes, as though some kind of palsy had stricken their penmanship. We didn't say anything to each other as we went back to the bungalow, but once inside, I began kicking the furniture and Elaine resorted to her dammits, interspersed with furious activity on the typewriter. George poured himself a glass of tomato juice and gobbled a ham-stack sandwich. "Eating is my panacea," he said. "I feel like I'm on the inside of a disaster."

When I arrived at his home that afternoon, Pappy was sitting at his piano, a cigarette burning in the ash tray, his pencil flying. "Sit down a minute, Ken. I have only one more bar to go, then I'm finished—literally."

I sat watching as he filled in the final chord, drew the double bar, and dropped his pencil in the rack.

"Look at this," he said, and shoved toward me a legal-sized stack of ruled yellow paper. I flipped the pages. The heading was "Vendetta" and there were twenty enumerated paragraphs in longhand. The notes alluded to a telephone conversation he had had that day with Stevens, and it was obvious that he had written them under stress. Several of the paragraphs dealing with the same subject were separated by widely disparate thoughts. I read the pages with growing incredulity while he went to the bathroom and returned with his Jameson's and a fresh cigarette. I lit it for him and one for myself.

"Who telephoned whom?" I asked.

"Stevens telephoned *me*," he said. "All very friendly at first . . . raved about the score, give or take a low note here or there—said it was by far the best thing I had done in this musical milieu—apologized for making so many changes, and hoped I could make them work. I said I'd do my best. Then he got down to telling me that word had come back to him that I had told someone that he had a lousy staff—that I had called the three Tonys 'his mafia' and 'his jury' and he didn't like that. He said a reliable source had suggested that I was out to sabotage my own score because my 'Hallelujah' had been removed from it. I asked him who had accused me of this and he named Frank Davis. I told him Frank was not only a liar, but a very frightened man, and that he wasn't the only one. I said, 'All of your people are afraid. I just want you to know I'm not one of them.' That enraged him.

" 'Who do you mean—*my* people?' And I said Dick Day and Nino Novarese, a couple of your editors, and your entire staff. Then he began to shout at me, accusing Harold Kress of being a spy and a gossip monger—of always being in our bungalow, telling tales and making trouble—said Kress was to blame for all the difficulty he was now having with United Artists, and even suggested that you and I should terminate our friendship with Harold. Right there I stopped him. I warned him never to raise his voice to me again—not ever! He changed his tone, but his next attack was even more devastating. He implied that you and I would deliberately slough off the recordings of the Handel music. He said, further, that he was terribly annoyed by phony compliments on *our* 'Hallelujah' from musicians, sound men, singers and visitors, and added, 'What do *they* know?' Then he paraphrased to me what he had said to you in the dubbing theater. 'Anybody who believes that I'll remove Handel's *Messiah* from the score just because *you* think it should *not* be used in this picture is crazy! That's final.'

"I asked him to allow me to finish my work with no more harassment, let me complete my contract and leave quietly. I begged him to remove my name from the screen credits as the composer of the score, adding a bit savagely that the credits should read 'Music by Tony, Tony, Tony, and G. F. Handel.'

"I told him Davis had quoted him (Stevens) as saying, 'Why should I use synthetic music when I can get the original?'—referring to *our* 'Hallelujah' versus Handel's. I asked him what the hell he meant by synthetic music—and he interrupted me right there, calling Davis all kinds of a liar, but I went right on talking. I told him Handel was already immortal before any of us now living had been born, and pleaded with him to relax his vendetta against me until my job was done. Then I assured him that my calling the Tonys 'Winken, Blinken and Nod,' and my reference to Baptist choirs, and my disagreement with him and his views on music did not automatically make me either a heretic or a Communist. I asked him what in God's name had gotten into him—and at that point I had a fit of coughing that forced me to put down the phone while I got some medication. When I picked it up again the line was dead, and now, from the looks of things, so am I."

"We both are," I said. "And the first station on our personal Via Dolorosa will be accompanied by Verdi's *Requiem*."

He looked at me strangely, stilled his cough with a neat shot of Irish, recovered, took the note Elaine had written out of my hand and said, "You're not kidding, are you." It was a statement, not a question.

I shook a negative at him. "Fact. No joking."

He read the account of Stevens' mandate for the *Requiem* and perused the fifteen listed scenes still to be scored, then dropped the note on the table, took off his reading glasses, pinched the bridge of his nose for a moment, and sighed.

"*You* do the *Requiem*," he said quietly. "Fred Steiner and I will do the rest—after I catch up on some sleep."

I took his sketches for the four revised music sequences and drove home dejectedly, hating the abrasive attrition that was threatening Pap's integrity, his musicianship, and his health, and thinking ugly thoughts about a reckoning.

Somehow, somewhere, someday, there had to be one.

SCENE IX

The logistics involved in preparing for an important recording session are enormous. Sixty singers, eighty instrumentalists, and all the music they are to sing and play must be at the same place at the same time on the same day. A crew of stage men must have the chairs in position, the music stands set up and wired for lights, a hundred earphones available at a moment's notice, and the microphones hung in place. Behind the scenes are the electronic experts who check and maintain all wiring to and from the patch bay—a marvelous maze of contacts connecting the microphones to the mixing panel by way of filters, echo chambers (if needed), and equalizers—from which point it patches the resulting mixture to the machine rooms, often in an adjacent building, where a cadre of technicians and recordists see that what comes out of the mixing panel is perfectly captured on magnetic film or tape. Then there are specialists who sit at the panel, receiving and controlling the sounds coming from the stage, mixing and balancing the information picked up by as many as fifteen microphones, blending the frequencies into a sonority of acceptable and often quite spectacular sound.

This was the kind of activity facing us as we prepared again to score the finales for Act I and the end of the film. Elaine booked the stages, alerted the sound department, notified Harry Taylor in the music library to have all parts for the orchestra and chorus on stage, sent memos to Stevens and his Tonys, and arranged for visitors. Rad Robinson, one of the original members of my King's Men quartet, was the choral contractor and called the singers. Bobby Helfer, the union contractor for the orchestra, earned the Newman death ray for employing a few second-raters on the call, but was forgiven because the music was within the range of their capabilities.

So there we were, with two versions of Handel to record, replacing forever the unusual and exciting work Alfred had so expertly created. The version for "The Raising of Lazarus" ran two minutes forty-four seconds; my cuts in the great old war horse worked without making anyone wince. The version of "The Resurrection and Ascension" ran four minutes and sixteen seconds—a total of seven minutes, and again I had found a way to cut the material without butchery or bloodshed.

When I told my singers *why* we were recording it, most of them laughed and refused to believe me. When I finally convinced them that Stevens had thrown out Alfred's "Hallelujah" because he wanted "something familiar" to end each act, they were indignant and said so. I could hear Stevens say, "What do *they* know?" and I rehearsed them furiously. "We must give the best performance of this work ever recorded or we're all in trouble," I warned. "So don't let down even for an instant."

Cartoon by
Bill Cole, Tenor
Feb. 1965

Bill Cole, one of the best tenors in the business, was also especially talented as a cartoonist. During one of our ten-minute coffee breaks, Cole's captioned drawing was circulated among the singers, eventually arriving at my rehearsal piano. It engendered some appreciative mirth, but the laughter was ambivalent, salted with disappointment.

Alfred was not fully rested when he came to the podium, but he was smartly outfitted and wore a little pork pie hat at rehearsal. The orchestra performed the "familiar" music with fresh inspiration under his baton, and my singers outdid themselves in sincerity and jubilation. When they had performed to our satisfaction—and everyone else's—I expressed my pride and gratitude. They thanked me for the call, but did not remain after the session—as they had before—to hear the combined tracks in the theater. Quietly, they bypassed Stevens.

Vellani wore a look of benign joy, and he was the first to offer praise. Stevens was friendly and solicitous and told Alfred to go home and rest up for a few days—a clear invitation for Pappy to stay away from the dubbing room. Thankfully, the day ended without friction.

On the way home Pap said, "You know who'll get blistered for using the *Messiah* in this film, don't you! It won't be Stevens or the Tonys. It's *me* the critics will murder. The minute that music hits the theater speakers, audience involvement with the picture will go right out the nearest exit! And the cost! Our music budget was already grotesquely vulgar. After today's little *whim*, it will be positively obscene."

February was suddenly upon us, rushing toward our deadline at a savage pace, and there just weren't enough hours in the days. Timing, writing, revising cues, measuring deletions, orchestrating new sequences—all these were impossible to dispatch by daylight, so George Brand and I worked nights, leaving our notes on Elaine's desk for her to type early in the mornings. My jigsaw puzzle on the *Requiem* was barely solved when Stevens asked for another conference, this time in Harold's cutting room.

"Verdi's *Requiem*," he began, and I sat down abruptly. "It works so well in the long section toward the end of the Via Dolorosa scene that I want to do the same kind of interpolation with it in an earlier spot. Harold has marked the places on your music dupe so we won't have to run it again in the projection room. Good luck with it."

I didn't telephone Pappy. The news would only aggravate him. I just sat there in the cutting room with Harold Kress and George Brand and chewed my fingernails. Then George put the sequence on his Moviola and we timed the new interpolation at two minutes fifteen seconds. The one I had just completed ran over four minutes. Key relationships were critical, and I had to invent a small enharmonic addition at the end of the first insertion of the *Requiem* to make it slide back into Alfred's score without a mutilating collision.

Physically, there was no way to cut directly from Newman to Verdi and back again, so I devised a scheme of overlapping one with the other. Where Verdi began, it would match precisely to the harmony of Newman's score—at the point where Stevens had commanded it to enter. For this, I had to transpose Verdi up a half tone. At the moment of Verdi's entrance, Newman would be faded quickly out, leaving Verdi in charge. Later, by a simple extension of a phrase, Verdi would overlap a bar of Newman, the latter fading in quickly to match the level of the Verdi.

Complicated? Yes. And it would have to be recorded in exact synchronization so that later, in the dubbing room, the two tracks would meet, meld, and not bleed to death in the process. I prayed it would work. Then I felt guilty and prayed that it wouldn't. But I did succeed so well in one of the surgical sutures—in and out of Verdi—that Pap said, "Not even Giusseppe would detect that alteration. You can be proud of it. You and he make a good team."

A ray of light broke upon us on Monday, February 9th. Wally Sterling telephoned Elaine; he was in the southland and was available. We set up a luncheon party in the MGM cafe for the following day, and I telephoned Pap, who was delighted.

I picked him up early and we drove in together, determined to relax and enjoy the company of this great man, and we succeeded. It is absolutely impossible to be in the Sterling presence and not feel ennobled and enriched. We met his limousine at the gate and took him at once to our apartment. Elaine made Bloody Marys for Alfred and me—mine virgin—and Wally had his usual.

Alfred, who liked copious quantities of Worcestershire sauce in a Bloody Mary, passed the bottle to Wally, recommending that he try it, not noticing that Wally's usual was Scotch and water. Thereafter, and all through lunch, there was much byplay about it, and our conversation was alternately seasoned with laughter and Worcestershire. There were reminiscences of earlier days when Wally had been Director of the Huntington Library in Pasadena, and of a radio show on which Wally and Alfred had appeared as interviewer and interviewee. We heard shocking revelations of the turmoil among dissident and angry students on campuses across the country; of the drug scene in and around Haight-Ashbury in San Francisco; and there were lighter moments when we chuckled at Wally's stories about Winston Churchill. For three hours we felt respectable, sane, human, and uplifted. It was a pleasurable high.

Wally's departure brought us down with a thud, and we rushed off to turn over all remaining cues to orchestrators, including several bits and pieces that would be needed to complete the phonograph album. We had one day to orchestrate, a day to copy, and we would be back on the recording stage again.

Pappy didn't look well that morning when I drove him to the studio. He conducted the double session (six hours) perched on a stool atop the podium. He was feverish and coughing painfully by the end of the day, but he had recorded an astounding nineteen minutes of music, all of which would be ready for the dubbing room as soon as George Brand could cut it into reels.

We didn't go to the apartment or linger at the studio. I turned up the heat in the car and took him straight to Martha, then left immediately for home. Our phone was ringing when I came in the door. Vera answered it, motioned for me to hurry, and I grabbed the receiver.

"Ken? This is Irving.* Pappy has pneumonia, but I think we've caught it in time. He says for you to carry on tomorrow with the orchestra; go ahead and finish the recordings for both the film and the album. I've already talked to Stevens and Davis. They know Pap has complete confidence in you, so it's all set. And good luck."

"Take extra care of him, Doc," I urged. "He's not just an ordinary guy, so he may not have just ordinary pneumonia."

---

*Irving Newman, M.D., Alfred's brother and his family doctor.

Amazing, I thought, how we drive ourselves beyond the limit of endurance. Pappy was down, but not out, and his ego would *never* be stripped to the bare bones. Not by anybody!

When the orchestra arrived on stage the next afternoon at one o'clock, I explained to the musicians what had happened. They took part of their first ten-minute break to sign a card Elaine had bought wishing Pappy a speedy recovery, and it was dispatched by special messenger.

In the first hour, I rehearsed with an earphone. On it I heard the track of Alfred's "Via Dolorosa." At the appointed bar I began conducting the Verdi *Requiem*. George Brand sat at the music cutter's desk, ready to slate (number) each take, handling the fader controls of two soundtracks that fed my earphone. When I gave my downbeat to the Verdi, he canceled the New-man track and turned on a low click track which guided me to the exact beat where Verdi would meet and overlap Newman again. It worked, and on the second take we had a perfect match. All the alterations were smooth, and the orchestra gave me the restrained dynamics I wanted.

The four-minute section was trickier—and I had a very criti-cal audience. Stevens and Vellani stood, listened, and watched, then sat during the takes, wondering perhaps if I was going to sabotage their musical innovation.

Two rehearsals and two takes later I was still off base, but on the third recording it produced the miracle they were looking for, and I was ashamed for having committed it.

During a fifteen-minute break we all went next door to the theater and played back the stereo six-track tapes of both Newman and Verdi together. Lysle Burbridge let me sit at the console, and as the Verdi music made its entrance, I dropped Alfred's score completely. The crossover into Verdi was so smooth that I heard Vellani gasp. Four minutes and five seconds later, I lifted Alfred's track to meet the outgoing Verdi and the two blended without the slightest intimation of technical ma-neuvering. To a musician, however, the giant flaw was that the two pieces were anomalous! They did not belong together, but to Stevens and Vellani it was a fine example of a perfect marriage.

"There, you see?" Vellani purred to Stevens. "I told you it would work."

I walked back to the recording stage at war with myself, disgusted with an art form that could be operated by chain of command—where the output of a spectacularly gifted composer for hire could be thwarted, dismembered, debased, fragmented, and butchered by executive privilege. I apologized inwardly to Signor Verdi and Mr. Newman for this deforcement and rupture of their music by a non-musician's personal opinion, and angrily reasoned that when executive privilege and personal opinion become art forms, allowing a committee to wield the power to distort and mutilate, to funnel and filter an artist's work through a mesh of whims and prejudices—that artist is dead!

I put *that* thought hastily out of mind, knowing I was overreacting outrageously. I found the musicians in their seats waiting for me, and together we recorded all the bits and pieces, the introductions and endings that would round out the rough edges of the phonograph album.

The last note fell into place, and the day ended. I thanked the orchestra both for myself and for Alfred, and was pleased when they applauded. As I stepped down from the podium, George handed me the telephone.

"Ken? Doc. Pappy's obeying orders and is responding to treatment, but he won't rest easy until he knows how *you* are. I won't let him talk on the phone so you'll have to tell me. How did it go with the orchestra?"

"Fine, Irving, and I'm okay. Tell Pappy that it's all wrapped up and tied with a bow. In the words of Jesus, 'It is finished.' Stevens and Vellani are in Verdi heaven. All we do now is dub, dub, dub for the premiere next week, and Pap is not to be concerned about *that*! I'll be in the dubbing room from now on every day, and I'll stop by tonight on my way home to see him."

"Not tonight, Ken. And maybe not for a few more days. Just keep in touch with Martha or me by phone, and get some rest yourself."

"Thanks, Irv. You're the doctor. But tell Pappy that my love—and the affection of Elaine, George Brand, and all the people in the orchestra—is every bit as potent as your penicillin. Give him that."

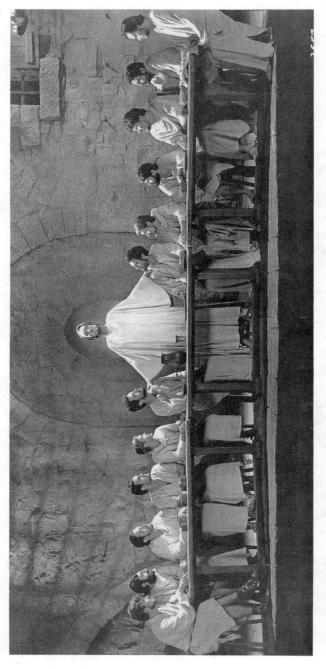

Left to Right: Matthew the Publican—Roddy McDowall; Thaddeus—Jamie Farr; James the Elder—David Sheiner; Andrew the Fisherman—Burt Brinkerhoff; James the Younger—Michael Anderson, Jr.; John the Beloved—John Considine; Jesus of Nazareth—Max von Sydow; Peter the Rock—Gary Raymond; Nathanael (Bartholomew)—Peter Mann; Simon the Zealot—Robert Blake; Thomas the Doubter—Tom Reese; Philip the Teacher—David Hedison; and Judas Iscariot the Betrayer—David McCallum. George Stevens' Production *The Greatest Story Ever Told* (Feb. 1965).

Above: Elaine supplied the groceries, Darby head griller! Note the folder on the desk full of manuscripts to be copied (1964/5). *Below:* Assistant Music Editor Milton Lustig with our principal Music Editor George Brand, reacting to the recording chart (1964/5).

Above: Alfred Newman and George Stevens in the Culver City screening room, ready to run ACT ONE of TGSET. *Below:* Three Tonys—Perris, Van Renterghem, and Vellani—in the dubbing room at Culver City during a recording session.

Above: Tony Vellani registers a preoccupied enigmatic reaction to the recording of Alfred's new music for the Resurrection, later replaced by Handel's "Hallelujah Chorus" from the *Messiah* (Dubbing theater, 1964/5). *Below*: Harold Kress, award-winning film editor (for *How the West Was Won*) in his Culver City cutting room. Notice the absence of any film to edit! (1964).

Florence Williamson, script editor, with projectionist Charles McCleod in the projection booth of Stevens's Culver City viewing room.

Above: Alfred Newman composing his score for *The Greatest Story Ever Told* in his studio at home (1964). *Below:* Fred Steiner taking notes on music he is asked to develop from Alfred's thematic material (1964).

Above: Hugo Friedhofer, composer and dear friend, listening to music he is asked to develop for *TGSET* (1964). *Below:* Top orchestrators Jack Hayes and Leo Shuken share a good moment with Alfred Newman, *center*.

M-G-M Music Mixer Bill Steinkamp, who complained that George Stevens had given him only one lesson on how to meld music with dialog.

Above: Ken Darby and Elaine Thompson, our secretary for ten years. Alfred, Elaine, and I comprised a troika for interrelated activities from *Flower Drum Song* through many films, ending with *Airport* in 1969. She was, in fact, captain of the ship and the crew, too! *Below*: Alfred Newman in his study (1962).

Above: Ken Darby, Angie Dickinson, Alfred Newman, and Gene Kelly at the Academy Awards Presentation in 1968. The Oscars are for music adaptation of *Camelot*. *Below*: Alfred conducting his last score, for the film *Airport*, on the recording stage of Universal Studios (1969). The score was nominated posthumously.

SCENE X

We dubbed day and night on the picture right up to the deadline. George Brand shuttled to and from his cutting room carrying film cans of completed music tracks. Harold Kress was now the editor of record, Stevens having tired of making all the decisions as I had prophesied. Elaine and I phoned Martha every day, and every day we were told that Pappy was recovering—but very slowly. "He's depressed," Martha confided. "He's listless about food, and hates it because he is not allowed to smoke."

"It's a very depressing disease," I said. "It dropped me flat, back in the early Forties, and I know how it feels. But look out when he revives. He'll chase you around the house."

She laughed and said, "Don't worry, I'll be ready."

On the first weekend I took all of the music tracks to United Artists Recording Studio and sat with the mixers and record producer Alan Douglas while the master of the stereo LP was made. With the time left over on Sunday, I had them make a quarter-inch stereo two-track tape of the entire score, omitting only the music of Verdi and Handel. I planned to make a copy for myself and present the original to Pappy on his birthday, March 17th.

Then the deadline arrived. The album and the picture were released simultaneously, and I still wonder how the last reel ever made it to New York's Warner Cinerama Theater on time for the premiere the night of February 15th. It must have been by jet and police escort, but it got there. And UA was selling the album in the lobby!

Philip K. Scheur ran a review-interview in the *L.A. Times* the day before the film opened. He hadn't even seen the picture when he wrote it, so we decided it was a publicity stunt—a

Valentine to George Stevens—but it should be included in this
chronicle. In many ways it is revealing.

Los Angeles Times, February 14, 1965*
by Philip K. Scheur

George Stevens is probably the best moviemaker in
Hollywood, and his "Greatest Story Ever Told" will probably remove the "probably." If, as a man, he is a paradox,
he is a perfectly consistent paradox. Interviewing him
requires a great deal of patience and even more intuitive-
ness, for whatever he says, he says very much as he would
create a big scene—planning it, shooting it, revising it,
then editing it, and listening to himself as he might to a
playback. As the editor of *Cinema Magazine* commented,
"He is a diverse man. He is composed of many parts, but
with Stevens the only time they all converge is on a strip
of film. That's when you say that's him, that is George
Stevens." And again: "Discovering in conversation with
him just how Mr. George Stevens makes his films is
virtually impossible!"

In my own case I have been interviewing Stevens for
thirty years and more, and always I have come away real-
izing that I understood what he was saying *behind* what he
was saying, but that it wasn't going to be easy to tell the
reader what it was. So on this occasion I started by asking
him point-blank what he thought of "The Greatest Story
Ever Told." Stevens threw up his hands—half humor-
ously.

"I'd rather keep silent, let it speak for itself. I'd rather
have you look at it and tell *me*. Film is a very strong thing
from where I sit. One must wait for that moment when it
confronts an audience, for it is the audience that brings it
to life. It is an audience that can articulate all this, we can
only wait. Film is a very precise medium. If the interpretation is loose enough an audience can apply a certain
interpretation to it, and we did allow tolerance for this—
that we, as the communicator, could come up with information and, hopefully, insight. Our aim was to bring to
the foreground the universality of the subject matter in its
relationship to all people. Having been made in our time
it is related to our time; and today, as no man can be an

island, so no religion can. A great part of our purpose, I feel, is like that of the Ecumenical Council. Its recent moves, such as the Pope's going to India, were particularly gratifying to us, for in the religious world they set the stage for the widest reception of the point of view of our picture. It can offend or disturb only those people who already have preconceived, well-defined religious beliefs, or perhaps those who suffered misfortune prior to 1945. Yet all of it is a plea for harmony, humanity and kindness and understanding among people. I am quite sure it will be heartwarming to people who find in it an opportunity to be exposed to more complete knowledge of the Judaic-Christian philosophy. For, remember, our principals are all Hebrew; this is a completely Hebraic work, and so if you want to damn, you've got to damn people who created the Christian Religion! It is completely impossible to separate Judaism and Christianity."

Having read this far, I decided Stevens should have stuck with his opening sentence—and kept silent. He had used this kind of double talk in the projection room often enough, but seeing it in print boggled my mind and I had to read it twice. That was when I noticed how slyly he had slithered out from under any directorial responsibility for making a bad movie, and I underlined the quotation and had Elaine mail it to Pap. "... *this is a completely Hebraic work, and so if you want to damn, you've got to damn people who created the Christian Religion.*"

The article went on, and for a man who wanted to let the picture "speak for itself" he still had one hell of a lot to say. Scheur continued:

While he expects the film to cause discussion on all levels, Stevens emphasized, "It is a film of a *story* not of a religion—a story told on film in a clean wholesome manner. We are not making a cause of it." His hope, he said, is that the film will appear to the contemporary mind as what he called "a happening." Stevens said:

"Remember, the written accounts were developed long after the Happening. Most of our conceptions stem from the Renaissance. We tried to get to the heart of the subject matter and suggest, to reasonable minds, this is the way it happened."

Stevens shrugged philosophically. Some criticism, he said, was to be expected. Anything on film can cause "great disturbance; greater than anything in life, in the newspapers or on television. The medium is quicker to be derided than any other. This is caused by fear; a strange sort of fear inspired by the knowledge that film presents an easy means of communication, almost a weapon, that *could* come into the hands of the wrong people. Perhaps the word is not 'derided'—but it does show an awareness of the power of film."

I asked him to comment on the structure of "The Greatest Story Ever Told." He said:

"In a way it's a very active film, although it dramatizes ideas of both mind and spirit. It plays like a play, was designed as a play . . . well then, a film-play—in two acts. The hazard was to keep the aspects of pageantry from getting in the way of the architecture of the play, which was carefully designed for the two acts. The picture will run around four hours."

The boastful title, he admitted, presented a problem in itself. It is underplayed in the lettering and a narrator delivers "the greatest story ever told" softly, even sotto voce. Stevens spoke sadly of the manifold responsibilities that confront the producer today when he is already head-deep in the logistics of a film.

"You want to do something light or delicate and you have to do it with an armored division. The day has long passed when you can go off and make a film by yourself and hope for an outlet. Take some of the older veterans! Who is to say, suddenly that they no longer have any value? D. W. Griffith wandered around town for ten years and couldn't get a job! For myself, I was grateful to have the opportunity to make this film. It was always exciting. I worked seriously and earnestly and asked the people with me to do as much. I think you'll find that they did."

Alfred smuggled a phone call through to me when he had read the article. He came right to the point.

"Ken, will you kindly tell me what possible bearing D. W. Griffith being out of work for ten years has on Stevens making a movie about the life of Christ?"

"I think it's a hedge against the future, Pappy. It may well be that one of Vellani's archangels has told Stevens he is doomed

to wander around Hollywood for the next ten years without
being able to get a job, and he's exonerating himself in advance
by comparing himself with the great Griffith."

"That's pretty complicated—but it's also funny. I think somebody should remind George of that old epigram, 'A closed
mouth gathers no foot.' Uh-oh! Here comes Marth. G'bye."

Everybody in both studios who had worked on the picture
now held their breath, waiting in a kind of static limbo for the
reactions of the critics. The first blast came from Judith Crist
after she had seen the New York premiere. Pappy read it and
began immediately to get well even though she gave him a
pasting.

The New York Herald Tribune, February 16, 1965*
by Judith Crist

"The Greatest Story Ever Told" succeeds in a number
of areas where other Hollywood spectaculars have failed
in detailing the life of Christ.

But it is unfortunate that it does *not* succeed ultimately
in elevating its theme visually or intellectually beyond the
dime-store-picture-Sunday-school-holy-primer level to
which its predecessors have accustomed us.

The disappointment is keen in view of the film's fine
auspices. Beyond the 20 million dollar investment,
George Stevens devoted more than four years to the
movie, for which he served as producer, director and
co-author, with even Carl Sandburg working in "Creative
Association" with the production. Most important, Mr.
Stevens has set a certain standard of taste and has almost
austerely avoided the orgies, the milling masses, the
pomp, circumstance and circus atmosphere that have
been the hallmark of the Hollywood Biblical. The result,
however, is what might be called a Hollywood Reverential, a film so in awe of its subject that it dares approach it
only in the most traditional terms at a slow and solemn
pace.

Mr. Stevens' primary achievement is in casting Max von
Sydow (pronounced Sea-dove) as Jesus. Even for those of
us who had seen him as the leading man in a number of
Ingmar Bergman films, this brilliant Swedish actor brings

*Reprinted by permission of Judith Crist.

an unfamiliar face to the role, as well as a striking presence and finely modulated voice. [Thanks to Vandraegen] He is a figure of grace and godliness and speaks Scripture with much eloquence and authority. If after a time his words inevitably assume the edge of pomposity it is because he is given a constant flow of familiar quotations to mouth; if—ultimately—the illusion of mystery and of the spiritual with which he enhances his Christ is shattered, it is because we are given a constant flow of familiar faces in the crowd.

Mr. Stevens has vitiated the power of his unknown Christ and disciples by casting any number of too-well-known players in less-than-barely-flash-in-the-pan bit parts; we get the impression that any performer passing through the location sites—or just visiting the Hollywood set between trains decided to don a hood and/or wig and get on camera, with or without dialogue.

At this point I began to underline the word "familiar" because it had been the catchword in Stevens' decision to supplant Alfred's score with Handel's *Messiah*. I went back and found two, and there were more to come.

The Hollywood tone is cast from the start with Claude Rains as a rheumy-eyed choleric Herod, Jose Ferrer as his heir and Dorothy McGuire a picture-book (and oddly unaging) Madonna; Charlton Heston is literally crying in the wilderness, and we get the whining British accents of Donald Pleasence as the hermit demanding, "If you are the Son of God, turn these stones into bread." Ed Wynn plays Ed Wynn straight as the sightless Aram; Telly Savalas and Victor Buono do their familiar "heavy" bits respectively as Pilate and as Sorak, and up pops Joseph Schildkraut to lend a folksy neighborhood synagogue tone to the councils.

And before you know it you're caught in a game of spot-the-stars: there's a black-wigged Shelley Winters shouting "I'm cured, I'm cured" and Pat Boone carefully enunciating "He is risen"; hey—that's John Wayne, the old centurion . . . and there's Sydney Poitier helping with the cross—and did you catch Angela Lansbury as Mrs. Pilate, and Van Heflin looking awestruck, and Sal Mineo saying "Look, I'm walking" and—well, five will get you ten

if you spot Carroll Baker black-wigged on the road to
Calvary as Veronica!

The game comes easily because our attention wanders.
The greatest story is perhaps the most familiar, and Mr.
Stevens has offered only restraint hour after hour through
literal depictions of each detail. Not that there is a lack of
technical exercise in sight or sound: voices come booming
out of various sides of the screen at high pitch whether the
speakers are far or near or silent; there are newsreel-and-
still-photo sequences, montages, endless panoramic
views . . . even an "Op Art" effect in latticework shadows
on the disciples' robes, all in colortoning that makes each
sequence seem like a separate slick magazine layout.

There are several beautiful sequences, but the special
effects seem to intrude more often than they enhance the
desired and occasionally lofty simplicity of the
theme . . . and much is mediocre. The beautiful Nativity
scene itself—two boyish shepherds peering in, the kings
unattended, the mood shattered by a far-off cry and the
silhouette of Herod's horsemen on the distant dune—is
lost between a Christmas-card approach and an arty after-
math. Salome dances in solitary white-veiled grace—but
to no point or purpose. The disciples' communal spirit in
the household chores of preparing the Last Supper seems
to have evaporated at table as the camera must linger and
figures freeze to emulate the stalest of lithographs. Most
often the very sense of time and place dissolves as the
camera draws back for huge pretentious display and we
are free to see that despite the painted city battlements in
the background and constructed villages in the foreground, we are in Monument Valley, Utah, land of high
rock and Redskin, and not Israel. The familiar places
shatter what little illusion the familiar faces have left us
with, and the dialogue pounds the pieces to dust.

Mr. von Sydow sustains the stature of Christ in sermon
and soliloquy; he is immediately diminished in colloquy,
trapped by the screenplay switch from Scripture to
script . . . from the Gospel to the vernacular. Most disas-
trous is the attempt to make James the Less the comic
relief juvenile among the disciples, with his remarks on a
constant gee-whiz level. We get the heavy underlining
with "I am Judas—Iscariot," "I am Jesus—of Nazareth"
and a handshake; we get the banality of Pilate remarking
to Herod Antipas, "You know, he's actually telling people

to love their enemies!"; a messenger reports " . . . and that's not all, he walked on water!" and Pilate retorts, "Get out!"; and we are not spared the ultimate cliche, with one official remarking, after the Resurrection, "Anyhow, the whole thing will be forgotten in a week" and another riposting, "I wonder."

It should not take us four hours to arrive at this point in such simple-minded fashion, without the refreshment of a point of view, a dramatic interpretation of some sort. The blandness is underlined throughout by an ordinary music-to-feel-religious-by score by Alfred Newman, who at least eschews carols at the outset but has to turn somehow helplessly to hallelujahs from Handel to celebrate the raising of Lazarus at intermission time. One might say the rest of the score suffers by contrast thereafter.

Elaine heard me butting my head against the wall and rushed in. "You're putting dents in that wallboard," she accused. "What's the idea?"

I showed her the paragraph mentioning Alfred's score. She read it quickly and asked, "May I join you?" And put a dent into the wall next to mine.

It broke me up—we laughed, and I read the final paragraph of the review aloud.

This is an oddly dispassionate story of Christ, told somehow in a social vacuum with no temper of the time, no sense of a popular pulse. If the focus is the individual, and certainly Mr. von Sydow provides us with one worthy of such concentration, it has been distorted by the requirements of the superscreen. The inescapable conclusion is that the story of Christ is too great to be captured in a spectacular, too personal to be told in the box-office vernacular. Although superior to what we have had before, at least in its restraint, its *taste* nevertheless fails to rise to the level of its theme.

At that moment, George Brand came charging in waving the newspaper. "Have you seen the review by Judith Crist?"

"We've just finished reading it."

"Well, what do you think Stevens is going to do about that last line where she casts insults on his taste?"

"I think he'll hurt for a while, George, and then I bet he'll tumble to the fact that his biggest error in taste was letting himself be masterminded by Vellani."

Elaine said, "I think we should all go home and pray."

SCENE XI

Usually, after a picture has been completed and theatrically released, the services of salaried and contract people are terminated. Mysteriously, we were all being retained on the payroll, and dismissal notices had never been mentioned. So here we were—loaded with unaccustomed leisure—with not a thing to do but read the reviews and critiques, an activity that developed into an important part of the daily agenda.

Our little music bungalow became a comfortable oasis for George Brand, Harold Kress, Charlie McCleod, Frank O'Neill, and, surprisingly, Frank Davis. They dropped in at odd moments to speculate on how this morning's critic would affect the box office, and came back in the afternoon with the latest newspapers and magazines to hash over the plaudits and insults. Frank Davis told us that Stevens and the Tonys were doing the same thing up in the executive suite, and from his presence in *our* group we concluded that Frank was—for the moment at least—persona non grata in the inner sanctum.

The *New York Times* gave Bosley Crowther a thousand words. He used them all. Mike Connelly, in the *Reporter*, needed only seventy-eight. The Hollywood papers: *Variety* and the West-Coast *Reporter* gave bland notices. The local press does not alienate a producer like George Stevens who has the professional clout to change your address. This was proven in a correlative way when Stevens attacked the use of "Musical Director" as a screen credit for the composer of a film score.

"There is only one 'Director' on a film, unless two or more 'Directors' collaborate." And he convinced the guilds, producers, and studios, by lobbying and legal means, to erase the appellation "Musical Director" from the screen. From that time to this the designation "Music Director" has been changed to

"Musical Supervisor," or "Music Composed and Conducted by——!" One does not write reviews that incite to action this kind of power—if one wants to stay in business.

Still, there were significant attacks (in a left-handed way) by some of the trade papers that became widely quoted by others, e.g., "It is said that people who don't believe in George Stevens' Jesus are people who don't believe in God." And there were snide remarks about Salome's veil dance as being so pure it could have been danced at a church social.

Variety and *The Hollywood Reporter* came out with short reviews, followed by longer ones in *Newsweek, Time* magazine, and *The New Yorker*, as well as many others. Some publications (if mentioning the music at all) panned Alfred for falling back on the masterworks of Verdi and Handel to salvage a sagging score.

Alfred, meanwhile, was being cured by righteous anger, looking at life with a warming eye, and even though critics were lambasting him, he refused to let their ignorance of the facts abort his recovery. The reviews were supporting his own prophetic conclusions, and although he was taking no joy in that knowledge, he felt his judgment was being vindicated.

On Friday, February 19th, George Brand came flying into the bungalow with startling news. "Guess what! We're all to be in Stevens' projection room tomorrow at 9 a.m. prepared for an all-day session. He's going to review the entire film. Guess why."

"The critics," Elaine offered.

"The picture is too long," I said.

"I think you're both right, but we'll know for sure by tomorrow night."

I couldn't get to the phone fast enough to relay this development to Alfred. He started to chuckle, but ended the conversation with a spasm of coughing. Martha came on the line and said, "He only coughs when he laughs. You're not to worry. Pappy is really doing a lot better. He received a cheerful letter from Wally Sterling today, and I'm sending it on to the studio."

It began to rain at 7 p.m. and continued all night, quite heavy at times. It was still raining lightly on Saturday morning when George Brand and I entered the damp, soggy projection room. Present were Harold Kress, Frank O'Neill, Tony Perris, Argyle

Nelson, Tony Vellani, and Stevens. Elaine was at the editor's desk with her note pad, Charlie McCleod was on duty in his booth, but Davis and Tony Van Renterghem were conspicuously absent.

Stevens stood up and delivered a short opening statement:

"The two gala premieres here and in New York have served as excellent previews. The general reaction is that the film runs too long. We will start with reel one and go through the picture scene by scene with the purpose of paring it without in any way emasculating it. Please make notes."

He had a fistful of reviews and clippings, and at every stop he kept refreshing his memory by referring to them. So Elaine and I had both been right: The picture was too long, and the critics had him bugged.

During this running, which lasted from nine in the morning to six in the evening (with twenty minutes out for sandwiches and drinks brought in by Tony Perris), eleven reels were studied and editing notes decided upon—and out of these eleven reels only eight minutes were cut—a few frames here, a few frames there, at the beginning of a scene or at the end of it . . . or at both ends. No big chunks were removed, and in nearly every case, music was affected.

After each decision to cut out a piece of the picture, Stevens asked George Brand, "That will work all right for the music, don't you think, George?"

And George would answer, "I really can't tell until I've put the track and picture together on the Moviola."

Not once did Stevens direct a question or a comment to me. Harold Kress was also ignored. He sat silently, absorbed and shaken by the prospect of pulling back into the studio forty-two completed prints, resizing the reels, recutting negative, and going through the entire dubbing-room process again with *thirty* reels of film!

At one point, where Stevens had used Ovadia Tuvia's music of the Inbal's hit tune "Watchman, What of the Night?" a big cut was made. George Brand asked, "Shall I leave the flute music in and just move it earlier, Mr. Stevens?"

"I suppose so."

"You can shift the position of the track to whatever place you think it sounds best when you get into the dubbing room."

Stevens' answer was a flat statement. "I won't *be* there."

I heard a stifled gasp from Kress and Nelson.

As I drove home through the rain that night, I decided that since Stevens hadn't even acknowledged my presence, I'd make no further appearances in the projection room unless he called me specifically. It was a good decision.

George Brand phoned at 6 p.m. on Sunday the 21st. "Man, are you smart! We've been running Act One all day long."

"Did he ask for me?"

"Not once. Does that mangle your feelings?"

"I'm crushed. Any scuttlebutt?"

"Yes. I found out why we're hacking this picture up in such a panic. United Artists put the screws on. Either Mr. Stevens cuts an *hour* out of the film, or UA *will*! Should I phone Alfred and give him the news?"

"By all means. He will want to know. How many minutes were cut out of Act one?"

"Twelve. And tomorrow we start on Act Two. Stay home. And get plenty of rest because when I start cutting Alfred's music to fit these new scenes I want you right beside me, and I won't cut it unless you are!"

And so it went, day after day, night after night, until the picture had been shortened to a running time of three hours and thirteen minutes. Stevens then called a halt, and United Artists said that would be acceptable.

Meanwhile, Elaine and I had dismantled our bungalow, moved out, turned in our parking passes and packed our glassware, filed our papers and the conductor parts, all against the day when we might set up shop on another film. In the process, we found Wally's letter of February 17th, and we read it together.

Letter From Wally Sterling, February 17, 1965 (typed)

Dear Al:

Many, many thanks for the pleasure of your company and for the good lunch. My omelette was delicious and the whiskey first-rate, even without Worcestershire. Please

tion

Book Two

heaven you will have early, successful and final release from "The Greatest Story Ever Told." If memory is correct, the doleful Job once remarked: "Oh that mine enemy had written a book." Bear that in mind as you select your targets for any fusillades you may be contemplating.

Yesterday afternoon I decided that I'd had enough of the world's troubles, so took to my garden and then early to bed. This passing declaration of independence massaged my ego and, in consequence, I feel better this morning.

I'm told that one benefits from serenity. Perhaps so. But how does one know unless one finds it? I'll keep looking, and promise to share with you any beneficial discovery I make.

Once again my thanks and, as always, my best wishes.
Yours,
Wally

Elaine and I sat in the only two chairs left in the bungalow, looking at each other disconsolately and listening to the rain gusting against the windows and pounding on the roof. Gone were the copy machine, the sandwich grill, and the refrigerator. The piano had been returned to David Abell's rental service; even the walls were bare of Mr. Woolworth's fine art. This is the letdown, I thought. We should be feeling relief, not dejection or bereavement. We had been on the project too long. All the people, the programs, the frictions, the plannings and accomplishments had become members of a big concentrated family, and now they had moved away, the concentration was dissolved, the glue had melted and split the big family into fragments, and the rain was conducting a wake.

Elaine said, "It's all over! Do you know that this is the first time we have finished a picture where we three didn't all celebrate the end of it and walk out together? I feel like bawling."

I got up quickly. "Come on, girl. Let's not have it as wet in here as it is outside. No tears! I'll get my umbrella and walk you to your car."

She looked up at me solemnly. "Mr. Newman was right. I never quite understood what he meant before, but I do now. He said, 'Every time we finish a picture it's like a little death.' And it's true."

"I know—and I feel it too. But this little death hurt us the most. He's not here to walk out with us. What we need now is not a bad case of the blues, but a miraculous resurrection from post-production depression. Come on."

And we walked out into the rainy night.

SCENE XII

Of the 47 minutes cut from *The Greatest Story Ever Told*, music was involved in less than half. But how do you slice 20 minutes from 142 minutes of score—bits and pieces at a time—and have it still sound like the original music? It can't be done. It comes out as trickery.

George Brand got his new music dupe from Harold Kress in early March, and I received a phone call from Frank Davis on the same day. Would I come back to work—at my regular contract salary—to assist George Brand in tailoring, editing, cutting, and fitting Alfred's music to the revised picture?

"Starting when?" I asked.

Frank cleared his throat. "I know it's short notice, but could you make it tomorrow?"

"On one condition, Frank. I'll need a complete set of new conductor parts from MGM. You authorize the printing of them through Harry Taylor in the music library and I'll pick them up on my way in tomorrow."

"Okay," he said. "And thanks. Brand says he'll quit if you aren't here to help him."

When I told Pappy what was happening, he groaned. "If anybody can do it, you can. But will it be music, or just a lot of splices? I'm going to forget it."

"It won't be exactly as you conceived it, Pappy, but I vow we won't hack it up into unintelligible fragments."

"It won't matter," he said. "It's not my music now, it's Stevens' property. Just do the best you can, and if it gets too tough, let *him* cut it. Keep in touch."

So began twenty-one days of agony in the garden by the swimming pool. Every morning we'd charge onto the lot, walk from our parking spaces past the pool into the cutting building and load up the Moviola.

George had an adding machine that did all manner of fine weird mathematics. He would time the new footage, then time the original music track and feed both bits of information into his machine. It would start a cackling, chuckling conversation with itself and twenty seconds later up would pop a piece of paper telling us how many bars, or beats, or frames, or feet we would have to cut out of the music to make it come out even with the film. This would send me on a note-by-note, bar-by-bar search through the conductor part, hunting for the bars or beats that might be eliminated without creating a monstrous scar. Sometimes I found it, and we'd make the cut and move on to the next scene. Sometimes there was simply no way to lose the necessary bars out of the body of the music, and then I'd look for a way to cut it from the beginning, giving the music a new start, or try to find a long sustained note near the end that could be faded out in the dubbing room.

And all the while, day after day, we both felt like mad Frankensteins bending over and mutilating an innocent victim, operating, stitching, and praying that we were not building a monstrosity. Some of the drastic incisions would not work at all by splicing, although they were perfectly logical cuts on paper. When this happened we tried overlapping—putting the severed, truncated tracks on two machines, letting the outgoing meet the incoming at exactly the correct level, and this worked on several sequences. But it hurt. The natural flow of the musical exposition was disturbed and thwarted.

"Don't worry about it," Alfred said.

But I did.

Suddenly, an order came down from the executive suite. Alfred's "Hallelujah" was to be restored to the end of Act One! We held a guessing contest to see who could come closest to the reason for such a restoration. Harold Kress won. The critics, worldwide, had finally broken through Stevens' armament with jibes, insults, and wisecracks about the *bad taste* he had displayed in using Handel's *Messiah*.

Harold finished his account with, "But Stevens insists that he'll keep Handel's music at the end of the picture, no matter *who* criticizes it."

At this point I was past caring. We just did as we were told, and a day came when we were down to the last cue. There was no possible musical cut to be found, and the music was almost eight bars too long for the shortened scene. But there *was* a pause—in musical terms a fermata—near the end that fell short of our picture footage by only seven seconds. The following scene was ominous and played without music. I thought of Stevens' aversion to low notes, and decided to give him a last parting shot.

"Do we have any timpani rolls in the library?"

"Not here," George said, "but they must have at MGM."

I got on the phone. Harry Taylor told me that Bobby Armbruster was scoring with a sizeable orchestra at that moment. I told him to grab a piece of music paper.

"All set," he said.

"Write out a timpani roll on a low E-flat. Make it start *mezzo forte* and gradually decrescendo to pianissimo. Mark it 'sustain for ten seconds' and see if Bobby will record it as soon as possible on three-track stereo. I'll send a driver over for the tape."

Later, in the dubbing room, that sequence played exactly as Alfred had written it, except for the ending. As the scene drew to its foreshortened close, the orchestra arrived at the fermata, but before it could conclude with the next eight bars, our new timpani track took over—we dialed out Alfred's music—and the low rumble remained suspended for the seven seconds required and faded under the incoming scene.

But what price such a victory?

Elaine was called to Alfred's home on March 19th, just two days after his birthday. He was up and about, feeling fit again, and sneaking a cigarette now and then when Martha or the children weren't watching. "They spy on me," he grumbled, "and I'm spooked by their gestapo tactics. I have to hide my cigarettes the way Ray Milland hid his bottles in *Lost Weekend*. Plus I feel guilty every time I smoke one. All I want to do today is dictate a few letters. I won't ask you *not* to smoke, my girl, but if you won't *I* won't."

Two of those letters are worth more than any words of mine. The first was to his attorney.

March 19, 1965

Dear Henry:

   You have read my contract with George Stevens Pro-
ductions, Inc. Do I have any recourse? Can I force United
Artists to remove my name from the film credits of TG-
SET?

   There are fifty witnesses to the fact that Stevens masterminded everything. Not one of the greatly respected
people connected with the film was permitted to perform
his function without interference and manipulation.
Harold Kress was ridiculed and nearly broken. Elisofon,
Novarese and Day were countermanded and subjected to
insult. My own music, good or bad, was interpolated,
deleted and displaced. Music designed for sensitive scenes
was removed and inserted into other sequences where it
actually damaged the dramatic content.

   The critics have no knowledge of this, so, while Stevens
had his way with the score, putting in music from *The
Robe, The Messiah*, and Verdi's *Requiem, I* am the one who
is being excoriated and criticized. It is *my* name on the film.

   Now Stevens is back in his projection room cutting and
patching. Most of the remaining music is being sliced up
like pastrami (or bologna, which it now is) to fit the new
shortened length. Some of it is still my music, but it is no
longer my score, and I desperately need a redress of this
grievance. What can I do? What can *you* do?

   What can anybody do with a producer who says, "Anyone who criticizes this film simply doesn't believe in God."

   I am disturbed. Please call me.

   Regards,
   A.N.

Letter to J. E. Wallace Sterling, March 20, 1965

Dear Wally:

   Many thanks for your letter and for the great pleasure
of your company at our MGM lunch. Perhaps the next
time you won't mind a drop or two of my Worcestershire
in your whiskey, just for the hell of it. I assure you there is
nothing erotic in such a concoction. Since I don't believe

there is such a thing as an aphrodisiac, we have nothing to lose—except, perhaps, our lunch.

I have left heaven, and I'm securely (more or less) back on earth. Unfortunately for Ken, he was called back to heaven, or hell—depending on how you look at it—by the author of the Fifth Gospel. His mission is to help edit the music for sizeable cuts which are being made in the film. This is somewhat like leading the horse out of the barn (charred to the bone) after the barn has burned down. I'm afraid our dear Ken isn't too happy about this assignment.

It has been said by some local wag columnist—after seeing TGSET—that if the Messiah returns as prophesied, "G.S. had better take to the hills."

Please continue your search for serenity and do share with me any beneficial discovery you may make, but try to make it soon, won't you?

Yours, as ever,
Alfred

Pappy never did see any of the several versions of *The Greatest Story Ever Told* in any commercial theater. And there was no available legal action to assuage his distress. In his contract with Stevens there was the usual "for-hire clause" stating that "the product of the artist belongs to the employer as though the latter created, authored and/or composed it."

Stevens wielded his Olympian power in another medium just before the picture was released. This occurred when the great two-piano team of Ferrante and Teicher made a record of "Jesus of Nazareth" accompanied by a large orchestra. United Artists had approved the record and disseminated it without Stevens' knowledge. He happened to hear it on the radio. Angrily, he had his attorney seek restraining orders against the record company, United Artists, Ferrante and Teicher, their agent, the Musicians Union, and several John Does. To everyone's dismay, the disc was recalled from the record shops and withdrawn from the market. That's clout!

The official album, released with his benediction, was not immune to his directorial tampering. He changed all of the titles on the record except two: "Jesus of Nazareth" and "The Great Journey." The other selections were given new names, which he made up out of generalizations rather than keep the descriptive titles Alfred had given them on his original manuscripts.

Side one of the disc had six bands of music: "Jesus of Nazareth"; "A Prophecy"; "A Voice in the Wilderness"; "Come Unto Me"; "The Great Journey," and "A Time of Wonders."

Side two had five bands: "There Shall Come a Time to Enter"; "A New Commandment"; "The Hour Has Come"; "Into Thy Hands," and "The Triumph of the Spirit."

"The Triumph of the Spirit" identified the music of the "Hallelujah Chorus" from the *Messiah*. Apparently, even Handel's beautiful title wasn't up to Stevens' taste.

The liner copy of the album was also written by Stevens. It made no mention of the music—which is what the album was all about—except in the column of screen credits, listing everybody under the Utah sun, then offering the simple betrayal: "Music by Alfred Newman." The rest of the copy was a collection of philosophical rhetoric paraphrasing epigrams, one of which appears to be his credo: " . . . any work of art undertakes to provide answers from within the beholder."*

The actual answers from within the articulate beholders were both laudatory and crushing. Unfortunately, the crush outweighed the laud. In my own personal notes I found a few lines of summation:

"Work completed March 26, 1965. Picture now three and a half hours long. Alfred's 'Hallelujah' is back in the film at the end of Act One. All reviews are in. Retribution *does* exist. Time will deliver it."

---

*See Coda section.

SCENE XIII

The last film George Stevens directed before his death was *The Only Game in Town*, for 20th Century-Fox in 1969. In that same year, Alfred scored *Airport*, the Ross Hunter-George Seaton blockbuster for Universal Studios. I was in constant attendance as liaison between Pappy and the various departments. He was mortally ill and again required the assistance of his rescuers Hugo Friedhofer and Fred Steiner, and we all leaned on the strong orchestrational skills of Leo Shuken and Jack Hayes. Alfred honored me by asking that I develop his piquant theme for "Mrs. Quonsett," played by Helen Hayes with so much serenely sly confidence. Elaine made the office at Universal a home base for us, but Pappy only came in when it was necessary for him either to view the film or to conduct the orchestra, and I always picked him up in the mornings and took him home after our sessions, he no longer self-assured enough to drive his car. When the score was finally completed even his love of conducting was assaulted by overpowering weakness, so he asked me, and the late Stanley Wilson, to co-conduct and produce the record album.

The Academy of Motion Picture Arts and Sciences voted Alfred a posthumous nomination (his 45th) for best original score, and the Academy of Recording Arts and Science awarded him a posthumous "Grammy" for the "Gwen-and-Vern" love theme, which he had entitled "A Time to Cry." The stereo LP album of *Airport* has since become a collector's item.

From 1948 to 1970, Alfred and I worked *together*. To the end of my career, I could have been listed only as a *Vocal Arranger* or *Choral Conductor* had it not been for his spontaneous decision to share his screen credit with me as his Associate Musical Supervisor, an act of generosity unheard of in Hollywood! This made me eligible for Academy recognition, and together we won five nominations and two Oscars. I was at his bedside when he died of emphysema on February 17, 1970, one month short of his seventieth birthday . . . and two almost mystic revolts occurred within me in that moment: I rejected any thought of continuing a film career without him, and—I permanently gave up smoking!

Among the papers stored in boxes Elaine and I had packed that rainy day in 1965, I found a large envelope with my name on it. Inside was a manuscript in Pappy's handwriting, the title: *Christ the Lord (Adonai)—Rough Preliminary Sketch*. Apparently he had planned to give it to me on that long-ago December as a companion to the gold pencil. In the first bar was written (in red ink) "To Ken—with admiration, love, and undying gratitude. As ever, Pappy—Christmas 1964."

There is a happier ending here in 1991. The inspired music Alfred wrote for *The Greatest Story Ever Told* and *The Robe* dared me to create a cantata for symphony orchestra and mixed chorale. But someone's edict at MGM, where the music for *TGSET* was stored, ordered all manuscripts and orchestrations to be destroyed. They were burned! So all I had to go on in reconstructing the score were conductor parts and a good memory. It took me seventeen years, large amounts of money paid out for lawyer and copyist fees, interminable wrangling with copyright owners, revisions and decisions. Some of the lyrics are mine, but most have Biblical sources. Whoever was looking over my shoulder brought it all together on the night of October 1, 1987, in the de Jong Concert Hall of Brigham Young University under the determined auspices of James A. Mason, Dean of Fine Arts and Communications and the classic introductions by our cherished friend, Tony Thomas.

The world premiere performance of *Man of Galilee* was the final entry in an "All Alfred Newman Program" that night. The magnificent student symphony orchestra, together with the 90-voice oratorio choir of young and beautiful singers were greeted with an enthusiastic standing ovation by a large and important audience. No one missed Handel or Verdi!

The Bourne Company Music Publishers have already printed a simplified version of the five segments which I arranged for choirs and small choral groups; the symphonic parts for promulgation to the great symphony orchestras and master chorales are ready and available.

All of us who remember the thrilling experience on MGM's sound stage, so many years ago, believe that perhaps—just *perhaps*—the world of the future will come to know and love this exciting and beautiful work, created by the most honored film composer of the twentieth century. It is my hope that, through many performances, it may become at last . . .
. . . "familiar."

CODA: CRITICS, SOURCES, AND QUOTES

FILMS IN REVIEW, Mar. 21, 1966. "Sound Track"—Page Cook. "My choice for '65's best score is Alfred Newman's for *The Greatest Story Ever Told* ... the restoration of Newman's own "Hallelujah" chorus for the finish of act one (replacing Handel's) is a breathless, canonical version of the march for Jesus and His disciples, and is one of the most glorious chorales I have ever heard."

GLENDALE NEWS-PRESS, Feb. 27, 1965. Review by George Raborn. Movie epic of Christ should be longer. Voice of God wanted. More miracles needed. (John 21:25) "But there are many other things which Jesus did; were every one of them to be written, I suppose that the world itself could not contain the books that could be written." This review emphasizes the impossible work that Stevens tried to do in making such a picture.

LIFE, Feb. 1965. Review by Shana Alexander. "The scale of *The Greatest Story Ever Told* was so stupendous, the pace so stupefying, that I felt not uplifted—but sandbagged!"

LOS ANGELES TIMES, Feb. 21, 1965. Review by Religion Editor Dan L. Thrapp. "The Very Rev. Leonidas C. Contos ... said he was 'let down' and disappointed' by the picture, primarily by what he saw as a lack of motivation on the part of some roles, and a lack of subtlety."

LOS ANGELES TIMES, Feb. 25, 1965. Review by Jack Smith. "Unicorn 909 to London," he called. "Request permission to orbit London. We're trying to finish *The Greatest Story Ever*

Told. "Jolly good," answered London. "You may orbit at 20,000 feet, but mind you don't bump into Global 808, though, old chap. They're up there somewhere—trying to finish *Cleopatra.*"

MUSIC FOR THE MOVIES, book by Tony Thomas. A.S. Barnes & Co., 1973. " . . . the music score was trounced. The more snide among the critics sneered at Newman's 'attempting to glorify his own music by incorporating Verdi and Handel' but once again it was a case of the blame being laid at the wrong door."

NEWSWEEK, Feb. 22, 1965. Review. " . . . von Sydow . . . walks up the path . . . to the tomb of Lazarus, and Handel's Hallelujah Chorus comes thundering out at us. The picture is a farrago of such solecisms."

THE NEW YORKER, Feb. 18, 1965. Review. "If to devout Christians the life of the Saviour is the greatest story ever told . . . the latest attempt to do so—a Cinerama and Technicolor . . . spectacular called, with conventional self-serving aplomb, *The Greatest Story Ever Told*—is, not to mince words, a disaster."

THE NEW YORK TIMES, Feb. 16, 1965. Review by Bosley Crowther. "The most distractive nonsense is the pop-up of familiar faces in so-called cameo roles, jarring the illusion. . . . Alfred Newman's music is conventional and generally tasteful except when it bears down hard on the 'Hallelujah Chorus.' "

THE NEW YORK TIMES, Feb. 1965. Interview with Stevens by Joann Stang. "I have tremendous satisfaction that the job has been done—to its completion—the way I wanted it done; the way I know it should have been done. It belongs to the audiences now . . . and I prefer to let them judge."

THE PRESBYTERIAN MAGAZINE, Feb. 1965. Review by Malcolm Boyd. "Challenged by the subject of Christ's life and ministry, Mr. Stevens poured into the enterprise . . . years of research, his talents and many millions of dollars. Yet the film sadly does not succeed."

TIME, Feb. 26, 1965. Review. " 'Wide is the gate, and broad is the way, that leadeth to destruction, and many there be which go in thereat,' says the Bible (Matthew 7:13). The latest to go in thereat is Producer-Director George Stevens."

UNITED ARTISTS STEREO ALBUM, UAS 5120, "The Greatest Story Ever Told." Liner Notes by George Stevens. "The film, and the portrait achieved by the represented Christ, do not so much attempt to answer Pilate's question, 'What is truth?' as to intensify each individual's desire to discover for himself within his own experience."

VARIETY, Feb. 15, 1965. Film Review. "In New York's Warner Cinerama Theatre at last week's preview the sound volume was ear-splitting on occasion and so distractive as to prevent a calm assessment of Alfred Newman's musical score which, without the assault upon the nervous system, is generally competent and attractive."

MUSIC DEPARTMENT STATISTICS
The Greatest Story Ever Told
February 20, 1965

Original score composed by Alfred Newman ran a total of   2:22:00

Recording to 1-4-65
- Orchestra = 80 hours
- Voices = <u>10 hours</u>
- Total = 90 hours

FIRST CHANGES

Flight Into Egypt	1:32		
Matthew, the Tax Collector	1:30		
Jesus and His Mother	3:03		
Judas and Caiaphas	1:25		
Aram, the First Witness	<u>:54</u>		
TOTAL MINUTES OF MUSIC	8:24		8:24
RECORDING TIME TO MAKE FIRST CHANGES		5 hours	

SECOND CHANGES

The Three Magi	1:09		
New Trumpets at Dawn	:16		
Magi Leave Jerusalem	:50		
Magi Reach Bethlehem	:48		
Introduction To Egypt	:05		
John the Baptist	2:37	Orchestra =	9 hours
The Highest Summit	2:18	Voices =	8 hours
Jesus Leaves Nazareth	1:15		
Prayer by the Jordan	:31		
I Am the Son of God	:31		
Lazarus, Come Forth (*Robe*)	2:01		
Lazarus, Come Forth (Handel)	2:45		
Resurrection (Handel)	4:15		
Verdi's Requiem #1	2:15		
Verdi's Requiem #2	<u>4:00</u>		
TOTAL MINUTES OF MUSIC	25:36		25:36

Recording time on stage in 1962	Orchestra =	4 hours
Chorus recording time in 1962		<u>16 hours</u>
TOTAL RECORDING TIME FOR THE PICTURE		132 hours

Minutes of prerecorded track used in film:	<u>4:00</u>
TOTAL LENGTH OF SCORE	3:00:00

Recording time for Album	Orchestra =	6 hours
	Voices =	<u>2 hours</u>
TOTAL RECORDING TIME FOR PHONOGRAPH ALBUM	=	8 hours

GRAND TOTAL RECORDING TIME FOR   = 140 hours!
PROJECT
[or 23 days of double sessions (6 hours per day) plus 2 hours of overtime]

TOTAL MUSICIANS CALLED	1,057
TOTAL SINGERS CALLED	386

TOTAL MUSIC REWRITTEN OR REVISED MORE THAN ONCE = 35 minutes!
[George Brand and Elaine call this (in retrospect) "A glimpse of Gehenna"]

CAST AND TECHNICAL CREDITS

Max von Sydow . . . . Jesus
Dorothy McGuire . . . . Mary
Robert Loggia . . . . Joseph
Charlton Heston . . . . John the Baptist

Michael Anderson Jr. . . . . James the Younger
Robert Blake . . . . Simon the Zealot
Burt Brinkerhoff . . . . Andrew
John Considine . . . . John the Beloved Disciple
Jamie Farr . . . . Thaddeus
David Hedison . . . . Philip
Peter Mann . . . . Nathanael (Bartholomew)
David McCallum . . . . Judas Iscariot
Roddy McDowall . . . . Matthew the Publican
Gary Raymond . . . . Peter
Tom Reese . . . . Thomas the Doubter
David Sheiner . . . . James the Elder

Ina Balin . . . . Martha of Bethany
Janet Margolin . . . . Mary of Bethany
Michael Tolan . . . . Lazarus
Sidney Poitier . . . . Simon of Cyrene
Joanna Dunham . . . . Mary Magdalene
Carroll Baker . . . . Veronica
Pat Boone . . . . Young Man at the Tomb
Van Heflin . . . . Bar Amand
Sal Mineo . . . . Uriah
Shelley Winters . . . . Woman of No Name
Ed Wynn . . . . Old Aram

John Wayne . . . . The Centurion
Telly Savalas . . . . Pontius Pilate
Angela Lansbury . . . . Claudia

Johnny Seven . . . . Pilate's Aid
Paul Stewart . . . . Questor
Harold J. Stone . . . . General Varus

Martin Landau . . . . Caiaphas
Nehemiah Persoff . . . . Shemiah
Joseph Schildkraut . . . . Nicodemus
Victor Buono . . . . Sorak
Robert Busch . . . . Emissary
John Crawford . . . . Alexander
Russell Johnson . . . . Scribe
John Lupton . . . . Speaker at Capernaum
Abraham Sofaer . . . . Joseph of Arimathea
Chet Stratton . . . . Theophilus
Ron Whelan . . . . Annas

Donald Pleasence . . . . The Dark Hermit
Jose Ferrer . . . . Herod Antipas
Claude Rains . . . . Herod the Great
John Abbott . . . . Aben
Rodolfo Acosta . . . . Captain of Lancers
Michael Ansara . . . . Herod's Commander
Philip Coolidge . . . . Cuza
Dal Jenkins . . . . Philip
Joe Perry . . . . Archelaus
Marian Seldes . . . . Herodias
Richard Conte . . . . Barabbas
Frank de Kova . . . . The Tormentor
Joseph Sirola . . . . Dumaha

Cyril Delevant . . . . Melchior
Mark Lenard . . . . Balthazar
Frank Silvera . . . . Casper

Entire cast of the Inbal Dance Theatre of Israel

Presented in Cinerama . . . . . . Released by United Artists
Produced and Directed by . . . . George Stevens
In association with . . . . Carl Sandburg
Executive Producer . . . . Frank I. Davis
Associate Producers . . . . George Stevens, Jr.
                                   Antonio Vellani

Music Composed and Conducted by Alfred Newman

Screenplay by . . . . James Lee Barrett
                                  George Stevens
Sets Created by . . . . David Hall
Art Decoration by . . . . Richard Day/William Creber
Costumes designed by . . . . . . Vittorio Nino Novarese
Assistant Designer . . . . Marjorie Best

Screenplay based on the Books of the Old and New Testaments, other
ancient writings; the book, *The Greatest Story Ever Told* by Fulton
Oursler, and other writings by Henry Denker.

Photographed in Ultra Panavision 70
Color by . . . . Technicolor
Photographed by . . . . William C. Mellor
                                  Loyal Griggs
Color Consultant . . . . Eliot Elisofon

Choral Supervision . . . . Ken Darby
Set Decoration . . . . Paul Ray Moyer, Fred McLean
                                  and Norman Rockett
Make-up Created by . . . . Del Armstrong
Assisted by . . . . Keester Sweeney

Hair Styles by . . . . Carmen Dirigo

Property Master . . . . Sam Gordon

Construction Supervisor . . . . . Jack Tait

Second Unit Directors . . . . . . Ridgeway Callow
                                  William Hale
                                  Richard Talmadge

Supervising Film Editor . . . . . Harold F. Kress

Film Editors . . . . Argyle Nelson, Jr.
                                  Frank O'Neill

Special Visual Effects . . . . . . J. McMillan Johnson
                                  Clarence Slifer
                                  A. Arnold Gillespie
                                  Robert R. Hoag

Sound (On location & set) . . . . Charles Wallace

Recording Supervisors . . . . . . Franklin Milton
William Steinkamp

Production Projectionist . . . . . Charles McCleod

Research Supervisor . . . . Tony Van Renterghem

Script Supervisor . . . . John Dutton

Casting . . . . Lynn Stalmaster

Production Managers . . . . Nathan Barrager
Eric Stacey

Production Staff . . . . Tom Andre
Ray Gosnell
Lee Lukather
Saul Wurtzel

The effort put forth by all these people was enormous—though misguided—and the experience was searingly imprinted on the memories of all. Set Designer David Hall and Photographer Bill Mellor died before the Gala Premiere in New York. Florence Williamson received no screen credit, and in spite of Alfred's earnest request, no credits were given to Leo Shuken, Jack Hayes, George Brand, Fred Steiner, or Hugo Friedhofer.

It was obviously not the greatest picture ever made, but, for me, the life of Christ is still the greatest story ever told—K.D.

GLOSSARY

Bar Breakdown: A piece of music paper divided into 4 (sometimes 8) bars to the staff on which the music editor writes a description of the action taking place in the film based on the tempo given to him by the composer. This breakdown provides the composer with the exact beat in the bar(s) where action takes place which he may want to point up with an accent or a musical effect.

Bohemian Grove: Twenty-seven hundred acres of redwoods north of San Francisco where the Bohemian Club holds its annual summer encampment in celebration of music, literature, drama, art, and comedy—based on the twin foundations of participation and appreciation.

Channel(s): The wires *from* a microphone *through* the patch bay *and* a dubbing panel *to* a recording machine is called a recording channel. Likewise, the wires carrying information *from* a playback machine *through* a patch bay *and* a dubbing panel *to* a recording machine is called a dubbing channel. [see PATCH BAY and DUBBING PANEL]

Chart: A graphic layout of the scenes to be scored with music, including the names or initials of orchestrators, the REEL & PART NUMBER given the scene by the film editor, the title of the piece to be recorded, the size of the orchestra, voices used (if any), the length of each piece of music in minutes, and the date of recording.

Control Desk: A small desk between chairs (or directly in front of them) in a projection room. It has space for making notes and is equipped with a small light, a two-way communication system between the projection booth and whoever is at the control desk (operated by a button or a toggle switch), and a dial control for raising or lowering the volume of the track being projected.

Cue(s): An inaccurate but timeworn word used as a label for a pictorial scene where music has been composed to fit the action; it is sometimes used for the music itself.

Dailies: The selected product of one day's photography. All of the chosen film is processed overnight in a laboratory and a print made of each shot. These prints are sent immediately to the film editor who, without removing the slate marks, splices them all together for viewing. Ideally, each day's work is viewed by the director, producer, and the involved technicians not later than 24 hours after it was sent to the lab, giving opportunity to rephotograph unacceptable scenes before the set is struck or the company moves to a different location.

Dubbing Panel: A console, ten or more feet in length, containing highly technical equipment for mixing recorded material drawn from microphones or playback machines. The face of the desk-top slants downward toward the recordists and supports a maze of controls for raising and lowering volume, equalizing frequencies of speech, music and/or sound effects, and for adding reverberation. Metering devices monitor elapsed time, film footage, and the volume levels of the sounds being processed. A modern dubbing panel can accommodate as many as sixty-four channels and six sound mixers.

Dubbing Room: A soundproof room, separated from recording stages, having a projection booth and a dubbing panel at one end, and a screen at the other. Behind the screen are one or more loudspeakers connected to the dubbing panel. Prior to stereophonic sound, only one speaker was behind the screen. In CinemaScope, Cinerama (or other wide-screen systems) there are five speakers behind the screen with surround horns placed along the side walls of the room itself. It is in this room that dialog, sound effects and music are combined to produce the finished commercial sound track which will be printed on the release print.

Fader Control: A potentiometer for manually raising or lowering the volume of a sound track or any amplified signal.

FPM: Feet Per Minute. The speed with which film normally passes the aperture of a projection machine [90 FPM]. The FPM speed of a movie camera may vary from 1 frame every four hours (lapse-time photography) to 180 or more FPM (for slow motion). When projected at 90 FPM the former may show a flower growing from bud to full bloom in a few seconds; the latter is used to reveal movement that is too rapid for the naked eye to see, such as the wings of a humming bird in flight.

HTWWW: Symbol for *How the West Was Won.*

Long Shot: In recording music, a microphone placed at a great distance from orchestra or chorus gives perspective, blend, and room reverberation to instruments and voices. In the dubbing room, this long shot can be mixed with the closeup tracks and patched into the surround horns to add tonal dimension.

Mixer: A technician skilled in the recording of sound; one who mixes signals coming from microphones or sound tracks.

Moviola: A patented machine, started and stopped by a foot pedal, having as one component a sprocket-driven escape mechanism for running film at varying speeds. A hinged ground-glass magnifying viewer can be swung upward and aside, allowing the editor to mark any given frame with a grease pencil. A second component is a magnetic head unit for reproducing sound. By attaching this sound drive to the motor of the escape mechanism, a synchronous union is achieved. The machine can be reversed, and some of the models are equipped with additional sound heads so that as many as four sound tracks may be played against the picture. If no Moviola existed, one would have to be invented; it is the workhorse of the industry.

Music Cutter: Another name for music editor, who cuts and edits the music tracks to fit scenes which have been scored by the composer, times sequences, prepares the dupe for projection during the recording sessions, and keeps a log of all music takes and prints. Indispensable.

Music Dupe: A black-and-white print of the picture, reduced to 35mm film stock, given to the editors of sound effects, dialog and music after the director has approved the final cut of the film. Dupes are used to measure scenes for music, to place sound effects, and to synchronize the elements.

Music Spotting: The action taken by the composer in deciding where the music shall start and where it shall end in a given scene. His decisions are then listed by reel and part number and presented to the director for discussion and approval. Music spotting is done in a projection room.

Patch Bay: A terminal for wires that conduct electrical signals from microphones or playback machines. It is adjacent (or built in) to the dubbing panel and contains many dozens of sockets into which the plugs of patch cords are inserted. These cords lead the signals to various control positions: to and from equalizers, in and out of reverberation chambers, filters and noise reduction units and, eventually, to the fader controls on the main panel. In some complicated reels the patch bay, with its multiplicity of patch cords, can look like a fierce tangled mass of black worms.

Playback: Any recording made prior to photography—played back on the set through loudspeakers—to which actors, singers, or musicians synchronize their voices or movements while being photographed. Example:

In the film *South Pacific*, Rossano Brazzi played the role of Emile de Becque which Ezio Pinza had made famous on the stage. Rossano's voice, while mellifluous in speech, was not up to the demands of Richard Rodgers' music, so Giorgio Tozzi (opera star) *sang* the role, recording it with Alfred Newman's orchestra under perfect conditions at 20th Century-Fox. On the location set in Kauai, Rossano sang to

Tozzi's amplified playback while my music cutter, Bob Mayer, and I watched the synchronization.

Mitzi Gaynor sang all of Nellie Forbush's songs herself, recording under the same optimum conditions several weeks before she left for location. She, likewise, heard—and synchronized with—the playback of her *own voice* while being photographed later on the set. Complicated? Not at all. Consider the alternative:

Before playbacks were used, musicians and singers—at outrageous cost—waited for hours on the shooting stage while lights were adjusted, makeup was applied, costumes repaired, decor was touched up, furniture was moved, props were put in place, or until the director was ready to shoot. Then the singer stood before the camera—nailed to the spot—with a microphone dangling above his head out of camera range, and sang to the live accompaniment of an orchestra (located somewhere behind the camera) that he could neither see nor hear properly. The soloist and the musicians, picked up on several microphones, were recorded permanently on a single strip of film (no tape in those days) with no possibility of changing the balance. After each take, everyone crowded around an acetate machine to hear the disk which had been recorded simultaneously with the film while the director decided if the quality, style, and performance were good enough to print or if other takes should be made. They usually were!

This entire process, called "direct recording," is done beautifully today in concert halls and TV studios with state-of-the-art equipment. Nobody minds if people cough or shuffle their feet . . . but in movies the disadvantages of direct recording are enormous: all noises are recorded with the music; a good orchestra blend is strictly accidental; none of the shooting stages is soundproofed, and all of them have the acoustics of mammoth silos! Airplanes *still* halt photography.

If the director decides to move in for a closeup or to change angles, a second performance "take" may be faster or slower in tempo, higher or lower in recording level, all of which makes an intercut between the two *takes* a jarring collision—if not impossible.

Glossary

That priceless little reference acetate saved the film musical. One day, the actor-singer (call him Bing) said, "If we have to make another take, play back the acetate on the loudspeaker and I'll synchronize with it."

Recording Level: The optimum volume of sound that can be recorded on film or magnetic tape without producing distortion.

Sequence: Any scene having a definite beginning and ending.

Shtick: Show-business vernacular for a caprice, a stunt in a vaudeville act, or a comic piece of stage business.

Slate Mark: A slate with a clapstick used in front of a camera to start a take. Marked on the slate are data defining film title, production, scene and take number, and the names of director and cameraman. The clapper puts a sharp sound on the recorded film or tape. The editor now has both visual and audible signals for synchronizing the sound with the picture.

Stretchout: An elongated, multi-seat limousine.

Take: Any recorded or photographed sequence—whether completed or not—is termed "a take." Repeated takes are given consecutive numbers. When the director (or the composer) is satisfied with a performance, he may say, "Print Take 5 and Take 7; hold Take 4. We may intercut between them." The same word is applied to playbacks, scoring cues and vocal recordings. All are identified as Take 1, 2, 3, etc.

TGSET: The symbol for *The Greatest Story Ever Told.*

Timings: A scene has been spotted for scoring. The music editor threads the scene into his Moviola, sets the footage counter to zero, and dictates to a secretary the moment-by-moment action taking place on the film, e.g.:

2 2/3" The king bows his head;
5 1/3" He draws his sword Excalibur;

    8 2/3"   He raises it high above his head;
    10 2/3"   He throws it far out over the misty lake;
    15 1/3"   A hand rises from the water to catch it.
Some of the longer scenes in a picture run to 8 and even 10
minutes. Without timings the composer has no guide to the
substance of the scene.

Track(s): Any recorded piece of film or magnetic tape used in
a motion picture is called "a track." There are DIALOG
TRACKS (often 2 or 3); ORCHESTRA TRACKS (often
two—one blending into a second); VOCAL TRACK (soloist); CHORUS TRACKS (2 or 3); SOUND EFFECTS
TRACKS (several for gunshots, wind, wagon trains, crickets,
etc.); GUIDE TRACK (used by the conductor to hear on an
earphone the pre-recorded voice of a singer while he con-
ducts the accompaniment); CLICK TRACK (made to sound
like a metronome in an earphone, useful for military scenes
where armies are marching on screen in a definite cadence).

Wahweep: A small village on the rim of a desert valley occupied
in 1962 by a few settlers and a small tribe of Indians.

Windsock: A cap of foam rubber (or porous plastic) fitted over
a microphone to shield it from wind noise.

Wollensak: A monaural tape recorder originating in Germany,
bought and distributed by 3M Company in the 1960's as a
home unit for amateur recorders. It used quarter-inch tape
at 3 3/4 IPS [Inches Per Second], and was useful for recording
conferences, letters, conversations and personal journals, but
was barely adequate for test recordings of instrumental or
vocal music. Still, it served its purpose in demonstrating—
through its playback system—tape which had previously been
commercially and/or professionally recorded.

INDEX